Mark Carwardine's Guide to

WHALE
WATCHING
IN NORTH AMERICA

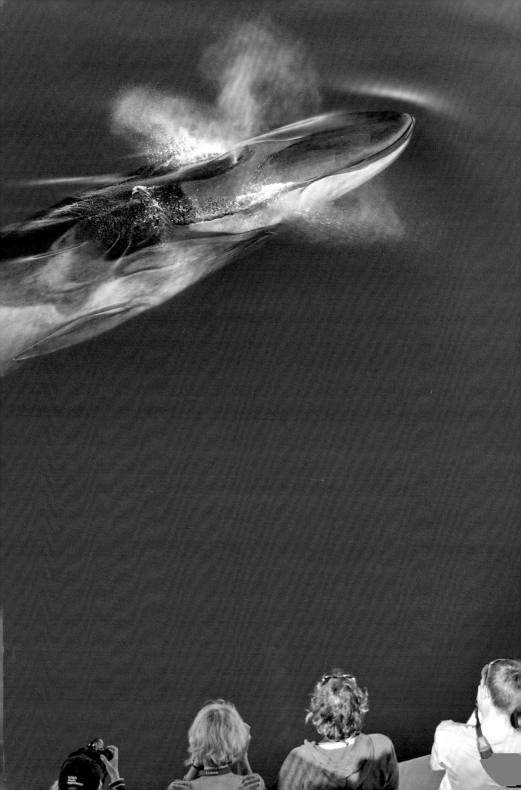

Mark Carwardine's Guide to

WHALE
WATCHING
IN NORTH AMERICA

United States, Canada & Mexico

WHERE TO GO, WHAT TO SEE

BLOOMSBURY

LONDON · OXFORD · NEW YORK · NEW DELHI · SYDNEY

CONTENTS

Bloomsbury Natural History
An imprint of Bloomsbury Publishing Plc

50 Bedford Square   1385 Broadway
London   New York
WC1B 3DP   NY 10018
UK   USA

www.bloomsbury.com

BLOOMSBURY and the Diana logo are trademarks of
Bloomsbury Publishing Plc

First published 2017

A catalogue record for this book is available from
the British Library.

Library of Congress Cataloging-in-Publication data
has been applied for.

ISBN: PB: 978-1-4729-3069-9
      ePub: 978-1-4729-3070-5

2 4 6 8 10 9 7 5 3 1

Designed and typeset in UK by Susan McIntyre

MIX
Paper from
responsible sources
FSC
www.fsc.org   FSC® C008047

Printed in China by C&C Offset Printing Co., Ltd.

INTRODUCTION

The identity of the world's first real whale watcher has been lost in the mists of time. Arguably, it was the Greek philosopher and scientist Aristotle who made some impressively accurate observations about whales and dolphins more than 2,400 years ago. But organized whale watching as we know it today did not begin until surprisingly recently.

The first whale-watching enterprise on record began in British Columbia, Canada, in the early 1900s, when Humpback Whales in Howe Sound (stretching from Squamish to the Strait of Georgia, opposite the southern region of Vancouver Island) became an attraction for trail-blazing tourists from nearby Vancouver. They went on organized boat excursions specifically to see the whales. Sadly, the enterprise was short-lived, because whaling from the station at Page's Lagoon in Nanaimo, from 1907–10, completely wiped out the Howe Sound whale population.

Despite this early start, the industry didn't really take off until 1950, when Donald M. Robinson, superintendent of Cabrillo National Monument in San Diego, converted an old army gun station into the first public whale-watching lookout. It was a huge success: in just a few months no fewer than 10,000 people came to see Gray Whales migrating along the southern California coast. Then, in winter 1955, San Diego fisherman Chuck Chamberlin put out a sign that read 'See the whales – $1' and began to take people out for a closer look at the same Gray Whales. It was the first 'official' boat-based whale watching – and a new industry was born.

Worldwide, whale watching has grown from those humble beginnings in the mid-1950s to today's colossal industry. At the last count, in 2008, it was worth US$ 2.1 billion and involved 119 countries and overseas territories. There are an estimated 3,300 whale-watch operators around the world and no fewer than 13 million people now join their trips every year. North America is far and away the world's largest whale-watching destination, attracting more than half of these whale watchers.

The industry plays a valuable role in local economies, because museums, science centers, bookstores, gift shops, bus companies, hotels and guesthouses, restaurants and cafes, taxi companies and many other businesses can all benefit from the tremendous influx of visitors. That, in turn, encourages local communities to care for the whales that the whale watchers come to see. But, above all, it means we have a huge responsibility to ensure that whale watching really does benefit the whales – by increasing awareness and compassion and raising money for conservation and research – rather than causing them more problems than they already face.

An exceptionally close encounter with a gargantuan Blue Whale.

It's not surprising that whale watching has become so popular. No one ever says, 'I can't remember if I've seen a whale'. A close encounter with one of the most enigmatic, gargantuan and downright remarkable creatures on the planet is a life-changing experience for most people. Over the past 35 years, I've spent countless thousands of hours watching whales (and dolphins and porpoises – by 'whale' I am talking about all cetaceans) and yet I still remember my first encounter: I was 21 years old, on a half-day commercial trip from Long Beach, California, when a Gray Whale suddenly breached right in front of me. In my mind's eye, I can see this great leviathan leaping out of the water and remember deciding – at that very moment – that I wanted to spend as much of my life with whales as possible.

Approximately half of all the cetacean species known to science have been recorded in North America at one time or another. You have to search hard to find some, such as the Narwhal or Vaquita, while others have been recorded just once or a handful of times. But many are residents or regular visitors – including everything from Blue Whales and North Atlantic Right Whales to Killer Whales and Pacific White-sided Dolphins – and are surprisingly easy to see if you go to the right places at the right times of year.

It is even possible to choose how to watch them: from the air, from the shore, or from a host of different vessels, including yachts, rubber inflatables, motor cruisers, research boats, kayaks and expedition cruise ships. And there are tours to suit every taste, from comfortable one-hour, half-day or full-day excursions to adventurous two- or three-week expeditions. You can spend a day watching Bowhead Whales in the golden light of the midnight sun in Baffin Island, Nunavut, tickle a friendly Gray Whale under the chin in Baja California, Mexico, listen to a live concert of singing Humpback Whales in Hawai'i, snorkel with Belugas in the freezing cold waters of Hudson Bay, Manitoba, follow a family of Killer Whales against the spectacular backdrop of Vancouver Island, or be surrounded by an enormous school of Northern Right Whale Dolphins in Monterey Bay, California. And so much more.

WHALE WATCHING AND CARING FOR WHALES

 ## How to Watch Whales, Dolphins and Porpoises

In theory, it is possible to see whales, dolphins and porpoises almost anywhere in North American waters. They occur in the wilds of the high Arctic, in the warmest waters of the Caribbean, within sight and sound of towns and cities, along shallow coastlines, and in deep waters far out to sea. At the same time, of course, they have to come to the surface at regular intervals to breathe. So, all in all, you might expect them to be relatively easy to find.

But that's not necessarily true. Without some prior knowledge and research (not to mention a little luck) you could easily spend hours staring at an apparently empty sea. Many cetaceans (the collective term for whales, dolphins and porpoises) live only in particular areas at certain times of the year and their distribution varies weekly, daily and even hourly, according to sea and weather conditions, food availability and many other factors.

Fortunately, this can work to your advantage. It means that, to a degree, you can predict where and when to look. The trick is to do your homework: decide which species you would like to see, select the best region, research the peak time of year, and then consider the precise location and even the exact time of day (a pod of dolphins might be well known for swimming past a particular beach at a certain time of day, for instance). A little preparation will increase your chances substantially.

Choosing a whale-watch operator

The simplest answer is to join a commercial whale-watching trip. Most have a pretty high success rate because they tend to concentrate on well-known cetacean populations and, of course, are operated in the appropriate seasons. But it can be difficult to choose an operator when there are so many organized trips on offer. How do you pick the right one?

If you are unable to get a firm recommendation, there are a number of considerations. What is the boat like? Does it look well maintained? Is there plenty of deck space, with 360-degree views so you will not miss anything? Does it have shelter from the sun, rain, wind and spray? Are there lavatory facilities on board (something you will appreciate more and more the longer the trip)? Bear in mind that smaller vessels offer a more intimate experience (shared with fewer people and closer to the animals), while larger vessels tend to offer the most comfort and stability. What is the operator's success rate

Scanning for North Atlantic Right Whales in the Bay of Fundy, eastern Canada.

at finding whales? It is a good sign if they offer a free return-trip guarantee if there are no sightings.

There are a few more important considerations. First, do they have a naturalist on board? The best trips have knowledgeable naturalists who are skilled at finding the animals and provide interesting and informative commentaries to keep everyone well informed. Their knowledge can add tremendously to the experience.

Second, do they emphasize the fact that they adhere to local whale-watching regulations or guidelines? It is sometimes easy to forget that we are uninvited guests in the world of whales, dolphins and porpoises. We are privileged to see them and do not have a divine right. In fact, we have a responsibility to cause as little disturbance as possible – which is why whale watching should always be an eyes-on, hands-off activity.

Fortunately, many whale-watch operators really care about the whales, and their guests, and do a great job. They are well versed in whale etiquette, abiding by local regulations or codes of conduct and putting the welfare of the animals before everything else. They take care not to disturb or injure them by manoeuvring their boats carefully, slowly and not too close, and then leaving before the whales show signs of distress.

Some operators, however, are not so careful and cause a great deal of unnecessary stress. Not only are the animals forced to steer clear of boats, or possibly even to abandon their preferred feeding or breeding grounds, but collisions and other accidents can cause serious injury and even death.

The best whale-watch operators also put something back to benefit the whales. They help to raise money for whale conservation, for instance, or provide free places for biologists to do urgently needed research. The researchers help to find the whales, provide a running commentary and answer questions, in return for doing their own photo-ID research and collecting other valuable data; they also drum up public support for whale conservation. Running a dedicated research boat is beyond the budget of many research groups, so the arrangement benefits everyone.

A whale-watching code of conduct

Whether on their feeding or breeding grounds, or on migration, whales, dolphins and porpoises can all be sensitive to disturbance by intrusive whale watching and poor boat handling. In the worst cases, they can be injured or even killed by propellers or collisions.

Some operators form their own associations to devise self-imposed codes of conduct, but most rely on researchers or conservation groups to suggest guidelines or for governments to impose official regulations.

Whatever you do, don't be tempted to put pressure on the skipper to get closer and closer (and, finally, too close) to the whales.

Careful and considerate whale watching is not only better for the whales, it is also better for the whale watchers. The probability of a close and prolonged encounter increases the more relaxed the animals are. Do not feel shy about complaining if you think the skipper is stressing the animals: few places have 'whale police' so we must all help to make sure that whale watching is conducted responsibly and, if applicable, local guidelines are being followed.

CAREFUL AND SENSITIVE WHALE WATCHING

There is no universally accepted 'good practice' for whale watching and the details will inevitably vary according to the location and species. Some existing regulations are quite lenient, for example allowing an approach to within 100ft, while others are much stricter (no closer than 1,000ft). In very broad terms, here is a simple code of conduct:

- Observe the animals carefully before approaching, to evaluate their behavior and direction of travel.

- Approach from a position to the rear and slightly to one side.

- Never approach head-on, from immediately behind or from an angle of 90 degrees.

- Approach slowly (at a 'no-wake' speed) and continue along a parallel course.

- Do not go nearer than 300ft (let the animals come to you if they want to).

- Avoid sudden changes in speed, direction or noise (avoid gear shifts and reversing, unless it is absolutely necessary to back away slowly).

- Avoid loud noises.

- Never pursue, overtake, head off or encircle the animals, or cause groups to separate.

- If the animals show avoidance behavior, leave them alone.

- Exercise extreme caution if they are feeding, if there are calves present and around socially active groups.

- Never have more than three boats around a single whale or group of whales.

- Do not stay too long (20–30 minutes is a reasonable time, depending on circumstances, unless the animals choose to spend longer with you).

- If an animal approaches the boat (unless it is wake-riding or bow-riding, of course) keep the engine in neutral, especially if your propellers are unguarded.

- Avoid switching off the engine – especially if you are near large whales that are breaching – because it is important for them to know exactly where you are at all times.

- When leaving, move off slowly (at a 'no-wake' speed) until the boat is at least 1,000ft away.

A friendly Gray Whale with its human admirers in San Ignacio Lagoon, Mexico.

Preparing for a whale-watch trip

What you will need for your trip obviously depends on where, when and how you intend to watch whales. But here are a few suggestions:

Seasickness remedies Seasickness patches (placed behind the ear), wristbands or tablets should be applied or taken at least an hour before the trip, if you have any doubts about suffering from seasickness. If you'd rather not use medication, try eating ginger, which is a natural remedy for nausea; ginger ale containing real ginger can also be effective.

Anti-sunburn aids Suntan lotion and a sun hat are essential to avoid sunburn and sunstroke, especially around midday (you are more likely to burn at sea than you are on land).

Sunglasses Polarized sunglasses help to reduce the sun's glare and are excellent for seeing through reflections on the surface of the water, to see whales and dolphins underwater if they approach your boat.

Waterproof bags These are essential for keeping all your stuff dry (especially to protect binoculars, cameras and other equipment from salty spray).

Waterproof clothing A waterproof jacket and trousers are important if sea conditions are likely to be rough or if you are expecting rain (whale watching often involves getting wet).

Warm clothing Warm and windproof clothing is vital if you are whale watching in cold weather. Remember that it is often

A Killer Whale spyhops in the Salish Sea, near Vancouver Island, Canada.

windier, and therefore much colder, at sea than it is on shore. Be careful not to underestimate how many layers you are likely to need. Even if it is T-shirt weather in the harbor, take plenty of warm clothes regardless (wear layers, which you can add or remove as necessary).

Shoes Rubber-soled deck shoes are important in case the deck gets wet and slippery.

Writing aids A field notebook and pen are invaluable – keeping notes is a great way to improve your spotting and identification skills.

Field guides Identification guides are useful for identifying the whales, dolphins or porpoises you encounter. Consider taking

guides to the birds, seals, fish and other local wildlife as well.

Binoculars These are crucial for finding whales, dolphins and porpoises, as well as for identifying them, studying their behavior and simply getting better views.

Telescope One with a tripod can be useful when whale watching from shore, or from the relatively stable platform of a large expedition cruise ship (but the high magnification makes it virtually unusable on smaller boats).

Cameras Camera equipment adds a whole new dimension to the whale-watching experience. It is possible to take good pictures with the simplest equipment, but if you're going to take it seriously use a DSLR camera

Who is watching whom? A Humpback Whale with whale watchers off California.

with a variety of lenses (wide-angle, medium zoom such as a 70–200mm or 80–200mm, and a longer zoom or telephoto lens up to about 400mm). Always shoot on motordrive – the more frames per second the greater your chances of getting that perfect shot.

Hydrophone, or underwater microphone Few whale watchers carry hydrophones because they are quite expensive and can be tricky to use (to hear underwater clearly the skipper will need to cut the engines, for a start, and may even need to switch off the generator). But they can help to find some whales by sound, as well as adding a new and exciting dimension to the whale-watching experience.

Safety equipment This should be provided by all organized whale-watching trips. It should include life jackets, life rafts, flares, a VHF radio and first-aid equipment.

How to find whales, dolphins and porpoises

Searching a vast, seemingly empty sea for whales, dolphins and porpoises can be quite daunting at first, especially when you do not know exactly what you are looking for. It is easy to lose your concentration, or to get disillusioned. There is a lot of luck involved, of course, but equally there is no escaping the fact that people with more experience tend to see more. They instinctively recognize all the tell-tale signs – the slightest clues that give the presence of cetaceans away.

With a large whale, the first clue is often its blow or spout. This is more visible in some weather conditions than others, but it can be surprisingly distinctive. It may look like a flash of white (especially against a dark background), a smudge or a more gradual puff of smoke. Blows are easy to miss, however, especially since there is often a considerable gap between each one, and just a little wind can literally blow them away.

Alternatively, you may catch a glimpse of the head and back of a whale as it breaks the surface. This often resembles a strange wave that, somehow, does not look quite right. Anything suspicious, even if nine times out of ten it does turn out to be a wave, is worth investigating. Or, sometimes, your eye catches a brief glint of light, which could be the sun bouncing off the head or back of a whale as it surfaces. As soon as you notice anything unusual have a closer look with your binoculars.

Splashes are also good clues. They can be caused by a large whale breaching, flipper-slapping or lobtailing, or by dolphins. A group of dolphins in the distance frequently looks like a patch of rough water, resembling lots of whitecaps and little breaking waves.

The presence of seabirds can be another tell-tale sign, particularly if they seem to be feeding or are concentrated in one particular area. They can usually be seen from a great distance and it makes sense that, if they have found a school of fish, there could be whales or dolphins feeding underneath.

When you are searching for cetaceans, get as high above sea level as possible, by standing on the highest deck. The higher your vantage point, the farther away the horizon and the more you can see. Don't forget to look *everywhere* – in front, behind and to both sides. Scan the horizon with binoculars and use the naked eye to check nearer the boat. While many cetacean encounters begin with distant sightings, it is not uncommon for them to sneak up on boats and ships totally undetected. It is amazing how often people miss dolphins bow-riding right in front of them, or are suddenly surprised by a whale surfacing alongside the boat, because they are too busy looking far out to sea.

Finally, whatever you do, do not stop looking. An occasional glance out to sea, followed by a cup of coffee and a chat, is unlikely to produce many sightings. Even the ride back to shore can be interrupted with unexpected encounters, so don't give up until you are actually back in the harbor. Slowly scan the sea with binoculars... and then do it again, and again, and again. Keep searching the same area of water, even if you did not see anything the first time. There can be long gaps between surfacings (many species dive for several minutes and a few for more than an hour) and even a large whale can be surprisingly easy to miss.

The golden rule is to be patient. The more you look, the more you will see.

Don't forget to look down – for bow-riding dolphins.

The Challenges of Identification

Identifying whales, dolphins and porpoises at sea can be enormously satisfying, but also quite challenging. In fact, it can be so difficult that even the world's experts are unable to identify every species they encounter: on most official surveys at least some sightings have to be logged as 'unidentified'.

The trick is to use a relatively simple process of elimination. In the early 1990s, while researching and writing one of the first cetacean field guides, the artist Martin Camm and I spent a huge amount of time in the field and meeting with cetacean experts all over the world, specifically to develop a workable identification technique. We came up with a mental checklist of 14 key features to run through every time a new animal is encountered at sea. It is not often possible to use all of these features together and one alone is rarely enough for a positive identification. The best approach is to gather information on as many as possible before drawing any firm conclusions.

Geographical location There is not a single place in the world where every cetacean species has been recorded. In fact, there are not many places with records of more than a few dozen, so this immediately helps to cut down on the number of possibilities.

Habitat Just as Cheetahs live on open plains rather than in jungles, and Snow Leopards prefer mountains to wetlands, most whales, dolphins and porpoises are adapted to specific marine or freshwater habitats. In this respect, marine charts can be surprisingly useful identification aids. Knowing the underwater topography could help to tell the difference between a Minke Whale (normally found over the continental shelf) and a superficially similar Northern Bottlenose Whale (more likely to be seen over submarine canyons or in deep waters offshore).

Size It is difficult to estimate size accurately at sea, unless a direct comparison can be made with the length of the boat, a passing bird or an object in the water. Remember that only a small portion of the animal (the top of the head and back, for example) may be visible at any one time. Larger species don't necessarily show more of themselves than smaller species, so size can be quite deceptive. Therefore it is better to use three simple categories: small (up to 10ft), medium (10–30ft) and large (more than 30ft).

Unusual features Some cetaceans have very unusual features, which can be used for a quick identification. These include the extraordinary long tusk of the male Narwhal, the enormous dorsal fin of the male Killer Whale and the wrinkly skin of a Sperm Whale.

Long-finned or Short-finned? This is a Short-finned Pilot Whale.

Dorsal fin The size, shape and position of the dorsal fin varies greatly between species and is a particularly useful aid to identification. Don't forget to look for any distinctive colors or markings on the fin.

Flippers The length, color and shape of the flippers, as well as their position on the animal's body, vary greatly from one species to another. It is not always possible to see them, but flippers can be useful for identification in some species – in the Humpback Whale, for example, they are unmistakable.

Body shape Much of the time, whales, dolphins and porpoises do not show enough of themselves to provide an overall impression of their shape. Sometimes, however, this can be a useful feature. The shape of the melon (forehead) can also be distinctive.

Beak The presence or absence of a prominent beak is a particularly useful identification feature in toothed whales. Broadly speaking, river dolphins, beaked whales and half the oceanic dolphins have prominent beaks, while porpoises, Belugas and Narwhals, Killer Whales and their allies, and the remaining oceanic dolphins do not. There is also great variation in the beak length from one species to another. Try to see if there is a smooth transition from the top of the head to the end of the snout (as in Rough-toothed Dolphins, for example) or a distinct crease (as in Atlantic Spotted Dolphins).

Color and markings Many cetaceans are surprisingly colorful, and have distinctive markings such as body stripes or eye patches. Bear in mind that colors at sea vary according to water clarity and light conditions, and the animal can appear much darker than normal if viewed against the sun.

Flukes The flukes can be important features for identifying larger whales. Some species lift their flukes high into the air before they dive, while others do not, and that alone can help to tell one from another. It is also worth checking the shape of the flukes, looking for any distinctive markings and noticing whether or not there is a notch between the trailing edges.

Blow or spout The blow is particularly distinctive in larger whales. It varies in height, shape and visibility between species and can be extremely useful for identification, especially on calmer days.

But identifying a blow is not easy – if it is raining or windy it can be bent out of shape, there are variations between individuals – and the first blow after a deep dive tends to be stronger than the rest. However, experienced observers can often tell one species from another just by the blow, even from a considerable distance.

Dive sequence The dive sequence can be surprisingly distinct in many species. Variations include: the angle at which the head breaks the surface; whether or not the dorsal fin and blowhole are visible at the same time; whether the animal arches its back to dive (and how much it arches) or whether it merely sinks below the surface; the time interval between breaths; and the number of breaths before a deep dive.

A Humpback Whale's distinctive blow can be seen from miles away.

Behavior Some species are more active at the surface than others, so any unusual behavior can sometimes be useful for identification purposes.

Group size Since some species are highly gregarious, while others tend to live alone or in small groups, it is worth noting the number of animals seen together.

It is often tempting to guess the identification of an unusual whale, dolphin or porpoise that you have not seen very clearly. However, working hard at identification – and then enjoying the satisfaction of knowing that an animal has been identified correctly – is what makes a real expert in the long term. It is perfectly acceptable to record simply 'unidentified dolphin' or 'unidentified whale' or 'unidentified beaked whale', if a more accurate identification is not possible. If you write detailed notes at the time and then see the same species again in the future, it may be possible to turn a sighting previously recorded as 'unidentified' into a positive identification, days, weeks, months or even years later.

Part of the fun is that cetaceans are unpredictable. Never say 'never' on a whale-watching trip: just because the distribution maps suggest you're unlikely to see a particular species in a particular area doesn't mean that it couldn't pop up anywhere at any time; and just because the guidebooks say that one species of whale doesn't fluke, doesn't mean that the particular individual next to your boat won't prove everyone wrong by lifting its tail high into the air.

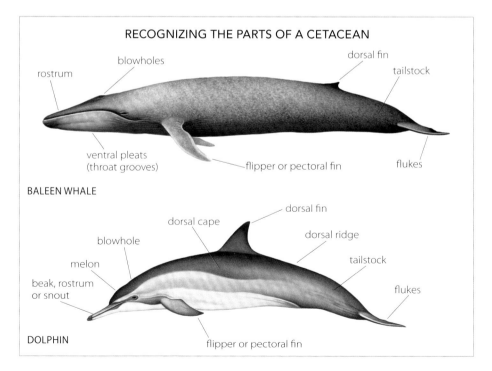

RECOGNIZING THE PARTS OF A CETACEAN

blowholes
rostrum
dorsal fin
tailstock
ventral pleats (throat grooves)
flipper or pectoral fin
flukes

BALEEN WHALE

dorsal cape
dorsal fin
blowhole
dorsal ridge
melon
tailstock
beak, rostrum or snout
flukes

DOLPHIN
flipper or pectoral fin

How to Recognize Whale Behavior... and what it all means

While most of their lives are spent underwater, many whales, dolphins and porpoises are active in full view at the surface. They slap the water with their flippers or flukes, ride in the bow waves and wakes of boats, lift their heads above the surface and even leap high in the air before falling back into the water with a tremendous splash.

We do not fully understand the meaning of many of these activities and it is quite possible that there are different explanations for different occasions, according to the species, the age and sex of the animals, and the context in which the behavior is taking place. For all we know, they might even be doing several different things at the same time.

The greatest challenge is trying to interpret what is happening at the surface when we have little or no clue about what the animals are up to when they are hidden out of sight underwater (which, of course, is where they spend most of their time). Sometimes it is even difficult to tell whether they are feeding, travelling, resting, socializing, courting or simply milling about, let alone what they are doing in more specific terms.

However, the good news is that a great deal of research has been done in recent years and at last we are beginning to unravel some of their secrets.

Blowing or spouting

All whales, dolphins and porpoises have to come to the surface to breathe. As their blowholes, or nostrils, break the surface they breathe out and then rapidly breathe in, before disappearing back into the depths. When large whales breathe out, they appear to blow a puff of steam into the air. This 'blow' or 'spout' is a misty cloud of water droplets with three main ingredients: condensed water, formed when warm air from inside the whale's body meets the cooler air outside; a fine spray of mucus from inside the lungs (rather like a sneeze); and seawater trapped in the blowholes as the whale surfaces. The term 'blow' refers both to the act of breathing – the explosive exhalation followed immediately by an inhalation – and to this mighty cloud of water vapor.

Bow-riding

Many small- and medium-sized toothed whales enjoy swimming or 'riding' on the pressure wave created in front of a boat or ship. They jostle for the prime location in the center of the bow, then fine-tune their body posture and position so as to be pushed along entirely by the force of the wave (often with no tail beats needed). Dominant individuals in a group edge others to less favorable positions, where they need to beat their tails to varying degrees to keep up.

The speed of the vessel is critical – too fast and the bow-riders can't keep up, too slow and they have to beat their tails too much and quickly get bored. But if there are no suitable boats or ships around, some small cetaceans will ride the bow waves of large whales in the same way; they annoy the whales, enticing them to surge ahead to produce a short-lived bow wave (one whale is 'good' for 5 to 10 surges, before it tires of the whole shenanigans).

Why do they do it? Despite some claims to the contrary, it is highly unlikely that bow-riders are simply hitching a free ride (especially since they actively go out of their way, and even change direction, for a chance to join the bow of a passing boat or ship). Bow-riding is far more likely to be nothing more than exuberant play, albeit with added benefits such as strengthening social bonds.

Wake-riding

Swimming in the frothy wake of a boat or ship seems to be a favorite pastime for many oceanic dolphins, as well as some whales and porpoises. They surf, twist and turn in the waves, or swim upside-down in the bubbles.

Breaching

When a large whale leaps completely (or almost completely) out of the water, it is breaching. In a classic breach the animal shows most of its body, twists in mid-air and lands back in the water on its back or side with a tremendous splash. There are many variations on this theme: Humpbacks and Sperm Whales, for example, sometimes do belly-flops, and a few individuals leave the water entirely.

A Gray Whale calf learning to breach next to its mother.

Breaching is perhaps the most impressive behavior of all and provides a rare opportunity for whale watchers to see the entire animal. The splash can be seen from some distance away and it can often be the first sign of a distant whale's presence.

Most species have been seen breaching at one time or another, although some do it much more often than others. A few have been known to breach nearly 200 times in a single display (though as the sequence progresses they tend to show less and less of themselves, visibly appearing more and more tired). It's a phenomenal achievement, given the sheer size of some of the breachers and the speed at which they have to launch themselves out of the water.

Although it is a common behavior, breaching is one of the great mysteries of the animal kingdom. Why do they do it? It is difficult to pinpoint a single explanation from the available evidence: both sexes and all ages breach; they breach at any time of year, on the breeding and feeding grounds; they breach when alone and in groups (although they breach more often when groups are merging or splitting); they can breach just once or many times in succession; when one animal breaches, it often triggers other individuals in the area to follow suit (rather like giggling in humans); sometimes two whales breach simultaneously, with perfect coordination – a spectacular double-breach; and they breach more often in windy conditions (breaching rates tend to increase with wind speed).

Many theories have been proposed over the years: it may be a courtship display, a form of signalling or communication, a show of strength or a challenge, a way to herd fish or even to stun them, a form of stretching, a sign of extreme annoyance or frustration, a way of gaining height to look long distances above the water (perhaps to search for flocks of feeding seabirds, for example), or it could simply be a way of inhaling water-free air in rough weather. Most likely, it has several of these functions, and possibly others, depending on circumstances.

One interesting clue is that, among large whales, the most frequent breachers are the stouter, slower species (in particular, Humpback, Right, Bowhead, Gray and Sperm Whales), while the slimmer, faster species (such as Bryde's, Sei and Fin Whales) tend to breach less often. Intriguingly, this may be less to do with their body shapes and more to do with the fact that the stouter whales tend to live in larger groups (and are therefore more social). Or it could be that they also tend to be more heavily infested with ectoparasites, in which case breaching might be a way of dislodging their unwanted hitchhikers. Another interesting clue is that breaching is often observed together with other behavior, such as lobtailing or flipper-slapping, so it could be used to add dramatic emphasis to something else (termed a 'behavioral exclamation mark').

Alternatively, recent research suggests an entirely different possible explanation, at least for repetitive breaching, that may work at the cellular level. Whales need to make long dives and, in order to do so, they need to be able to hold their breath for as long as possible. They employ a range of mechanisms to help increase their breath-holding abilities: reducing their heart rate, diverting oxygenated blood from non-essential organs to those that need it most, carrying exceptionally high levels of hemoglobin (the protein that carries oxygen within red blood cells) in their blood, and so on. Their muscles are rich in another oxygen-carrying protein called myoglobin, which gradually releases its store of oxygen as the whales dive. But

One Humpback Whale was observed breaching nearly 200 times in a row.

what has this got to do with breaching? Well, studies suggest that high levels of myoglobin play a large part in a whale's breath-holding abilities and there is a tenuous – but highly compelling – link between exercise and increased amounts of myoglobin in the cells. In other words, breaching may enable the whales to stay underwater for longer.

But here is the best possibility: many experts now acknowledge that some whales, at least, breach purely for fun.

Lunging

Officially, if more than 40 per cent of the whale's body leaves the water, it is termed a 'breach', otherwise it is a 'lunge'. Lunges are sometimes called 'half-breaches' or 'belly-flops' – which describe the behavior perfectly. The animal lurches forward through the water surface, showing less than 40 per cent of its body, and lands on its belly. Lunging can be the result of feeding near the surface, but it can also be an aggressive display between competitive males.

Peduncle-slap or tail-breach

Otherwise known as a 'peduncle-throw, 'rear-body throw' or 'tail breach', this is when the whale throws the rear portion of its body, including its flukes, high out of the water and sideways across the surface, creating a huge splash. It usually happens without warning and typically only once.

Tail extending

The whale raises its tail slowly into the air (usually high enough that the genital area is above the surface) and holds it there for some time. Right, Bowhead and Gray Whales may do this for several minutes at a time. It may be associated with activities underwater, although there is some evidence that Southern Right Whales, at least, do this when it is windy for 'recreational sailing'.

Leaping

When dolphins and smaller toothed whales leap out of the water it is usually termed 'leaping'. Some spend a lot of time in the air and can leap impressively high. They often do complete somersaults, twists and turns in mid-air, or make 'clean-entry leaps', returning to the water smoothly, beak first. Large whales never re-enter head-first like this.

Flipper-slapping

Otherwise known as 'flipper-flopping', 'flippering', 'pectoral-slapping' or 'pec-slapping', this is when the animal lies on its back or side, raises a flipper out of the water and then slaps it onto the surface. It may slap one or both flippers and it may do it once or many times in succession. There are many possible theories to explain flipper-slapping – the best being similar to some of the explanations for breaching.

Fluking

When some cetaceans embark on a deep dive, or 'sounding dive', they lift their tails into the air. This is called 'fluking'. Larger, more rotund whales, such as Humpback, Right, Bowhead, Gray, Sperm (and some Blue) whales fluke regularly, especially when diving into water that is deeper than at least two of their own body-lengths; however, slimmer whales never fluke or do so only

rarely. Fluking is the natural extension of a dive – the whale simply bends its body toward the seabed and, as it rolls forward and down, the tail automatically rises above the surface. But it may also have a practical advantage by giving extra thrust and helping to propel the whale into a more steeply angled descent to deeper waters.

Once they have disappeared, all whales leave a 'flukeprint' at the surface – a circular swirl of smooth water that looks rather like a sheen of oil – made by the downward movement of the tail creating a vortex.

Head-slap

Also known as a 'chin-slap', this is when a whale lunges partially out of the water and forcefully slaps the underside of its head down onto the surface with a large splash.

Lobtailing and tail-slapping

The term 'lobtailing' is used when a large whale lifts its tail clear of the water and then slaps it down onto the surface, usually repeatedly and often quite forcibly. Also known as 'tail-lobbing' or 'fluke-slapping', this impressive behavior often creates a tremendous splash. 'Tail-slapping' is a similar behavior, though normally associated with smaller cetaceans, in which the animal vigorously slaps its tail against the surface, often many times in a row.

As with breaching, lobtailing and tail-slapping probably have different functions depending on the species and the circumstances. It is used mainly in a social context, since relatively few animals lobtail or tail-slap when they are alone (and species with complex social systems tend to lobtail the most). It is often contagious and may be accompanied by breaching.

Above: An exceptionally rare photograph of a breaching Sowerby's Beaked Whale.

Left: A Humpback Whale flipper-slapping.

Below: A Sperm Whale fluking as it begins a deep dive.

Long-beaked Common Dolphins porpoising with perfect symmetry.

Logging

Logging is the habit of lying horizontally and still at or near the surface. It is a form of rest. Very often a pod of whales will all face the same direction while logging.

Porpoising

When members of the dolphin family – and, less commonly, some other cetaceans – travel at high speed they often leap clear of the water every time they take a breath, before re-entering headfirst. This is called 'porpoising' or 'running'. It is believed to reduce friction on their bodies when they break the surface, which may help to conserve energy.

Spyhopping

A 'spyhop' is when a whale remains stationary and upright while raising its head vertically out of the water, before sinking smoothly below the surface without much splash. It is sometimes known as a 'head rise' or an 'eye-out'. The animal often rises just to the level of its flippers, and its eyes may or may not appear above the surface. If the eyes are visible, it is quite possible that the whale is looking around (most species can see reasonably well above and below the surface); if the eyes are not visible, a recent theory suggests that spyhopping may help the whales hear better (for example, with Gray Whales on migration, it may be to hear the surf – since their route follows the coastline).

Caring for Whales, Dolphins and Porpoises

Human impact has now reached every square mile of the Earth's oceans. In particular, commercial whaling and other forms of hunting, myriad conflicts with fisheries, pollution, habitat degradation and disturbance, underwater noise, entanglement in or ingestion of marine debris, ship strikes and climate change are some of the main threats being faced by whales, dolphins and porpoises around the world.

To the best of our knowledge, one cetacean has become extinct in modern times: the Yangtze River Dolphin, or Baiji, from China. But a frightening number of other species are in serious trouble, while others have all but disappeared from many of their former haunts. At the same time, the number of survivors is not the only consideration. The Blue Whale, for example, is not one of the rarest cetaceans in the world but, after decades of intensive whaling, its chances of recovery are limited because it is a particularly slow breeder and its remnant population is widely dispersed.

It is also rather simplistic to talk about conservation of entire species. In many ways, it is more important to talk about distinct populations. For example, Gray Whales are – for all intents and purposes – extinct in the North Atlantic, but there are still a few survivors in the western North Pacific (fewer than 130) and they are back to their pre-whaling numbers in the

eastern North Pacific. Each population has a different story to tell.

Protecting cetaceans is no easy task: they are mobile and ignore political boundaries, and they face many quite complex, insidious and cumulative threats. These days the odds are firmly stacked against them and, for some at least, the future is undoubtedly bleak.

Whaling

Coastal communities around the world have killed whales for centuries. The blubber and meat provided a welcome source of light, heat and food that were sometimes essential for human survival.

In the old days, this small-scale subsistence hunting probably had only a local impact on whale populations, but by the end of the seventeenth century the character of most whaling had changed beyond all recognition. In an age before petroleum or plastics, whales provided valuable raw materials for thousands of everyday products, from soap and candles to whips and corsets. There were huge profits to be made and whaling rapidly became big business.

The slaughter reached its worst excesses around the middle of the twentieth century, thanks largely to a series of technological advances in whaling vessels,

The Yangtze River Dolphin, or Baiji, is now considered extinct.

killing equipment and processing methods. Literally millions of great whales were killed and, one by one, without pity, many of them were pushed almost to the point of extinction. By the time the worst of the slaughter was over, we were left merely with the tattered remains: in many cases, no more than 5–10 per cent of their original populations.

The good news is that some populations are showing signs of recovery (although we do not have sufficiently accurate estimates for many to determine whether numbers are increasing or not). But, incredibly, we still have not learnt the lessons of the past. Norway, Iceland and Japan persist in hunting whales in the North Atlantic, the North Pacific and the Antarctic – in blatant defiance of world opinion and of a 1986 moratorium on commercial whaling agreed by the International Whaling Commission.

There has been some progress in recent years, albeit with inevitable setbacks. In March 2014, for example, after a four-year court case brought by Australia, the UN's International Court of Justice (ICJ) – the highest court in the world – ruled that Japan's so-called scientific whaling in the Antarctic was illegal because it was not conducted 'for purposes of scientific research'. Despite claims by Tokyo, it was nothing more than commercial whaling in disguise. This once-in-a-generation decision – it was the first time an environmental issue had ever made it to the ICJ – meant that Antarctic whaling could end for good.

There was a brief pause in whaling. But this lasted for just one year before Japanese whalers presented a pitifully weak justification for carrying on (basically,

Inupiaq subsistence whalers hunting a Bowhead Whale off Barrow, Alaska.

a revised 'research plan') and suddenly announced in a declaration to the UN that Japan would no longer be bound by ICJ jurisdiction regarding living marine resources. The following season, in 2015/16, Japanese whalers were again slaughtering whales in the Antarctic. They took 333 Minke Whales (over 200 of them pregnant females). Then the whaling ships set sail again in November 2016, for another Antarctic season. For some reason, Japan holds whaling to be so important that it will risk further international criticism and condemnation to pursue it.

As well as commercial whaling, so-called aboriginal subsistence whaling continues in North America (as well as in Russia, Greenland and St Vincent and The Grenadines), with catch limits set by the International Whaling Commission. In the US, there is just one official aboriginal hunt. A total of up to 336 Bowhead Whales can be landed from the Bering-Chukchi-Beaufort Seas stock, in the period 2013–18, with no more than 67 whales struck in any one year. In theory, the hunt is shared between the native people of Alaska and of Chukotka, Russia, but in practice the vast majority are taken by Alaska. The IWC has also approved a hunt of Gray Whales in the Eastern North Pacific, with a total catch of 744 whales (no more than 140 in any one year) allowed for the same period, 2013–18. Officially, this is shared between the people of Chukotka and the Makah tribe in Washington State, although the US government is still considering an official – and highly controversial – request from the Makah Tribe to take up to five Gray Whales per year from this quota.

Canada withdrew from the International Whaling Commission in 1982 after the vote to impose the moratorium, although it continues to ban commercial whaling in its own waters. However, it does still allow aboriginal whaling, and very small numbers of Bowhead Whales are taken by the Inuit in the eastern Arctic and by the Inuvialuit in the western Arctic.

Apart from conservation concerns, another major issue with whaling is that it is virtually impossible to kill a large whale humanely at sea (although it is possible to kill stranded animals humanely). In some cases, it can take as long as an hour for them to die agonizing deaths after explosive harpoons have blown huge, gaping holes in their bodies (even longer if traditional harpoons or rifles are used). As one ex-whaler commented: 'If whales could scream, whaling would have stopped many years ago.'

Large whales are not the only cetaceans to be hunted. It is believed that tens of thousands of small whales, dolphins and porpoises are killed every year in seas and oceans around the world, although the true extent of the problem is unknown. They are killed for human consumption, to reduce the perceived competition with commercial fisheries, and for bait. Nets, knives, rifles, hand-held harpoons and even explosive harpoons are used for the slaughter.

Narwhal are hunted by the Inuit in Canada, for example. The vitamin C-rich muktuk (which is the skin and adhering blubber) is highly valued by Arctic residents who have little access to fresh fruit and vegetables, and the meat is usually used as dog food. Narwhal tusks still command a high price, too, despite many limitations on international trade. Currently, about 1,240 Narwhal are officially landed in Canada every year (they are shot with rifles). But despite official harvest limits – which may or may not be sustainable – there are doubts about the accuracy of these figures. There is also major concern about the significant (but unknown) number struck and killed, but lost (so not counted); many Narwhal in Arctic Canada bear bullet wounds in testament.

Some small cetacean hunts are called 'drive fisheries' – although it would be more accurate to call them 'drive hunts' – and, again, they are not subject to any form of international control. One, in particular, has been in the news a great deal since the release of the Oscar-winning documentary *The Cove*. Every winter, from September to April, more than 1,000 dolphins are slaughtered in a cove at Taiji, on the south coast of Japan. Another couple of hundred are kept alive for sale to marine parks and aquaria around the world (although many die of shock before they get to their final destinations). Most of the animals killed are Bottlenose Dolphins, but Risso's Dolphins, Striped Dolphins, Pantropical Spotted Dolphins, Short-finned Pilot Whales and other species also get caught up in the hunt.

The Taiji fishermen have responded to international public abhorrence by constructing an elaborate structure of tarpaulin curtains that they draw across the shoreline to hide the killing from the press, conservation and animal welfare campaigners, and the public. But you can still see the blood-red seawater draining out of the cove (although the fishermen are even attempting to hide this, by ramming wooden plugs into the dolphins' wounds to stop the blood flow – something that actually prolongs the time it takes for them to die).

Capture for live display

Whales, dolphins and porpoises are the unfortunate stars of aquariums, marine parks and zoos around the world. Every year, millions of people flock to see them 'kissing' their trainers, fetching balls, jumping through hoops, performing somersaults and making synchronized leaps in choreographed shows often accompanied by loud music. But their permanent 'smiles' often hide an awful inner suffering and many people – myself included – believe that keeping them in captivity is ethically indefensible.

Since the first – largely unsuccessful – attempts to capture and exhibit Belugas and Bottlenose Dolphins in the early 1860s, many different cetacean species have been held in captivity at one time or another. The only real limitation is size: apart from two young Gray Whales, which were kept for about a year each, no one has managed to exhibit great whales. Nowadays, four species dominate: Common Bottlenose and Indo-Pacific Bottlenose dolphins, Beluga and Killer Whale. These are the ones that tend to survive longer in captivity, perform well in shows and are relatively easy to capture.

They are kept in a bewildering range of establishments, from hotel swimming pools and badly run zoos, where they are poorly treated, to more natural sea pens and professional marine parks. In most cases, the animals have nowhere to go in bare and featureless concrete tanks, they can no longer hunt or hear the sounds of the sea, they are unable to dive into the murky depths and they may even be deprived of natural sunlight. They have to acclimatize to a diet of dead fish, the presence of noisy

In North America, 65 zoos and marine parks keep whales and dolphins in captivity.

human observers and a severe lack of familiar company. Shy animals cannot escape from aggressive ones and they may have to live with several different species in groupings that would seldom, if ever, exist in the wild; or, of course, they are forced to live alone.

Often, they simply cannot cope. They repeatedly circle their small tanks, develop stereotyped behavior, stop vocalizing, become aggressive or depressed, and often die prematurely. Yet facilities are still opening around the world – and they all need new animals to stock their tanks. Some Bottlenose Dolphins and small numbers of other species are bred in captivity. But many are still being taken from the wild in places like the Caribbean, Japan and Russia. Russia still captures live Killer Whales and Belugas for export and captive display.

The people who keep cetaceans argue that captivity is a simple trade-off. The animals lose their freedom and natural companions in return for escaping the two biggest challenges faced in the wild: going hungry and being eaten. They also claim that their choreographed shows are educational.

But the reality is entirely different. Most dolphinaria are run primarily as commercial enterprises in which the whales and dolphins are nothing more than financial assets. The shows are just entertainment for profit (whales and dolphins are worth a lot of money), and do little more than perpetuate the domineering and manipulative attitude we tend to have toward nature.

There are currently no fewer than 65 dolphinaria in North America (32 in the United States, 2 in Canada and 31 in Mexico), displaying 950–1,000 cetaceans of 10 different species. The vast majority of these animals are Common Bottlenose Dolphins, but there are also significant numbers of Belugas and Killer Whales, as well as Short-finned Pilot and False Killer Whales, Pacific White-sided, Atlantic Spotted, Rough-toothed and Commerson's dolphins, and Harbor Porpoises.

Many of these were caught in the wild. No fewer than 56 Killer Whales, for example, were captured for public display in British Columbia–Washington State waters during the late 1960s and early 1970s. So many Bottlenose Dolphins were captured in Mexican waters that they were officially classified 'at risk' under Mexican law.

Nowadays, in theory, in the United States it is still possible to capture wild cetaceans for public display, but in reality no permits have been issued since 1993. Similarly, the import of wild cetaceans from elsewhere in the world was last permitted in 1992. In June 2012, Georgia Aquarium applied for a permit to import 18 Belugas captured in the Sea of Okhotsk, Russia, which would have been divided up among several aquariums, but the application was denied. Meanwhile, SeaWorld recently signed a pledge to never again take whales and dolphins from the wild.

The situation is similar in Canada, where a permit is needed to capture wild cetaceans, but none has been issued since 1992. Currently, there is no specific legislation that prevents the importation of wild cetaceans caught elsewhere in the world, but the last time that happened was in 2001. Mexico was still capturing Bottlenose Dolphins until 2002 when, following a particularly scandalous and violent capture in La Paz Bay, no more cetaceans were allowed to be taken unless for 'scientific or educational' purposes (an intentionally vague term). Importing cetaceans from other countries (again, except for scientific or educational purposes) has been banned since 2006.

At the end of the day, it is not essential to see whales and dolphins in real life to understand and appreciate them; after all, it is possible to learn about the Moon without actually standing on it. So that is not an argument for keeping them in captivity. But the biggest irony is that it is almost as easy to see them in the wild as it is in concrete tanks – in fact, in some parts of the world you can see whales and dolphins, wild and free, from the steps of dolphinaria that are holding their hapless counterparts captive.

Conflicts with fisheries

Since the 1950s, the staggering growth of many modern fisheries and the introduction of increasingly destructive fishing methods have spelt disaster for cetaceans around the world. Fishing is currently the most serious conservation threat to most marine mammals. There are two main issues: bycatch (when they get caught in fishing gear intended for other species) and overfishing (leaving less prey available for them).

In some parts of the world fishermen also intentionally kill cetaceans and other marine mammals, either to use as bait or because they view them as competition for 'their' fish. Yet whales are not responsible for declines in fish stocks – humans have to take responsibility for that – and research shows that culling them will not help commercial fisheries to recover.

Bycatch

Hundreds of thousands of whales, dolphins and porpoises – one estimate suggests 308,000 every year – die slow, lingering deaths in fishing nets and other fishing gear. Entanglement can lead to drowning, injuries, infection and starvation. This bycatch is a significant problem for most, if

not all, cetaceans. And it is probably the most pressing and acute threat to small cetaceans. It is not a new problem – conservationists have been ringing alarm bells for more than 25 years – but it is nowhere near solved. The bottom line is that bycatch is the biggie.

Driftnetting is one of the worst culprits and, indeed, is one of the most indiscriminate methods of fishing ever devised. Hanging in the water near the surface, unseen and nearly invisible, driftnets are carried freely with the ocean currents and winds. Dubbed 'walls of death', or 'curtains of death', they catch everything in their path from seabirds and turtles to whales and dolphins. The United Nations took action by calling on all member nations to agree to a moratorium on large-scale high seas driftnets over 1.5 miles long by the end of 1992 (before the moratorium some driftnets reached lengths of 31–37 miles). The global ban has had a very positive impact, but it is still being violated by many commercial fishing operations. So progress is being made, albeit much too slowly.

Gillnets are similar to driftnets in design, although much smaller, and pose another serious threat. Since they are relatively inexpensive, these death traps are used along coastlines and in major rivers worldwide, from New Zealand and Sri Lanka to Canada and Britain. Tens of thousands of small cetaceans are believed to drown in them every year.

But perhaps the most infamous culprit, responsible for killing more dolphins in the past 50 years or so than any other human activity, is the tuna-fishing industry. In the eastern tropical Pacific, a stretch of ocean extending from southern California to Chile and covering an area roughly the size of Canada, tuna fishing has directly caused the deaths of more than 6 million dolphins.

Quite simply, the tuna boats deliberately encircle dolphin schools to catch the tuna beneath them. The Eastern Spinner Dolphin stock was reduced to 44 per cent of its original size in just a few years. Fortunately, public outrage forced the authorities to introduce new rules and regulations, which include releasing dolphins from the nets when they are captured, and the scale of the slaughter has dropped to thousands of deaths a year rather than hundreds of thousands. It is still too many, however, and the effects of stress from capture are an ongoing concern. There is also mounting evidence to suggest that dolphins are being set upon by tuna-fishing fleets in other parts of the world.

Solutions to the bycatch problem fall into two main categories: altering the behavior of the fishing industry and altering the behavior of the cetaceans. Conservation efforts include reducing fishing effort, which is good for the long-term sustainability of the fisheries as well as cetaceans; implementing changes to fishing gear and practices; seasonal closures of fishing grounds; the establishment of marine sanctuaries and other no-fishing areas; and the use of 'pingers' – acoustic alarms to alert the animals to the presence of nets, which work for some species under some circumstances. There has been progress – though nowhere near enough – and it is hindered by an almost complete lack of reporting on a global scale.

Overfishing

Cetaceans are also threatened by the sheer scale of modern fisheries, which over-exploit fish stocks with scant regard for the future health of the world's oceans. One estimate suggests that there were at least six times more fish in our oceans a century ago than there are today.

Increased human demand for fish, and loans and subsidies for fishing fleets, have resulted in too many industrial-scale boats chasing too few fish. Large, profit-seeking commercial fleets – which have supplanted local fishermen as the world's source of seafood – are extremely aggressive, scouring the world's oceans and developing ever more sophisticated methods and technologies for extracting their target species.

Worldwide catches reached a peak in the late 1980s, when about 90 million tonnes of fish were being taken from the oceans every year. But many large-fish populations collapsed and yields have declined or stagnated in the years since. Instead of pulling back – which would be the sensible thing to do – commercial fleets are becoming increasingly aggressive and cut-throat in their determination to make a profit.

Not surprisingly, two-thirds of the world's fish stocks are now either fished at their limits or over-fished. Experts grimly predict that, if fishing rates continue apace all the world's fisheries will have collapsed by 2048.

There is only one possible long-term solution: we have to re-build over-exploited stocks, by relieving fishing pressure. And the only way to do that is with aggressive fisheries management. In other words, there needs to be a zero tolerance policy on the illegal fishing and unsustainable harvesting that still plague the industry.

Pollution

Pollution is a silent, insidious and widespread killer. Given that we dump staggering quantities of industrial waste, agricultural pesticides, herbicides and fertilizers, radioactive discharges, untreated sewage, oil, detergents, plastics and a wide

A dead Minke Whale tangled in fishing line.

variety of other pollutants directly into the sea every day, it's not really surprising.

Over 80 per cent of these pollutants come from land-based activities. For instance, there is an area of floating plastic debris – estimated to be the size of Texas – in the central North Pacific. It has been dubbed the Pacific Trash Vortex because all the pollutants have been trapped by the currents of the North Pacific Gyre. However, its more popular (and perhaps more appropriate) name is the Great Pacific Garbage Patch. A similar garbage patch has recently been described in the North Atlantic and there are believed to be plastic debris convergence zones in the three other sub-tropical gyres. Another example is the Mississippi River Delta: each summer it is dominated by a vast 'dead zone' – the size of New Jersey – caused by phenomenal quantities of nitrogen and phosphorus being washed out to sea from far inland (the Mississippi River Basin drains much of the United States).

Sometimes, such as during an oil spill, the impact of marine pollution is obvious. And some pollutants are so toxic, or are present in such huge quantities, that they result in immediate death. But the consequences are often more subtle and it can be difficult to evaluate the precise details of the damage caused. The pollutants may be responsible for weeks, months or even years of prolonged suffering. Among marine mammals, in particular, there has been a dramatic rise in a host of devastating illnesses – such as problems with their nervous and digestive systems, liver disease, and growth and development issues – as well as a general lowering of disease resistance and a loss of fertility. Worst of all, there has been an alarming growth in cases of cancer among whales, dolphins, porpoises, seals and sea lions.

Clean-up operations after the 2010 Deepwater Horizon Gulf of Mexico oil spill.

Unfortunately, cetaceans and other top predators are particularly vulnerable to pollution, because the toxins are passed along the food chain: minute quantities are picked up by marine plankton, which are then eaten by fish and squid, and these in turn are eaten by cetaceans and pinnipeds. The farther up the food chain, the higher the concentration of toxins. Worse still, much of this build-up is passed from one generation to the next. A lactating female, through her milk, can deliver the toxins in highly concentrated doses to her young calf. Consequently, many cetaceans have contamination levels millions of times higher than the water in which they live.

It is hard to believe but, despite all the warnings, many governments continue to pretend that the world's seas and oceans have an infinite capacity to absorb the waste products of human activities. The severely declining health of ocean-going mammals sends us an undeniable message – they are showing us our own future, unless we change our ways.

Habitat degradation and disturbance

It's well known that one of the greatest threats to terrestrial wildlife is habitat degradation, whether it be tropical rainforest destruction, desertification, wetland drainage or road building across important grasslands and heathland. Whales, dolphins and porpoises also suffer from habitat degradation and disturbance, although in different ways.

The main problem areas are rivers, areas close to shore and anywhere near human activities farther out to sea. Coastal and riverbank development, land reclamation, deep-sea dumping, oil, gas and mineral exploration, dredging, commercial fish farming, heavy boat traffic, and the effects of land-based activities such as deforestation and river damming are all to blame. Their consequences can be quite subtle, such as increased amounts of sediment, changes in salinity or electromagnetic disturbance, but they can also be extremely dramatic by forcing changes in prey availability or literally scaring cetaceans away from preferred foraging or breeding areas.

One solution to the problem is to provide the animals with special sanctuaries, or marine reserves, in which they can feed and breed in relative safety. These critical areas need to be quite extensive – to protect the cetaceans throughout their range – and must take into account fluctuating oceanographic conditions. Some already exist (although they frequently need better legislation to be truly effective) and, of course, many more are needed.

Noise pollution

Even marine sanctuaries cannot protect cetaceans from underwater noise pollution. Caused by a variety of human activities, from coastal development and seismic surveys to piledriving for wind farms, heavy shipping and military-related activities, this is a particular problem for cetaceans because they rely on sound for many of their day-to-day activities. Being able to hear is a life-or-death matter for them – in the way that being able to see or smell is a life-or-death matter for most animals on land – and yet we are drowning out the noises that marine mammals rely on for their survival.

Impacts of excessive noise include temporary and permanent hearing loss; abandonment of preferred feeding and breeding grounds; disruption of communications, mating and hunting;

immeasurable amounts of stress; and even beach strandings and death. But identifying how much noise is too much can be surprisingly difficult. It is not only the loudness of a noise that is important, but its frequency as well. Some frequencies are likely to be more disturbing than others, depending on the operating range of different species. There are other considerations, too, such as whether the noise is continuous or intermittent.

There are solutions, but these can be extremely difficult to introduce and enforce. Take wind farms, for example: today's wind farms are large and require long and continuous construction periods – piledriving, in particular, produces a huge amount of underwater noise. But there is a possible solution – to surround the construction area with curtains of bubbles – that can reduce noise levels by up to 65 per cent. Meanwhile, the International Maritime Organization (IMO) has recently adopted voluntary guidelines to reduce underwater noise from commercial ships, specifically to reduce impact on marine life. These include: guidance for designing quieter ships and on reducing noise emitted by existing ships (everything from slowing down to polishing ship propellers).

Two sources of noise are believed to be particularly damaging: seismic testing and military sonar.

Seismic testing is used to find oil and gas reserves deep underneath the seabed. Industrial high-pressure airguns, which are towed behind ships, direct a series of loud booms toward the seabed to reveal the structure of underlying rock formations. The noise from these airguns is louder than the noise of oil and gas production itself. Imagine dynamite going off in your living room every 10 seconds, 24 hours a day, for

Like all cetaceans, Long-beaked Common Dolphins are highly vulnerable to noise pollution.

days or weeks at a time, and you begin to understand why seismic testing is a colossal problem for marine mammals. This is not an exaggeration – hydrophones placed in the middle of the North Atlantic were able to record the sounds of seismic airguns from more than 1,800 miles away. And, of course, seismic airguns are just the first step toward dangerous and dirty offshore drilling, with all its associated problems.

Military sonar has been in the news a great deal recently – and deservedly so. Used to detect enemy submarines, it is a dangerous technology that deafens, disorientates and kills cetaceans with the loudest sounds ever emitted in the world's oceans.

Two active sonar systems are currently being deployed by navies around the world to detect ultra-quiet submarines that are not audible to other listening systems. The Mid Frequency Active Sonar (MFAS) has been in use since the late 1980s and is operational on more than 150 ships; it is effective over a relatively short range of tens of miles. The newer Low Frequency Active Sonar (LFAS) is operational on a handful of ships (owned by the US and the UK) and is effective over a range of hundreds of miles.

Both systems work in a similar way. They emit extremely loud sounds into the sea, which are generated by massive transmitters towed behind ships, and listen for echoes returning from submarines and other targets. By the US Navy's own estimates, even 300 miles from the source, low-frequency sonic waves can retain an intensity 100 times higher than the level known to alter the behavior of large whales. During testing off the coast of California, the noise was detected on the other side of the North Pacific.

The US Navy has been leading the way in sonar testing – frequently running tests in defiance of federal law and without conducting sufficient environmental impact assessments – but other NATO countries, including the UK, France, the Netherlands and Germany, have developed (or are developing) similar systems.

Whatever the source of the noise, there is one clear solution: to decrease the sound levels and exposure to cetaceans.

Ship strikes

Many whales, dolphins and porpoises are injured, or even killed, after being hit by everything from large commercial ships to recreational speedboats and jet skis. The obvious solutions are speed limits, route changes and no-go areas, according to season and locality. These can be difficult to introduce – and even more difficult to enforce – but experience in Boston Harbor, Massachusetts, and the Bay of Fundy, Canada, for example, prove them to be very effective.

Climate change

Ultimately, the effects of climate change could trump all other threats to cetaceans. Global warming is likely to result in an increase in sea temperature, a corresponding retreat of sea ice, a rise in sea levels, higher oceanic acidity and changes in upwellings and other ocean processes. It will shift the state of the world's oceans toward a future of reduced productivity and biodiversity.

How these changes will affect different species of whales, dolphins and porpoises is difficult to predict, especially as there simply is not enough data and it does not go back far enough. Also, the impacts are likely to vary from location to location. A simple rise in sea temperature, for example, might even benefit some species, though it is more likely to have a deleterious effect on many others. It could alter their migrations and local movements, expand or contract their breeding and feeding ranges, and change the timings of their seasonal cycles. It might also influence what they eat, their reproductive success, their susceptibility to disease and, ultimately, their abundance. We are already seeing evidence of such changes in many parts of the world.

Ship strikes and propeller injuries are a serious hazard – even to Blue Whales.

Then there are changes associated with the impact of global warming on people. Melting ice, for example, will also open up more areas to industrialization, fishing and shipping. And that, inevitably, will bring its own problems.

The Intergovernmental Panel on Climate Change (under the auspices of the United Nations, the leading international body for the assessment of climate change) predicts a further temperature rise of between 1.4–5.8°C by the end of the century. Climate change could therefore be the knockout punch for many species that are already under stress from hunting, conflicts with fisheries, noise pollution and the myriad other threats they face.

The upshot is quite simple. Unless we wake up – and dramatically alter our approach to marine conservation very soon – the outlook for whales, dolphins and porpoises is rather bleak.

NORTH AMERICA'S WHALES, DOLPHINS AND PORPOISES

Comparison of species (not to scale)

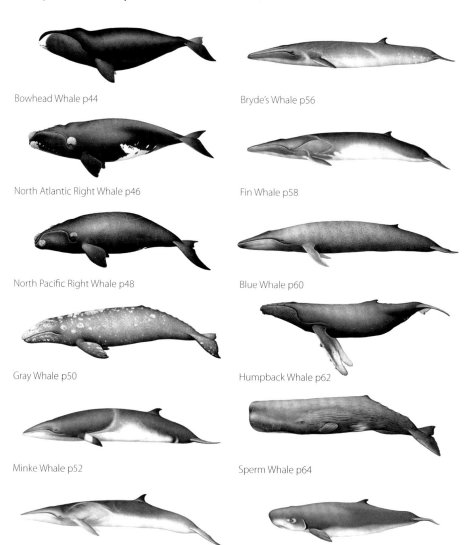

Bowhead Whale p44

Bryde's Whale p56

North Atlantic Right Whale p46

Fin Whale p58

North Pacific Right Whale p48

Blue Whale p60

Gray Whale p50

Humpback Whale p62

Minke Whale p52

Sperm Whale p64

Sei Whale p54

Pygmy Sperm Whale p66

Dwarf Sperm Whale p68

Sowerby's Beaked Whale p82

Narwhal p70

Blainville's Beaked Whale p84

Beluga p72

Ginkgo-toothed Beaked Whale p86

Baird's Beaked Whale p74

Perrin's Beaked Whale p88

Unnamed Beaked Whale p76

Hubbs' Beaked Whale p90

Cuvier's Beaked Whale p78

Pygmy Beaked Whale p92

Northern Bottlenose Whale p80

Gervais' Beaked Whale p94

True's Beaked Whale p96

Melon-headed Whale p110

Stejneger's Beaked Whale p98

False Killer Whale p112

Longman's Beaked Whale p100

Rough-toothed Dolphin p114

Killer Whale p102

Short-beaked Common Dolphin p116

Short-finned Pilot Whale p104

Long-beaked Common Dolphin p118

Long-finned Pilot Whale p106

Atlantic Spotted Dolphin p120

Pygmy Killer Whale p108

Pantropical Spotted Dolphin p122

Spinner Dolphin p124

Pacific White-sided Dolphin p138

Clymene Dolphin p126

Fraser's Dolphin p140

Striped Dolphin p128

Northern Right Whale Dolphin p142

Common Bottlenose Dolphin p130

Dall's Porpoise p144

Risso's Dolphin p132

Vaquita p146

White-beaked Dolphin p134

Harbor Porpoise p148

Atlantic White-sided Dolphin p136

Bowhead Whale

Named for its enormous and distinctive bow-shaped skull, the Bowhead is the only large whale that lives exclusively in the Arctic. With a layer of blubber up to 16 inches thick and an ability to create its own breathing holes by breaking through the ice, it is well adapted to life in its freezing home. When lying at the surface, most adults show two distinct humps in profile. The triangular hump in front is the head, the depression is the neck and the rounded hump in the rear is the back. The Bowhead has the longest baleen plates of any whale – many have been recorded over 9ft long and there is a disputed claim of one measuring 17ft. It is also renowned as one of the longest-lived animals on Earth – the record, so far, is 211 years; that particular whale was killed by whalers and, since it was fit and healthy, may have lived much longer. Heavily hunted by commercial whalers for several centuries, a relatively small number of bowheads are still being taken each year by native peoples of Alaska, United States; Chukotka, Russia; West Greenland; and Nunavut, Canada.

Identification

- V-shaped blow
- No dorsal fin
- Black, rotund body
- Irregular white patch on chin (with black spots)
- Two distinct humps in profile
- Huge head with strongly arched mouth
- No callosities or barnacles
- Often raises flukes when diving

Surface profile

Fluking

Spyhopping

Breaching

At a glance

Alternative names: Greenland Right Whale, Greenland Whale, Arctic Right Whale, Arctic Whale.

Scientific name: *Balaena mysticetus.*

Adult size: 45–65ft (14–20m); 65–110 tons (60–100 tonnes); females larger than males.

Diet: mainly krill, copepods and other small- and medium-sized crustaceans.

Behavior: slow swimmer but may breach, lobtail, flipper-slap and spyhop.

Breeding: single calf born late April–early June, after a gestation period of 13–14 months.

Distribution: cold Arctic and sub-Arctic waters, generally between 55°N and 85°N, and rarely far from pack ice; normally migrates to the high Arctic in summer, but retreats southward with advancing ice edge in winter.

World population: best estimate 23,000.

Best places to look in North America: Nunavut, Inuvik.

Distribution Map

North Atlantic Right Whale

With no dorsal fin, a dark rotund body and an enormous head covered in raised patches of rough skin, the Right Whale is easy to identify. The patches of skin are known as callosities and, although their function is still a mystery, each whale has a different arrangement on its head that enables scientists to tell one individual from another. The North Atlantic Right Whale was once common on both sides of the Atlantic, but was a popular target for commercial whalers for many centuries and is now among the rarest large whales in the world. Since it was protected in the late 1930s, it has shown slow signs of recovery in the west, though not in the east. The vast majority of the 525-odd survivors live in the western North Atlantic, with no more than a handful left in Europe. It is unclear whether Europe has a remnant population or occasional sightings are stray animals from the west. North Atlantic Right Whales are virtually identical to two other species – the North Pacific Right Whale, which also occurs in North America, and the Southern Right Whale – but the three never meet on their ocean travels.

Identification

- V-shaped blow
- Black, rotund body
- Irregular white patches on underside
- Broad back with no dorsal fin
- Large head covered in callosities
- Strongly arched mouthline
- Large paddle-shaped flippers
- Usually raises flukes when diving

Surface profile   Fluking   Spyhopping   Breaching

At a glance

Alternative names: Northern Right Whale, Black Right Whale.

Scientific name: *Eubalaena glacialis*.

Adult size: 49–52ft (15–16m); 34–78 tons (30–70 tonnes); females larger than males.

Diet: tiny crustaceans – mainly copepods and krill.

Behavior: slow swimmer but surprisingly acrobatic and frequently breaches, flipper-slaps and lobtails; can be very inquisitive and will approach boats.

Breeding: single calf born December–March, after a gestation period of 12–13 months.

Distribution: main population in the western North Atlantic, but occasional sightings in Europe.

World population: about 500 in the western North Atlantic (plus low tens in Europe).

Best places to look in North America: Bay of Fundy.

Distribution Map

North Pacific Right Whale

There are no significant differences in appearance between the North Pacific Right Whale and its close relative the North Atlantic Right Whale, though North Pacific individuals can grow a little larger. Recently split into two separate species (they were previously known together as Northern Right Whales), they are both exceptionally stocky animals with enormous heads. Named for being the 'right' whales to catch – they were easy to approach, slow swimmers, lived close to shore, normally floated when dead, and provided large quantities of valuable oil, meat and baleen or whalebone – Right Whales are now extremely rare in the North Pacific. Indeed, they are considered to be one of the most critically endangered of all the great whales. There were probably at least 11,000 of them at one time (possibly as many as 30,000) but, as a result of more than a century of heavy exploitation, barely 400–500 survive today. Most of these are in the western Pacific (there are believed to be no more than 30–50 in the eastern population). Sightings in North America are extremely rare, except during summer and early fall in a small area in Alaska.

Identification

- V-shaped blow
- Black, rotund body
- Irregular white patches on underside
- Broad back with no dorsal fin
- Large head covered in callosities
- Strongly arched mouthline
- Large paddle-shaped flippers
- Usually raises flukes when diving

Surface profile

Fluking

Spyhopping

Breaching

At a glance

Alternative names: Northern Right Whale.

Scientific name: *Eubalaena japonica*.

Adult size: 49–56ft (15–17m); 34–90 tons (30–80 tonnes); females larger than males.

Diet: tiny crustaceans – mainly copepods and krill.

Behavior: slow swimmer, but surprisingly acrobatic and frequently breaches, flipper-slaps and lobtails.

Breeding: little known; gestation period probably 12–13 months.

Distribution: main population in the western North Pacific, with dangerously low numbers in the east.

World population: possibly about 400–500 (including only 30–50 animals in eastern North Pacific).

Best places to look in North America: nowhere for reliable sightings. Occasional sightings in Aleutian Islands & Pribilof Islands.

Distribution Map

Gray Whale

The Gray Whale is an inveterate traveller: the round-trip distance between its winter breeding grounds in Baja California, Mexico, and its summer feeding grounds in the Bering, Chukchi and Beaufort Seas, can be as much as 12,400 miles. It also has a reputation as one of the friendliest whales in the world, sometimes allowing itself to be stroked and tickled by enthusiastic whale watchers. But by the time Gray Whales were given full official protection in 1946, whaling had driven them dangerously close to extinction. They once occurred in the North Atlantic, but that population was wiped out sometime in the late 1600s or early 1700s. Astonishingly, in May 2010, a single Gray Whale unexpectedly appeared in the Mediterranean Sea – no one knows whether a small, remnant population survives, previously undetected, or if this individual broke all migration records and swam from the North Pacific via the Northwest Passage. Bizarrely, in 2013, a different individual appeared in Walvis Bay, Namibia – the first Gray Whale ever recorded in the southern hemisphere. Only a small number survive in the western North Pacific but, thankfully, in the eastern North Pacific, they have fared much better: the current population matches or even exceeds pre-exploitation levels.

Identification

- Low V-shaped or heart-shaped bushy blow
- Mottled gray, slate blue or gray-brown color
- Narrow head encrusted with barnacles and whale lice
- At surface head looks like top of shallow triangle
- Low hump instead of dorsal fin
- 'Knuckles' between hump and tail
- Usually raises flukes when diving

Surface profile   Fluking   Sailing   Spyhopping   Breaching

At a glance

Alternative names: California/Pacific Gray Whale; rarely – Mussel-digger, Grayback, Scrag Whale, Devilfish (by American whalers).

Scientific name: *Eschrichtius robustus.*

Adult size: 36–49ft (11–15m); 18–40 tons (16–35 tonnes); females larger than males.

Diet: mainly benthic amphipods, but also mysids and polychaete tube worms; opportunistically takes small schooling fish, red crabs, crab larvae and other prey.

Behavior: lots of surface activity; often exhibits 'friendly' behavior toward small whale-watching boats on the breeding grounds.

Breeding: single calf born late December to mid-February, after a gestation period of 12–13.5 months.

Distribution: North Pacific and adjacent waters; in recent years, at least one individual in the North Atlantic and another in the South Atlantic.

World population: about 18–21,000 in the eastern North Pacific; probably fewer than 130 in the western North Pacific.

Best places to look in North America: Southeast Alaska, Northwestern Gulf of Alaska, Aleutian Islands & Pribilof Islands, Westport & the Olympic Coast, Oregon, California (including Monterey Bay), Vancouver Island (west coast), Baja California (breeding lagoons, Pacific Coast, Los Cabos & Gorda Banks).

Distribution Map

Minke Whale

The Minke is the smallest and most abundant of the rorqual whales. It is slim, with a sharply pointed head, and shows relatively little of itself as it blows, surfaces and rolls through the water. Its smaller size compared with other great whales provides the first indication of the species, and the way the tip of its snout breaks the surface first and at a slight angle is another useful identification feature. It was reputedly named after a novice eighteenth-century Norwegian whaler, called Meincke, who misidentified it as a much more valuable Blue Whale and was ribbed by his shipmates for his mistake. These days it is the baleen whale most hunted by commercial whalers from Norway, Iceland and Japan. It can be nervous and is difficult to see well in many parts of the world, but in some areas it has learnt to recognize whale-watch vessels and will sometimes approach to within a few yards. Three sub-species are recognized – North Atlantic, North Pacific and Dwarf Minke Whale (which is found only in the southern hemisphere). An entirely separate species, the Antarctic Minke Whale (*Balaenoptera bonaerensis*), was officially recognized in the late 1990s.

Identification

- Low, indistinct blow
- Small and slender
- Sharply pointed snout breaks surface first
- Relatively large, falcate dorsal fin
- White bands on flippers in some populations
- Single longitudinal ridge on head
- Tailstock strongly arched when diving
- Does not raise flukes when diving

Surface profile

Spyhopping

Breaching

At a glance

Alternative names: Common Minke Whale, Northern Minke Whale; rarely – Little Finner, Little Piked Whale, Pikehead, Lesser Finback, Lesser Rorqual.

Scientific name: *Balaenoptera acutorostrata.*

Adult size: 21–30ft (6.5–9m); 5.5–10 tons (5–9 tonnes); females larger than males.

Diet: crustaceans (mainly krill) and small schooling fish.

Behavior: sometimes spyhops and breaches.

Breeding: single calf born throughout the year, with peaks in January and June (in the North Pacific – different elsewhere) after a gestation period of 10–11 months.

Distribution: widely distributed from the tropics to the edge of the polar ice (mainly in warmer waters in winter and cooler waters in summer); primarily coastal and inshore, but can be seen offshore.

World population: no accurate figures, but hundreds of thousands.

Best places to look in North America: Southeast Alaska, Northwestern Gulf of Alaska, Aleutian Islands & Pribilof Islands, San Juan Islands & Puget Sound, California, New England, Eastern Seaboard (New York to Georgia), Vancouver Island (Johnstone Strait, Salish Sea), Bay of Fundy, Newfoundland, St Lawrence River & Gulf of St Lawrence.

Distribution Map

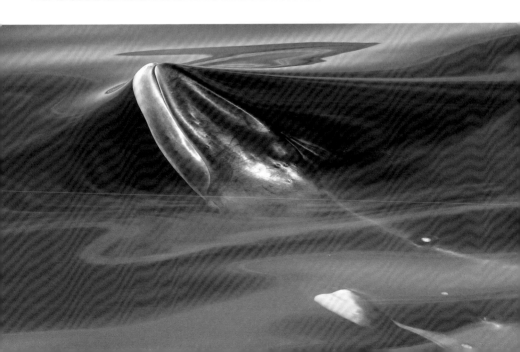

Sei Whale

The least known of all the rorqual whales, the Sei Whale usually lives far from shore, tends to be elusive and does not seem to gather in the same specific areas season after season or year after year. No commercial whale-watch operation is dedicated to observing this unpredictable species, although it is sometimes encountered opportunistically during tours specializing in Minkes, Humpbacks and other large whales. Named after a Norwegian word for the fish we call Pollock, for many years it was confused with the superficially similar Bryde's Whale (which has three ridges on the top of its head instead of the single ridge characteristic of the Sei Whale). As with all members of the rorqual family, individuals in the southern hemisphere tend to be larger than those in the northern hemisphere; Sei Whales in each of the two hemispheres are considered to be separate sub-species and differ subtly in the number of throat grooves and baleen plates. Sei Whales were heavily exploited by commercial whalers, especially during the 1960s and early 1970s, and the population has been severely depleted. The name 'sei' is normally pronounced 'say'.

Identification

- Mostly dark gray or brown
- Fairly tall, prominent blow
- Large, slender body
- Single longitudinal ridge on head
- Both sides of head and lower jaw same color
- Prominent, falcate dorsal fin
- Does not arch tailstock or raise flukes when diving
- Appears to sink into dive

Surface profile   Breaching

At a glance

Alternative names: rarely – Sardine Whale, Pollock/Pollack Whale, Coalfish Whale, Japan Finner, Rudolphi's Rorqual, Northern Rorqual.

Scientific name: *Balaenoptera borealis.*

Adult size: 39–59ft (12–18m); 17–45 tons (15–40 tonnes); females larger than males.

Diet: more varied diet than most other baleen whales, including krill, copepods and other small crustaceans, and schooling fish.

Behavior: blowhole and dorsal fin usually visible simultaneously; seldom breaches; tends to be shy of boats.

Breeding: single calf born in mid-winter, after a gestation period of 10–12 months.

Distribution: widely distributed from the tropics to the poles in both hemispheres and in all major oceans (though most common in mid-latitude temperate zones); mainly in warmer waters in winter and cooler waters in summer.

World population: no recent estimate, but probably at least 80,000; 74,000 taken by whalers in the North Pacific (mainly between the 1950s and the 1970s).

Best places to look in North America: nowhere for reliable sightings. Occasional sightings in Northwestern Gulf of Alaska, Aleutian Islands & Pribilof Islands, California, New England, Eastern Seaboard (New York to Georgia), Newfoundland, St Lawrence River & Gulf of St Lawrence, Nunavut, Baja California (Pacific Coast).

Distribution Map

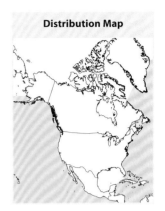

Bryde's Whale

Unlike most other large whales, Bryde's Whales do not migrate long distances between separate feeding and breeding grounds each spring and summer, preferring to stay in warm tropical and sub-tropical waters with temperatures higher than 16°C (61°F) year-round. They make only short migrations – or none at all – and rarely visit cold waters. Named after a Norwegian consul, Johan Bryde, who helped to build the first whaling factory in Durban, South Africa, in 1909, the Bryde's Whale is unique in having three parallel, longitudinal ridges on its head (other members of the rorqual family have just one). There may be separate inshore and offshore populations, differing slightly in appearance and behavior, and there seem to be distinct variations from one geographical locality to another. A new species, called Omura's Whale, was named in 2003 – it was previously referred to as the 'Pygmy Bryde's Whale' – and it is possible that other variations of Bryde's Whales will be recognized in the future (a very small but genetically distinct population in the Gulf of Mexico, for example, may be assigned sub-species or even species status). In the meantime, they are lumped together in the 'Bryde's Whale complex'. The name 'Bryde's' is normally pronounced 'Broo-dess'.

Identification

- Large, slender body
- Fairly tall, prominent blow
- Three parallel ridges on head
- Prominent, falcate dorsal fin
- Both sides of head and lower jaw same color
- Irregular dive sequence
- Tailstock arched when diving
- Does not raise flukes when diving

Surface profile

Breaching

At a glance

Alternative names: Tropical Whale, Eden's Whale (possibly a separate species).

Scientific name: *Balaenoptera edeni.*

Adult size: 38–54ft (11.5–16.5m); 13–45 tons (12–40 tonnes); females larger than males.

Diet: mainly schooling fish such as anchovy, mackerel and herring, but also crustaceans, pelagic red crabs, squid and other invertebrates.

Behavior: sometimes inquisitive and may approach whale-watch boats; breaching known in some areas (the whale often leaves the water almost vertically and may arch its back in mid-air).

Breeding: single calf born at any time of the year, after a gestation period of 11–12 months.

Distribution: warm waters worldwide, mainly between 40°N and 40°S, but does sometimes occur outside this broad range.

World population: no recent estimate, but possibly around 70,000–90,000 (including 20,000–30,000 in the North Pacific).

Best places to look in North America: Baja California (Gulf of California).

Distribution Map

Fin Whale

left side

right side

Fin Whales are unusual in having asymmetrical pigmentation on their heads (the only other species in which this is also true is the newly described Omura's Whale). The lower 'lip', mouth cavity and some of the baleen plates are white on the right side, but they are uniformly gray or black on the left side. This may be an adaptation for feeding, perhaps to confuse small prey (Fin Whales often roll onto their right sides when they feed). The second-largest living animal on Earth, after the Blue Whale, the Fin Whale is a sleek and fast swimmer, capable of speeds of over 19 miles per hour. It tends to be more social than some other members of the rorqual family and is often seen in small groups typically of three to seven individuals. Once one of the most abundant of the large whales, it was hunted ruthlessly by commercial whalers – more than 1 million individuals were killed altogether – and today we are left with little more than 10 per cent of the original population. Some populations seem to be resident year-round (such as in the Gulf of California), but most migrate between warmer waters in winter and cooler waters in summer; their movements are less predictable than in some other large whales. There are reports of hybrids between Fin Whales and Blue Whales.

Identification

- Very tall, narrow blow
- Exceptionally large and streamlined
- Backward-sloping dorsal fin
- Single longitudinal ridge on head
- Asymmetrical coloration on head
- Creamy-white chevron between flippers and shoulders
- Rarely raises flukes when diving

Dive sequence

Breaching

At a glance

Alternative names: Finback, Finner; rarely – Razorback, Herring Whale, Common Rorqual.

Scientific name: *Balaenoptera physalus.*

Adult size: 59–88ft (18–27m) (maximum 79ft (24m) in northern hemisphere); 34–100 tons (30–90 tonnes); females larger than males.

Diet: variety of schooling fish, krill and other crustaceans and, to lesser extent, squid (varies seasonally and locally).

Behavior: usually indifferent to boats, neither avoiding them nor approaching them; rarely breaches or spyhops.

Breeding: single calf born in mid-winter, after a gestation period of 11–12 months.

Distribution: deep, mainly oceanic water in tropical, temperate and polar regions worldwide (when seen near shore it is usually where deep water approaches the coast) but most common in cooler waters.

World population: unknown for certain, but possibly as many as 140,000 (including several thousand off the US west coast).

Best places to look in North America: Northwestern Gulf of Alaska, Aleutian Islands & Pribilof Islands, California, New England, Eastern Seaboard (New York to Georgia), Bay of Fundy, Newfoundland, St Lawrence River & Gulf of St Lawrence, Baja California (Pacific Coast, Gulf of California).

Distribution Map

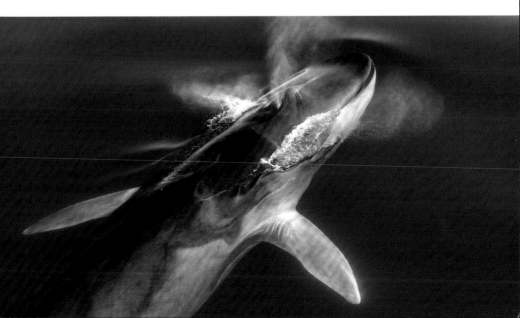

Blue Whale

The largest animal ever to have lived on Earth, the Blue Whale is almost as long as a Boeing 737 and weighs nearly as much as 2,000 people. A length of more than 110ft and a weight of 213 tons (190 tonnes) have been reported, although these are exceptional. The Blue Whale needs so much food that, in terms of weight, it could eat a fully grown African Elephant every day. It also has the loudest voice in the animal kingdom, emitting low-frequency sounds that can travel literally hundreds or even thousands of miles underwater. Sadly, its sheer size made it one of the most sought-after whales during the heyday of modern whaling and as many as 360,000 Blue Whales were killed worldwide. As a result, some populations may never recover. It lives up to its name and picks up the reflected blues of the sea and sky, adding an extra dimension to its basic blue-gray body color; it often looks light blue or even turquoise when it is just beneath the surface. The characteristic mottling on the back and sides of all Blue Whales is used by researchers to recognize individuals.

Identification

- Very tall, slender blow
- Exceptionally large size
- Mottled blue-gray body color
- Tiny, stubby dorsal fin set far back
- Broad, flattened, U-shaped head
- Huge blowhole splashguard
- Extremely thick tailstock
- Often raises flukes when diving

Surface profile

At a glance

Alternative names: rarely – Sulphur-bottom, Sibbald's Rorqual, Great Northern Rorqual.

Scientific name: *Balaenoptera musculus.*

Adult size: 69–95ft (21–29m) (rarely more than 89ft (27m) in northern hemisphere); 90–150 tons (80–135 tonnes) exceptionally 213 tons (190 tonnes); females larger than males.

Diet: mainly krill; some pelagic crabs and very occasionally squid, amphipods and copepods.

Behavior: usually ignores boats, but can be inquisitive and will sometimes approach; breaching is known occasionally in juveniles, but very rarely observed in adults.

Breeding: single calf born in mid-winter, after a gestation period of 10–12 months.

Distribution: worldwide from the tropics to the poles in both hemispheres, although distribution is very patchy; some populations migrate between low-latitude winter breeding grounds and high-latitude summer feeding grounds, but others appear to be resident.

World population: unknown for certain, but possibly fewer than 10,000.

Best places to look in North America: California (including Monterey Bay), St Lawrence River & Gulf of St Lawrence, Baja California (Pacific Coast, Gulf of California).

Distribution Map

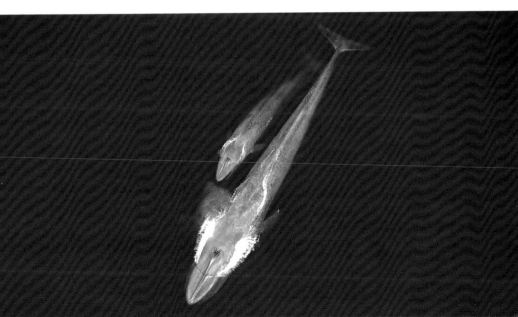

Humpback Whale

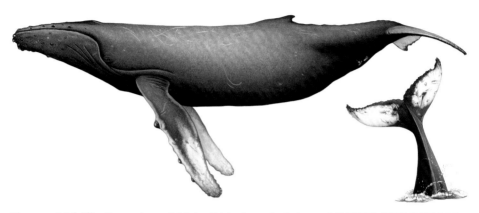

Herman Melville, the author of *Moby Dick*, described the Humpback Whale as 'the most gamesome and lighthearted of all the whales, making more gay foam and whitewater generally than any of them'. Its spectacular breaching, as well as lobtailing, flipper-slapping and spyhopping, make it particularly popular with whale watchers. It is also among the most studied of all the world's large whales, although many aspects of its life are still shrouded in mystery and we are only just beginning to unravel some of its best-kept secrets. Biologists use the distinctive black-and-white markings on the underside of the tail flukes to tell one individual from another, and they have prepared huge catalogs containing photographs of thousands of individually identified Humpbacks around the world. Humpbacks are easy to identify at close range, with their enormous flippers and the knobs or tubercles on the top of the head and lower jaw (these are golf ball-sized hair follicles, each with a single coarse hair growing out of its center). The scientific name, *Megaptera novaeangliae*, means 'big-winged New Englander' – New England being where the first individual was described.

Identification

- Tall, wide, bushy blow
- Stocky, predominantly black body
- Low, stubby dorsal fin sits on hump
- Long pectoral fins (up to one-third of body length)
- Knobs on rostrum and lower jaw
- Variable black-and-white markings on underside of flukes
- Usually raises flukes when diving
- Alone, small or large groups

Surface profile

Lobtailing

Breaching   Flipper-slapping

At a glance

Alternative names: rarely – Hump-backed Whale.

Scientific name: *Megaptera novaeangliae*.

Adult size: 46–56ft (14–17m); 28–45 tons (25–40 tonnes); females larger than males.

Diet: diverse diet of krill and small schooling fish such as herring, capelin and sand lance.

Behavior: often inquisitive and approachable, with lots of surface activity.

Breeding: single calf born in mid-winter, after a gestation period of 11–12 months.

Distribution: wide-ranging worldwide, but with distinct hotspots and seasonal changes; most spend the winter in low-latitude breeding grounds and the summer in high-latitude feeding grounds.

World population: increasing in abundance after decades of heavy exploitation; possibly as many as 110,000.

Best places to look in North America: Hawai'i, Southeast Alaska, Northwestern Gulf of Alaska, Aleutian Islands & Pribilof Islands, San Juan Islands & Puget Sound, Westport & the Olympic Coast, California (including Monterey Bay), New England, Eastern Seaboard (New York to Georgia), Vancouver Island (Johnstone Strait, Salish Sea, west coast), Bay of Fundy, Newfoundland, St Lawrence River & Gulf of St Lawrence, Baja California (Pacific Coast, Los Cabos & Gorda Banks, Gulf of California), Revillagigedo Archipelago, Banderas Bay, Bahía de Petatlán.

Distribution Map

Sperm Whale

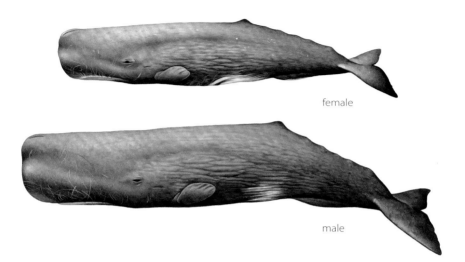

female

male

Easily recognized by their huge, squarish heads, wrinkly prune-like skin and uniquely angled, bushy blows, Sperm Whales behave more like submarines than air-breathing mammals. Capable of diving deeper and for longer than any other mammal (with the possible exception of some beaked whales), they have been tracked at depths of 6,500ft and there is circumstantial evidence to suggest that they may be able to dive to 10,500ft or even deeper. In exceptional circumstances, these amazing forays into the cold, dark ocean depths can last for two hours or more. The two sexes normally spend time together only during the breeding season. At other times, there are three main groupings: 'bachelor schools', containing non-breeding males; 'nursery schools', containing females with calves of both sexes; and solitary older males. No other cetacean shows such a marked difference in size between the sexes – males can be at least twice as large as females and lead very different lives. The Sperm Whale was once the mainstay of the whaling industry and as many as a million were killed over several centuries. It somehow survived, however, and is probably now the most abundant of all the great whales.

Identification

- Bushy blow projected forward and to left
- Dark gray-brown body with wrinkled skin
- Huge, squarish head
- Low hump in place of dorsal fin
- 'Knuckles' from hump to flukes
- Single, slit-like blowhole
- Often lies motionless at surface
- Usually raises flukes when diving

At a glance

Alternative names: rarely – Cachalot, Great Sperm Whale.

Scientific name: *Physeter macrocephalus*.

Adult size: 36–52ft (11–16m) exceptionally 62ft (19m); 15–50 tons (13–45 tonnes) exceptionally 78 tons (70 tonnes); males much larger than females.

Diet: mainly deep-water squid of all sizes, although octopuses and large fish also taken.

Behavior: often unconcerned about whale-watch boats; frequently breaches (especially juveniles).

Breeding: single calf usually born in summer and fall, after a gestation period of 14–16 months.

Distribution: patchy distribution in deep waters worldwide, from tropics to sub-polar waters; normally, only large males venture to extreme north and south of range.

World population: possibly 300,000–450,000.

Best places to look in North America: nowhere for reliable sightings. Occasional sightings in Northwestern Gulf of Alaska, Aleutian Islands & Pribilof Islands, Westport & the Olympic Coast, Oregon, California (including Monterey Bay), Eastern Seaboard (New York to Georgia), The Gully, Newfoundland, St Lawrence River & Gulf of St Lawrence, Baja California (Pacific Coast, Los Cabos & Gorda Banks, Gulf of California).

Distribution Map

Surface profile   Fluking   Breaching   Spyhopping

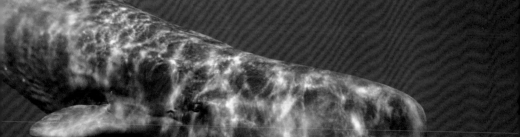

Pygmy Sperm Whale

With a preference for deep water far from shore, and rather inconspicuous habits, the Pygmy Sperm Whale can easily be overlooked in anything but the calmest conditions. However, it is one of the most frequently stranded small cetaceans in some areas (such as Florida), and may be more common than the lack of sightings currently suggests. It is often confused with the Dwarf Sperm Whale, which was not recognized as a separate species until 1966, although it can be identified at close range by its dorsal fin, which is much smaller, more rounded and set farther back on the body. Stranded animals have also been mistaken for sharks, because of their underslung lower jaws and some unusual creamy-white markings on either side of the head, resembling gill-slits. The Pygmy Sperm Whale is a deep diver. When resting between dives it tends to float motionless at the surface with part of the head and back exposed, and the tail hanging limply in the water. It usually sinks out of sight, but may roll forward to dive if it feels threatened. It is easily startled and may evacuate a reddish-brown fecal material, leaving behind a dense cloud in the water while it dives to safety; this may function as a decoy, like squid ink.

Identification

- Low, barely visible blow
- Small, robust body
- Squarish head
- Small, hooked, falcate dorsal fin behind mid-back
- Back more rounded in profile than Dwarf Sperm Whale
- False 'gill' behind each eye
- May float motionless at surface
- Simply drops below surface when diving

Surface profile

Breaching

At a glance

Alternative names: rarely – Lesser Sperm Whale, Short-headed Sperm Whale, Lesser Cachalot.

Scientific name: *Kogia breviceps.*

Adult size: 8.9–12.5ft (2.7–3.8m); 700–1,000lb (315–450kg; minimal size difference between sexes.

Diet: deep-water squid and octopus, but will also take variety of fish and crustaceans.

Behavior: sometimes permits close approaches by boats, but easily startles; usually undemonstrative, but occasionally breaches.

Breeding: single calf born March–August, after a gestation period of 9–11 months.

Distribution: deep water worldwide in tropical, sub-tropical and warm temperate seas, although never officially recorded across vast areas within this assumed range.

World population: unknown.

Best places to look in North America: nowhere for reliable sightings. Occasional sightings in Banderas Bay.

Distribution Map

Dwarf Sperm Whale

The Dwarf Sperm Whale is smaller than some dolphins. Its square head and slow, deliberate movements distinguish it from most dolphins, but it is often confused with its close relative, the Pygmy Sperm Whale. The two species were not officially separated until 1966, although they can be told apart at close range by their dorsal fins (the fin of the Dwarf Sperm Whale is usually larger, more pointed and more erect – rather like a Bottlenose Dolphin's dorsal fin – and it is set farther forward on the body). Also, Dwarf Sperm Whales have flatter backs (they look rather like upside-down surfboards when floating on the surface) and tend to be slightly smaller than Pygmy Sperm Whales. The two species share several intriguing characteristics: their underslung lower jaws and the creamy white arcs behind each eye (resembling gill slits) make them look superficially like sharks. When resting between dives, they tend to float motionless at the surface with part of the head and back exposed and the tail hanging limply in the water; and, when frightened, they sometimes evacuate a reddish-brown fecal material, which may function as a decoy, like squid ink. Dwarf Sperm Whales are very difficult to spot in anything but the calmest conditions.

Identification

- Low, barely visible blow
- Small, robust body
- Squarish head
- Prominent falcate dorsal fin midway along back
- Back flatter in profile than Pygmy Sperm Whale
- False 'gill' behind each eye
- May float motionless at surface
- Slight roll as drops below surface when diving

Surface profile   Spyhopping

Breaching

At a glance

Alternative names: rarely – Owen's Pygmy Sperm Whale.

Scientific name: *Kogia sima*.

Adult size: 6.9–8.9ft (2.1–2.7m); 300–600lb (135–275kg); minimal size difference between sexes.

Diet: mid- and deep-water squid and octopus, but will also take variety of fish and crustaceans; may feed in shallower water than Pygmy Sperm Whale.

Behavior: sometimes permits close approaches by boats, but easily startles; usually undemonstrative, but occasionally breaches.

Breeding: single calf born probably in summer, after a gestation period of about 12 months.

Distribution: deep water worldwide in tropical, sub-tropical and warm temperate seas, although never officially recorded across vast areas within this assumed range.

World population: unknown.

Best places to look in North America: Baja California (Gulf of California).

Distribution Map

Narwhal

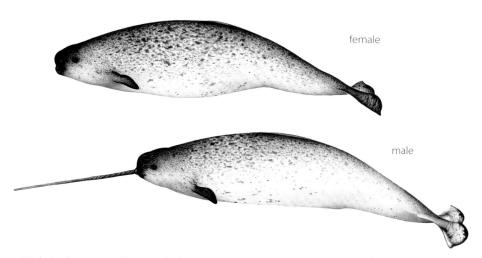

female

male

With its long, spiralling tusk, looking like a gnarled and twisted walking stick, the male Narwhal is unique and unlikely to be confused with any other cetacean. Until early in the seventeenth century the tusk was believed by many to be the horn of the legendary Unicorn, but it is actually a modified tooth. Its role has long baffled scientists: weird and wonderful theories proposed that it was used for spearfishing, grubbing for food along the seabed and even drilling through ice. Another is that it may be a sensory organ, used by the whales to measure the salt concentration of water as an early warning system that the sea is freezing. More likely, it is used as a visual display of strength, like the antlers of a stag – males have been seen 'sparring' with their tusks above water (broken tusks and head injuries support this theory). A small number of males have two tusks and, very rarely, females grow them as well. Narwhals change color as they grow older – blotchy gray or brownish gray when they are first born, then dark gray to black, then mottled light and dark, and finally very old animals can appear almost entirely white. They have been hunted for centuries by the Inuit and are still hunted today in Arctic Canada and Greenland.

Identification

- High Arctic distribution
- Medium size
- Long tusk of male
- Variable light and dark mottling
- Low ridge instead of dorsal fin
- Relatively small head with pronounced melon
- Very short beak
- Frequently logs with top of head and back showing above surface

At a glance

Alternative names: Narwhale; rarely – Sea Unicorn.

Scientific name: *Monodon monoceros.*

Adult size: 12.1–16.4ft (3.7–5m) not including male's tusk (up to 9.8ft (3m); 1,500–4,000lb (700–1,800kg); males larger than females.

Diet: variety of fish, squid and crustaceans.

Behavior: often shy and wary of boats, especially where hunted, but much less nervous of people standing on the floe edge or shore.

Breeding: single calf born May–August, after a gestation period of 14–15 months.

Distribution: High Arctic (mainly 70–80°N), living farther north than almost any other cetacean; mainly Atlantic sector of Arctic (few records for Pacific sector); winters in deep water under ice between Baffin Island and Greenland, and in deep waters of Greenland Sea; summers in ice-free bays, fjords and island passages closer to shore.

World population: possibly 80,000-plus, but this estimate has a huge margin of error and some experts consider it to be optimistic.

Best places to look in North America: Nunavut.

Distribution Map

Surface profile

Jousting males

Male tusk

Beluga

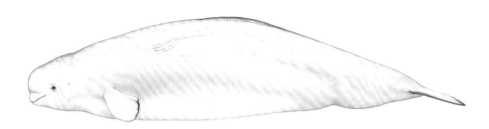

Ancient mariners used to call the Beluga the 'Sea Canary' because of its great repertoire of trills, moos, clicks, squeaks and twitters – once described by a Beluga scientist as sounding like a string orchestra tuning up before a concert – that can even be heard from above the surface. It also has an impressive array of facial expressions, thanks to a remarkable ability to alter the shape of its forehead and lips. Not all Belugas are white: their body color changes with age, from creamy, pale gray at birth, then dark gray to brownish-gray, to almost pure white when they are about 10 years old. Well adapted to living close to shore, they are able to maneuver in very shallow water and, if stranded, can often survive until they are refloated by the next tide (unless they are found by a Polar Bear first – many Belugas have scars caused by bear attacks). Belugas have been hunted for centuries and hunting is still a threat to some populations. They are also threatened by oil and gas development, global warming and chemical pollution.

Identification

- Arctic and sub-Arctic distribution
- Medium size
- Very pale to pure white, pale gray or yellowish
- No mottling
- Low ridge instead of dorsal fin
- Relatively small head with rounded melon
- Very short beak
- Distinct and flexible neck
- Surfaces often with distinctive slow rolling motion

Surface profile

Fluking   Spyhopping   Rolling

At a glance

Alternative names: Sea Canary, White Whale.

Scientific name: *Delphinapterus leucas.*

Adult size: 9.8–18ft (3–5.5m); 1,100–3,500lb (500–1,600kg); males larger than females.

Diet: wide variety of fish, as well as crustaceans and squid, octopuses and other molluscs.

Behavior: fairly easy to approach and may show curiosity toward boats, snorkellers and divers; frequently spyhops.

Breeding: single calf born April–September, after a gestation period of 12–14.5 months.

Distribution: cold waters of Arctic and sub-Arctic (mainly 50–80°N). Wide choice of habitat, including estuaries, coastal waters, continental shelves and deep ocean basins, in open water and loose ice. Some populations make extensive migrations with advancing and retreating ice edge, others spend summer in coastal areas and move offshore in winter (to avoid dense fast ice).

World population: no reliable global estimate, but probably more than 150,000 (although many parts of the range remain unsurveyed).

Best places to look in North America: Cook Inlet, St Lawrence River & Gulf of St Lawrence, Nunavut, Churchill, Inuvik.

Distribution Map

Baird's Beaked Whale

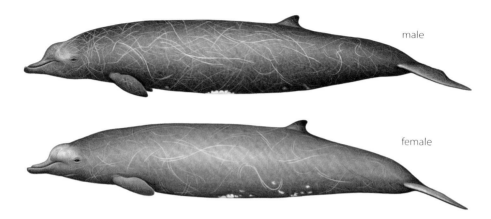

male

female

The largest member of the beaked whale family, Baird's Beaked Whale is very similar to Arnoux's Beaked Whale (which does not occur in North America). These two species are unusual among beaked whales in having four teeth which erupt in both males and females: two large ones at the tip of the protruding lower jaw (visible even when the mouth is closed) and a smaller pair just behind them. In some older animals, the teeth may be heavily infested with barnacles. Baird's Beaked Whale was discovered in 1882 when researcher Leonhard Stejneger picked up a four-toothed skull on Bering Island, off the Kamchatka Peninsula. He published his discovery the following year and named the new species after his colleague, Spencer Baird, who had just been appointed Secretary of the Smithsonian Institution. Like other members of the family, Baird's Beaked Whales are deep divers. They have been known to hold their breath for as long as 67 minutes, though most dives last around half an hour; they are believed to reach depths of at least 3,200ft on a regular basis. A new, closely related species of beaked whale has recently been discovered in the North Pacific.

Identification

- Large size
- Conspicuous low, bushy blow
- Long, dark slate-gray or brownish-gray spindle-shaped body
- Extensive scarring on older animals (especially males)
- Cookie-cutter Shark bites often evident
- Small dorsal fin two-thirds of the way along back
- Prominent, bulbous forehead sloping to long beak
- Anterior teeth may appear white in bright sunlight
- Tightly packed groups

Surface profile   Fluking   Breaching

At a glance

Alternative names: rarely – Giant Bottlenose Whale, Four-toothed Whale.

Scientific name: *Berardius bairdii.*

Adult size: 33–39ft (10–12m); 11–13 tons (10–12 tonnes); females may be slightly larger than males.

Diet: mainly deep-water and bottom-dwelling fish, squid and crustaceans.

Behavior: sometimes breaches and performs other aerial behaviors.

Breeding: single calf born late winter to early spring (peak March–April), after a gestation period of around 17 months.

Distribution: deep oceanic temperate and sub-Arctic waters in the North Pacific, especially along continental shelf edges and around seamounts; rarely close to shore except where deep water approaches coast.

World population: no reliable global figure, but possibly in the order of tens of thousands (including an estimated 1,100 in the eastern North Pacific); small numbers are taken annually by Japanese whalers.

Best places to look in North America: nowhere for reliable sightings. Occasional sightings in Monterey Bay, Baja California (Pacific coast).

Distribution Map

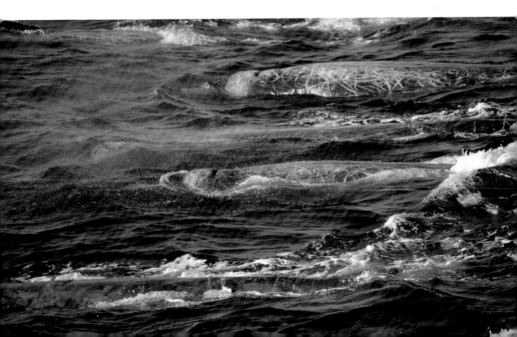

Unnamed Beaked Whale

Whalers in Japan have traditionally recognized two different kinds of Baird's Beaked Whale: the relatively common 'slate-gray' form (see page 74) and a rarer, smaller 'black' form. They often see groups of the 'black' form in the Nemuro Strait (near the northern tip of Hokkaido, in the Sea of Okhotsk). Although no scientist has ever seen one alive, it has long been suspected that these animals belong to a new, previously unknown species. Sure enough, recent DNA studies on eight 'black' specimens (three from Japan and five from the Bering Sea and eastern Aleutian Islands) found a significant genetic difference between the two forms. Amazingly, the skeleton of one of these specimens was found hanging in the gymnasium of Unalaska High School in the Aleutians (see the picture opposite), while another had been collected from the Aleutians in 1948 and held, unknowingly, in the Smithsonian Institution for many years. The new species has yet to be officially accepted by taxonomists and does not have a name, though the researchers have suggested *Berardius* (the same genus as Baird's Beaked Whale) *beringiae* (after the sea where it was found). Two possible common names have been proposed: Black Baird's Beaked Whale or Dwarf Baird's Beaked Whale. Meanwhile, the Japanese call it Karasu, or the Raven.

Identification

- Medium size
- Long, dark spindle-shaped body
- Fewer and less intense scars than on Baird's
- Cookie-cutter Shark bites may be evident
- Small dorsal fin two-thirds of the way along back
- Prominent, bulbous forehead sloping to long beak

At a glance

Scientific name: researchers have proposed *Berardius beringiae*.

Adult size: 20–26ft (6–8m); weight unknown; no information on size difference between the sexes.

Diet: unknown.

Behavior: unknown.

Breeding: unknown.

Distribution: temperate and sub-Arctic waters in the North Pacific; currently known only from northern Japan, the Bering Sea and the eastern Aleutian Islands (Alaska), though the sample size is very small; bite scars from tropical sharks suggest that it migrates south for part of the year.

World population: no reliable global figure.

Best places to look in North America: nowhere for reliable sightings.

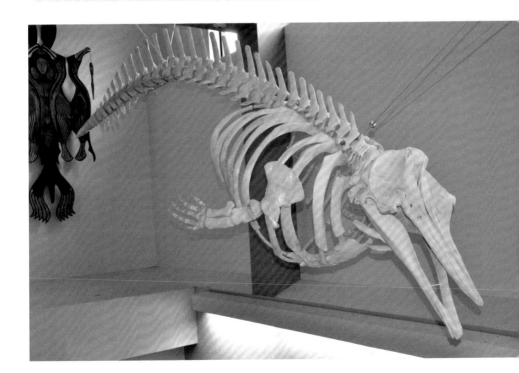

Cuvier's Beaked Whale

female

male

Cuvier's Beaked Whale was first described in 1823 by the French anatomist Georges Cuvier, from an imperfect skull that had been found on the Mediterranean coast of France some 20 years earlier. Cuvier believed it to be the remains of an extinct animal. But it is now recognized as one of the most widespread and abundant of the beaked whales and, despite its preference for deep offshore waters, is probably one of the most watched beaked whales in the world. Older males sometimes travel alone, but small groups of up to seven animals are more typical (rarely, as many as 25 have been seen together). The body color varies from individual to individual and according to age and sex. Younger animals are usually darker and grayer, for example, while males tend to have a more extensive pale area on the head than females and are often heavily scarred from the teeth of other males. The shape of the head and beak is sometimes described as resembling a goose's beak, which is why one of its alternative names is the Goose-beaked Whale. Dives of up to 9,800ft, lasting up to 138 minutes, have been recorded.

Identification (male)

- Medium size
- Robust body with scarring
- Dark gray to reddish brown body color
- Cookie-cutter Shark bites evident
- Head (often pale) with slight concavity behind
- Smoothly sloping forehead
- Indentation behind blowhole
- Small conical teeth at tip of lower jaw
- Small, falcate dorsal fin two-thirds of the way along back

Surface profile

Breaching

At a glance

Alternative names: Goose-beaked Whale; rarely – Goosebeak Whale, Cuvier's Whale.

Scientific name: *Ziphius cavirostris.*

Adult size: 18–23ft (5.5–7m); 2.2–3.9 tons (2–3.5 tonnes); minimal size difference between sexes.

Diet: deep-water squid, some fish and possibly crustaceans.

Behavior: normally avoids boats or indifferent to them, but can be inquisitive and approachable on occasion; known to breach.

Breeding: single calf (seasonality unknown) after a gestation period of about 12 months.

Distribution: widely distributed in cool temperate to tropical waters worldwide, especially around oceanic islands and in enclosed seas; mainly deep waters offshore and often associated with submarine canyons and escarpments on the continental shelf edge.

World population: unknown; over 90,000 believed to live in the eastern North Pacific.

Best places to look in North America: nowhere for reliable sightings. Occasional sightings in Hawai'i, Monterey Bay, Eastern Seaboard (New York to Georgia), Baja California (Gulf of California).

Distribution Map

Northern Bottlenose Whale

female

male

The Northern Bottlenose Whale is one of the better known beaked whales and is certainly one of the most inquisitive. It frequently approaches slow-moving or stationary boats and ships, and this behavior has made it more likely to be hunted, studied and, more recently, watched by whale enthusiasts than any other member of the family. More than 80,000 Northern Bottlenose Whales were killed (and many more struck and lost) between the 1850s and the 1970s. They are known for their habit of 'standing by' injured companions, which permitted whalers to kill large numbers of whales in the same group. Northern Bottlenose Whales are deep divers, known to venture to depths of 5,000ft or more (sometimes for at least an hour – though most dives last less than 10 minutes) and use their superb sonar system to pursue deep-water squid. Older males, in particular, are very distinctive with their large bulbous foreheads and prominent tube-like beaks; females are smaller, with less pronounced foreheads and beaks. Research in the western North Atlantic suggests that they are resident year-round, but at least some populations in Europe appear to be migratory.

Identification (male)

- Medium size
- Visible bushy blow
- Dark grey to brown color
- Robust, cylindrical body
- Falcate dorsal fin two-thirds of the way along back
- Bulbous forehead often pale and squared off
- Prominent tube-like beak
- Pair of teeth at tip of lower jaw (not always visible)
- May be curious

Surface profile

Spyhopping   Breaching

At a glance

Alternative names: North Atlantic Bottlenosed Whale; rarely – Flathead, Bottlehead, Steephead.

Scientific name: *Hyperoodon ampullatus.*

Adult size: 19–32ft (5.8–9.8m); 6.4–8.3 tons (5.8–7.5 tonnes); males significantly larger than females.

Diet: mainly squid, but also some other invertebrates and shoaling fish.

Behavior: often quite curious and will approach boats; sometimes breaches and lobtails.

Breeding: single calf born April–June, after a gestation period of 12 months or more.

Distribution: deep, cool temperate to sub-Arctic waters in the northern North Atlantic, mainly along or beyond the edge of the continental shelf and over submarine canyons.

World population: no reliable global estimate, but one evaluation for the eastern North Atlantic suggests a population of 40,000.

Best places to look in North America: The Gully.

Distribution Map

Sowerby's Beaked Whale

female

male

Sowerby's Beaked Whale was the first of the beaked whales to be described and named. A lone male was found stranded in the Moray Firth, Scotland, in 1800, and its skull was collected. Four years later the species was described by the English watercolor artist James Sowerby, who painted a picture of the skull and how he imagined the animal might have looked. It has one of the most northerly distributions of all the *Mesoplodon* beaked whales, although parts of its range do overlap with other closely related species and identification can therefore be extremely difficult. The position of the two teeth in the male is distinctive, lying roughly midway along the mouthline, and these are visible even when the mouth is closed – but only at close range. Sowerby's remains one of the more elusive members of the family and is still poorly known. It is sometimes called the North Sea Beaked Whale because, although its range extends across the North Atlantic, it is most likely to be found in the northern North Sea (based on strandings, northern Europe appears to be the center of abundance).

Identification (male)

- Medium-sized, spindle-shaped body
- Bluish gray, slate-gray or dark brown upperside, lighter underside
- Limited scarring (single scratches, not paired) and blotching
- Relatively small head
- Often lifts head at 45-degree angle when surfacing
- Long, slender beak with relatively straight mouthline
- Two flattened, triangular teeth roughly midway along lower jaw
- Prominent bulge in front of blowhole
- Small, curved dorsal fin two-thirds of the way along back

At a glance

Alternative names: rarely – North Sea Beaked Whale, North Atlantic Beaked Whale.

Scientific name: *Mesoplodon bidens*.

Adult size: 13–18ft (4–5.5m); 1.1–1.4 tons (1–1.3 tonnes); males slightly larger than females.

Diet: mostly deep-water fish; unlike most other beaked whales, rarely takes squid.

Behavior: has been known to approach boats; breaching, spyhopping and tail-slapping have been observed.

Breeding: single calf believed to be born in spring and summer, after a gestation period of possibly 12 months.

Distribution: cool temperate and sub-Arctic waters of the northern North Atlantic, with most records from the east and north of 30°N; mainly deep waters offshore.

World population: unknown.

Best places to look in North America: nowhere for reliable sightings. Occasional sightings in The Gully.

Distribution Map

Surface profile   Breaching

Blainville's Beaked Whale

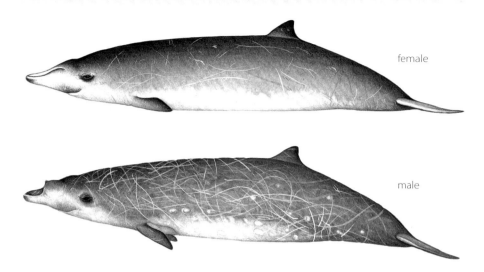

female

male

Blainville's Beaked Whale has a wide distribution and appears to be relatively common. Following a number of long-term studies, it is now one of the better-known beaked whales. The male is one of the oddest-looking of all cetaceans and is relatively easy to identify at sea. It has a pair of massive teeth that grow from substantial arches in its lower jaw, like a couple of horns, and these may be so encrusted with barnacles that the animal appears to have two dark-colored pompons on top of its head. The females have less prominently arched lower jaws and, as with most other beaked whales, their teeth do not erupt. This species was named in 1817 by Henri de Blainville, who described it from a small piece of jaw that was the densest bone structure he had ever seen (thus the scientific name '*densirostris*', meaning 'dense beak', and its alternative common name, the Dense-beaked Whale). Dives of up to 4,600ft and over 54 minutes have been recorded, although most dives are much shallower and shorter.

Identification (male)

- Medium size
- Robust, spindle-shaped body
- Dark (brownish or bluish-gray) upperside, paler underside
- Heavily scarred body
- Some populations have Cookie-cutter Shark bites
- Strongly arched lower jaw
- Huge, forward-tilting, horn-like teeth
- Flattened forehead with indentation at blowhole
- Thick, moderately long beak
- Prominent curved or triangular dorsal fin two-thirds of the way along back

At a glance

Alternative names: Dense-beaked Whale.

Scientific name: *Mesoplodon densirostris*.

Adult size: 13.7–15.4ft (4.2–4.7m); 0.8–1.1 tons (0.7–1 tonnes); minimal size difference between sexes.

Diet: mainly deep-water squid, but also some small fish.

Behavior: generally unobtrusive, but occasionally breaches and spyhops; on surfacing, beak may appear first at a sharp angle.

Breeding: single calf born after a gestation period of possibly 12 months.

Distribution: deep warm temperate to tropical waters worldwide, including many enclosed seas; mainly offshore but often around oceanic islands.

World population: unknown, but appears to be fairly common in most tropical seas.

Best places to look in North America: nowhere for reliable sightings. Occasional sightings in Hawai'i.

Distribution Map

Surface profile

Ginkgo-toothed Beaked Whale

female

male

The Ginkgo-toothed Beaked Whale is named for the male's strangely flattened teeth, which in juveniles (but not adults) are shaped like the leaves of a ginkgo tree – a common tree in Japan, where the first specimen of this whale was found and described in 1958. Their teeth are about 4 inches wide – they are wider than they are tall – making them the widest of any known *Mesoplodon* species; they do not erupt from the gums in females. The Ginkgo-toothed Beaked Whale has never been reliably identified alive at sea and is very poorly known. Most information comes from stranded animals found on shore and a handful of individuals killed by Japanese whalers. It was being hunted on an opportunistic basis by shore-based whalers in Japan and Taiwan even before it had been scientifically described. Unlike many of its relatives, the male has very few, if any, linear scars on its body – perhaps because of the small amount of tooth that erupts from the gums. However, some individuals do have white spots and blotches, which may be scars made by Lampreys or Cookie-cutter Sharks rather than true pigmentation.

Identification (male)

- Medium-sized, spindle-shaped body
- Dark upperside, possibly lighter underside
- Little or no linear scarring
- White spots and blotches
- Smoothly sloping forehead
- White anterior beak
- Small head with arched lower jaw
- Teeth barely visible on arch
- Small dorsal fin two-thirds of the way along back

At a glance

Alternative names: rarely – Ginkgo Beaked Whale, Japanese Beaked Whale.

Scientific name: *Mesoplodon ginkgodens.*

Adult size: 15.4–16ft (4.7–4.9m); possibly *c.* 1.1 tons (1 tonne); minimal size difference between sexes (females may be larger on average).

Diet: presumably deep-water squid, perhaps also some small fish.

Behavior: unknown.

Breeding: single calf, otherwise unknown.

Distribution: known from only a small number of widely scattered records in the tropical and warm temperate waters of the Pacific Ocean; possibly also in the Indian Ocean.

World population: unknown; does not appear to be common.

Best places to look in North America: nowhere for reliable sightings.

Distribution Map

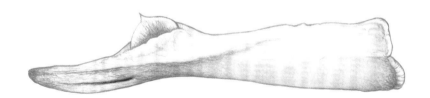

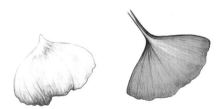

Perrin's Beaked Whale

female

male

Perrin's Beaked Whale is a recent addition to the cetacean list and was first described in 2002. It is known from just five animals, which stranded along the coast of California between 1975 and 1997, between Torrey Pines State Natural Reserve, just north of San Diego, and Fisherman's Wharf in Monterey. There was considerable confusion over their identity at first – four were initially believed to be Hector's Beaked Whales and the fifth a juvenile Cuvier's Beaked Whale – but, after detailed genetic studies, beaked whale experts realized that they belonged to a new species. With so little information, Perrin's Beaked Whale is an exceptionally difficult species to identify. It is strikingly similar to Hector's Beaked Whale, in particular, though the two probably do not overlap in distribution. However, it may have been overlooked at sea and it now seems possible that two sightings of small groups of beaked whales off southern California, in 1976 and 1978, may also have been Perrin's. These sightings, and experience with other beaked whales, suggest that it may prefer oceanic habitats more than 3,300ft deep. It was named after W. F. Perrin, who collected two of the known specimens.

Identification (male)

- Medium size
- Spindle-shaped body
- Dark gray upperside, paler underside
- Some body scarring
- Small head with slight bulge at melon
- Short beak
- Two triangular teeth near tip of lower jaw
- Small dorsal fin two-thirds of the way along back

At a glance

Alternative names: rarely – California Beaked Whale.

Scientific name: *Mesoplodon perrini.*

Adult size: 12.8–14.4ft (3.9–4.4m); possibly *c.* 1,500lb (700kg); females slightly larger than males.

Diet: probably mainly deep-water squid, possibly some fish and invertebrates.

Behavior: unknown.

Breeding: single calf, otherwise unknown.

Distribution: known only from five strandings in California, between approximately 33–37°N, suggesting a range in the eastern North Pacific. However, this is very limited evidence and it is possible that the true distribution is much broader.

World population: unknown.

Best places to look in North America: nowhere for reliable sightings.

Distribution Map

Hubbs' Beaked Whale

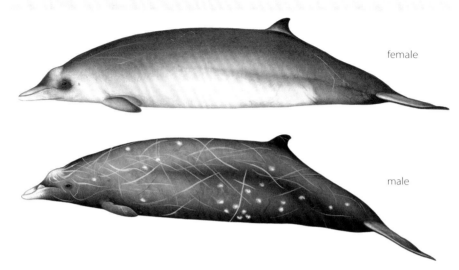

female

male

Hubbs' Beaked Whale is another poorly known member of the family and, although the adult male is more readily identifiable than most other beaked whales, there have been few reliable sightings at sea. Adult males are covered in a remarkable number of single and double linear scars, which are probably made by the teeth of other males during aggressive encounters over females or dominance hierarchies; other male beaked whales have similar scarring, but rarely as much as in this species. Hubbs' Beaked Whale is so similar in appearance and morphology to Andrew's Beaked Whale that, at one time, the two were believed to belong to the same species. However, recent genetic evidence confirms that they are separate. Hubbs' Beaked Whale was named after the American ichthyologist Carl Hubbs – in 1945, a live specimen stranded outside his office at Scripps Institution of Oceanography in San Diego, California. It appears to be most common along the California coast and north into British Columbia, but there are also records from Japan. No one knows whether it ranges right across the North Pacific, or if there are separate east and west populations.

Identification (male)

- Medium size
- Dark gray to black, spindle-shaped body
- Tangle of linear scars
- White 'cap' on fairly bulbous melon
- Stocky, fairly short beak, mainly white
- Strongly arched lower jaw
- Massive teeth visible on top of arch in center of beak
- Slightly falcate dorsal fin two-thirds of the way along back

At a glance

Alternative names: rarely – Arch-beaked Whale.
Scientific name: *Mesoplodon carlhubbsi.*
Adult size: 15.4–17.4ft (4.7–5.3m); *c.* 1.1–1.7 tons (1–1.5 tonnes); minimal size difference between sexes.
Diet: mainly deep-water squid, some fish.
Behavior: unknown.
Breeding: little known, but single calf believed to be born in summer.
Distribution: known only from temperate waters in the North Pacific.
World population: unknown.
Best places to look in North America: nowhere for reliable sightings.

Distribution Map

Pygmy Beaked Whale

female

male

The Pygmy Beaked Whale is the smallest member of the family. Scientists first became aware of its existence in 1976, when a skull was discovered at a fish market near San Andrés, Peru. The first complete specimen (a female) was found in 1985, at another fish market just south of Lima, Peru, and the first adult male was found three years later. In 1990, there were two strandings in La Paz Bay, Baja California, Mexico – the first outside Peruvian waters. The new species was officially named in 1991. Since then, it has been reliably identified at sea on a number of occasions – more frequently in recent years – especially in the Gulf of California, Mexico. Males and females are quite different in appearance – the males are light and dark, with a light swathe across the back that is readily identifiable at sea, while females are more uniformly colored brownish-gray above and lighter below. There is no information on abundance, but because many of the first specimens had been caught by fishermen off the coast of Peru, it raises alarm bells about what appears to be a high level of incidental catch.

Identification (male)

- Small, robust spindle-shaped body
- Light swathe across back
- Linear scarring
- Small head with slightly bulbous melon
- Short beak often with white tip
- Slightly arched lower jaw
- Teeth just visible in front of arch
- Small triangular dorsal fin two-thirds of the way along back

Surface profile

Breaching

At a glance

Alternative names: Peruvian Beaked Whale; rarely – Lesser Beaked Whale.

Scientific name: *Mesoplodon peruvianus.*

Adult size: 12.1–12.8ft (3.7–3.9m); *c.* 1,100lb (500kg).

Diet: probably deep-water squid, fish and possibly crustaceans.

Behavior: little known, though usually in small groups of two to five.

Breeding: single calf, otherwise unknown.

Distribution: limited evidence suggests deep oceanic waters of eastern Pacific (30°N–28°S); a single record of a stranding in New Zealand is thought to represent a vagrant individual.

World population: unknown.

Best places to look in North America: nowhere for reliable sightings. Occasional sightings in Baja California (Gulf of California).

Distribution Map

Gervais' Beaked Whale

female

male

The first recorded specimen of Gervais' Beaked Whale was found floating in the English Channel, between the UK and France, in the early 1840s (hence its scientific name, *europaeus*, and one of its alternative common names, European Beaked Whale). Since then, most of the information about this species has been gleaned from strandings and a small number of confirmed sightings at sea. It is extremely difficult to distinguish from other beaked whales and has only rarely been positively identified alive. However, Gervais' Beaked Whale is the most commonly stranded *Mesoplodon* beaked whale along the Atlantic coast of the southeastern United States and appears to be widely distributed in the Caribbean. Records from other parts of the world are so widely dispersed that it is difficult to tell if there is another important center of distribution. A stranded male can be identified by the single pair of triangular teeth on the lower jaw, which are located about 4 inches from the tip of the beak, although these can be difficult to spot at sea; as with most other beaked whales, the teeth do not erupt in females.

Identification (male)

- Medium-sized, spindle-shaped body
- Brown, gray or marine blue upperside, paler gray underside
- Limited body scarring (usually single scars, not paired)
- Small head with short beak
- May be a dark patch around each eye
- Two tiny triangular teeth set back from tip of jaw
- Flattened forehead with indentation at blowhole
- Small, shark-like dorsal fin two-thirds of the way along back

Surface profile

At a glance

Alternative names: rarely – Gulf Stream Beaked Whale, European Beaked Whale, Antillean Beaked Whale.

Scientific name: *Mesoplodon europaeus.*

Adult size: 13.8–17.1ft (4.2–5.2m); 0.9–1.3 tons (0.8–1.2 tonnes); females slightly larger than males.

Diet: mainly deep-water squid, but probably also some fish and possibly crustaceans.

Behavior: lack of sightings in relatively well-studied areas within range suggests it is likely to be inconspicuous; sometimes lifts head out of water upon surfacing; known to breach.

Breeding: single calf born after a gestation period of possibly 12 months.

Distribution: mainly deep tropical to warm temperate waters in the North Atlantic, with scattered records in the South Atlantic; may be closely associated with warm waters of the transatlantic Gulf Stream.

World population: unknown, but based on frequency of strandings probably relatively common along the east coast of North America.

Best places to look in North America: nowhere for reliable sightings. Occasional sightings in Eastern Seaboard (New York to Georgia).

Distribution Map

True's Beaked Whale

female

male

In 1913, the American biologist Frederick W. True named this species *mirus*, meaning 'wonderful'. True was a curator at the United States National Museum (now the Smithsonian Institution) and named the species from an adult female that had stranded in North Carolina the year before. As with most other *Mesoplodon* beaked whales, females and juveniles are probably unidentifiable, unless stranded specimens can be examined closely. If the teeth of an adult male are visible, it may be possible to make a positive identification. Not surprisingly, with few confirmed sightings at sea and relatively few strandings, little is known about True's Beaked Whales. There may be two genetically distinct forms – one in the North Atlantic and the other in the southern hemisphere – with significant morphological and pigmentation differences. In particular, southern animals have a large white or pale area on the rear of the body, between the dorsal fin and the flukes, which is not present in North Atlantic animals. In the future, these two forms may be classified as separate sub-species or even species.

Identification (male – North Atlantic form)

- Predominantly brownish-gray or bluish-gray upperside, lighter underside
- Medium-sized spindle-shaped body
- May be closely spaced parallel scarring
- Dark patch around each eye (often with darker line to top of head)
- Relatively short beak
- Two small teeth at tip of lower jaw
- Rounded melon with slight indentation at blowhole
- Small, falcate dorsal fin two-thirds of the way along back

At a glance

Alternative name: rarely – Wonderful Beaked Whale.

Scientific name: *Mesoplodon mirus.*

Adult size: 15.7–17.7ft (4.8–5.4m); 1.1–1.5 tons (1–1.4 tonnes); females may be slightly larger than males.

Diet: probably mainly deep-water squid, possibly some fish.

Behavior: with just a handful of possible sightings, virtually nothing is known about behavior at sea; reported to breach.

Breeding: single calf, otherwise unknown.

Distribution: in the North Atlantic, mostly known from temperate waters; in the southern hemisphere, known from southern Brazil, South Africa, Mozambique, Madagascar and southern Australia, but the full extent of its distribution is unclear; it is absent from the tropics.

World population: unknown.

Best places to look in North America: nowhere for reliable sightings.

Distribution Map

Surface profile   Breaching

Stejneger's Beaked Whale

female

male

For nearly a century, the only evidence for the existence of Stejneger's Beaked Whale came from a single skull found on Bering Island, off the Kamchatka Peninsula in Russia, in the mid-nineteenth century. But since the late 1970s information about this enigmatic whale has improved and there are now more specimens available for study. In particular, in 1994, a group of four adult females stranded in the Aleutian Islands, Alaska, providing the first Stejneger's Beaked Whales in good condition. Alaska – especially the Aleutian Islands – may be a key center of distribution. The Sea of Japan may be another hotspot. The male has extraordinary tusk-like teeth, second only in size to the teeth of Strap-toothed Beaked Whales, which are set about 8 inches from the tip of the jaw immediately in front of the apex. They are laterally compressed and tilt forward; sometimes, they converge inwards toward one another, cutting into the upper lip, and may actually restrict the opening of the jaws. The species was named in 1855 after the man who found the first skull, Leonhard Stejneger.

Identification (male)

- Predominantly brownish-gray to nearly black
- Medium-sized spindle-shaped body
- May be lighter around face
- Dark hood from each eye to around blowhole
- Relatively short beak with strongly arched mouthline
- Large tusk-like teeth on front of arch
- Closely spaced parallel scarring and white mottling
- Small, falcate dorsal fin two-thirds of the way along back

At a glance

Alternative names: rarely – Bering Sea Beaked Whale, North Pacific Beaked Whale, Sabre-toothed Beaked Whale.

Scientific name: *Mesoplodon stejnegeri*.

Adult size: 15.7–18.7ft (4.8–5.7m); 1.1–1.8 tons (1–1.6 tonnes); females may be slightly larger than males.

Diet: probably mainly deep-water squid, possibly some fish.

Behavior: little known, but tightly bunched groups of 5–15 reported in Sea of Japan.

Breeding: single calf, otherwise unknown.

Distribution: cool temperate to sub-Arctic waters of the North Pacific and in the southern Bering Sea. May also range into warm temperate waters, but the only evidence for this is the presence of scars inflicted by Cookie-cutter Sharks (the sharks are more abundant in warmer waters farther south).

World population: unknown.

Best places to look in North America: nowhere for reliable sightings.

Distribution Map

Longman's Beaked Whale

female

male

Until recently, Longman's Beaked Whale was one of the least-known cetaceans. The only evidence for its existence came from two weathered skulls: one discovered in 1882 on a beach near MacKay in Queensland, Australia, and the other in 1955 on the floor of a fertilizer factory in Mogadishu, Somalia (later traced to a beach near Danane, where it had been picked up by a local fisherman). But in recent years more specimens have been found – in South Africa, Kenya, the Maldives, Sri Lanka, the Philippines and Japan, as well as Somalia and Australia – and there have been quite a few confirmed sightings of live animals at sea from similarly widespread locations, especially in the Maldives. There is a significant population in Hawaiian waters, though they are rarely seen. Large beaked whales occasionally reported from the warmer waters of the Indian and Pacific Oceans – and dubbed 'Tropical Bottlenose Whales' for their similarity to Southern Bottlenose Whales – are now believed to have been Longman's. The species is named after Albert Herber Longman, director of the Queensland Museum, Australia, who recognized the 1882 skull as belonging to a new species.

Identification (male)

- Brownish to gray-brown upperside, lighter underside
- Medium sized spindle-shaped body
- Fairly conspicuous, low bushy blow
- Lighter face and bulbous melon
- Moderately long, tube-like beak
- Single pair of teeth near tip of lower jaw
- Distinctive crease between melon and beak
- May have linear scarring and white circular scars
- Relatively large, falcate dorsal fin two-thirds of the way along back

At a glance

Alternative names: Indo-Pacific Beaked Whale, Tropical Bottlenose Whale; rarely – Pacific Beaked Whale.

Scientific name: *Indopacetus pacificus*.

Adult size: *c.* 18–21.3ft (5.5–6.5m); *c.* 8.3 tons (7.5 tonnes).

Diet: probably mainly deep-water squid, possibly some fish.

Behavior: little known, but large tightly bunched groups of 10–100 (average 20) reported in the North Pacific (smaller groups in the Indian Ocean); breaching has been observed.

Breeding: single calf, otherwise unknown.

Distribution: limited evidence, but sightings and strandings at widespread locations indicates broad range in Indo-Pacific; believed to be more common in the western Pacific and western Indian Ocean.

World population: unknown; estimated may be low thousands around Hawai'i.

Best places to look in North America: nowhere for reliable sightings.

Distribution Map

Surface profile   Breaching

Killer Whale

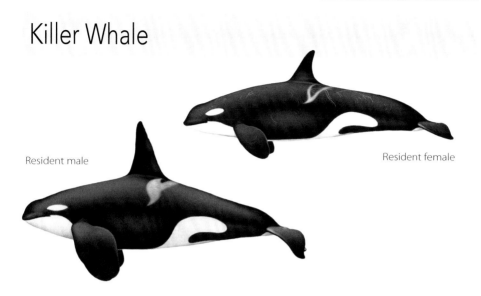

Resident male

Resident female

Two thousand years ago, Roman scholar Pliny the Elder described the Killer Whale as 'an enormous mass of flesh armed with savage teeth'. Even as recently as the early 1970s, US Navy diving manuals described it as 'extremely ferocious', warning that it 'will attack human beings at every opportunity'. But Killer Whales do not deserve their killer name any more than other top predators and they do not hunt humans (which is why some people prefer to call them Orcas). They live in close-knit matrilineal groups that, in many cases, are so stable only death or capture can break them apart, and these join forces to form extended family groups known as pods. These pods belong to a bewildering array of so-called ecotypes, which differ in appearance, social structure, behavior, ecology and vocalizations. Different ecotypes are ecologically distinct and do not appear to interbreed, even if they inhabit the same waters. Ultimately, they may be split into several different sub-species or even species. Killer Whales are the largest members of the dolphin family and, with their predominantly jet-black and brilliant white markings and the enormous dorsal fin of the male, are the most readily identifiable of all cetaceans.

Identification

- Medium size
- Distinctive black-and-white coloration
- White patch above and behind each eye
- Gray 'saddle-patch' behind fin
- Huge triangular dorsal fin of male (smaller and falcate in female)
- Robust, heavy body
- Large, paddle-shaped pectoral fins
- Usually in mixed family groups

Surface profile   Fluking   Breaching Spyhopping   Porpoising   Playing with prey

Transient (Bigg's) female

Transient (Bigg's) male

Distribution Map

At a glance

Alternative names: Orca; rarely – Blackfish.

Scientific name: *Orcinus orca.*

Adult size: 15–30ft (4.5–9m); 1.4–7.3 tons (1.3–6.6 tonnes); males larger than females.

Diet: includes squid, fish (including sharks), seabirds, sea turtles, seals and sea lions, sea otters and most cetaceans (including Blue Whales); different ecotypes tend to specialise.

Behavior: often inquisitive and approachable, with lots of surface activity such as spyhopping, breaching and lobtailing.

Breeding: single calf born year-round (peaks vary regionally), after a gestation period of 15–18 months.

Distribution: worldwide, in all depths and temperatures, from tropical to polar waters; and from the surf zone to the open sea; but distribution patchy and most common in inshore waters in cooler, high-latitude regions.

World population: no reliable global estimate, but likely minimum 50,000 (over half of these in the Antarctic).

Best places to look in North America: Southeast Alaska, Northwestern Gulf of Alaska, Aleutian Islands & Pribilof Islands, San Juan Islands & Puget Sound, California (including Monterey Bay), Vancouver Island (Johnstone Strait, Salish Sea).

Short-finned Pilot Whale

female

male

Short-finned Pilot Whales are almost impossible to tell apart from Long-finned Pilot Whales at sea but, fortunately, there is relatively little overlap in their range. The main differences are in the shape and length of the flippers, the shape of the skull and the number of teeth. They are very social animals and are almost never seen alone: a typical group contains 15–50 individuals, but sometimes there can be several hundred travelling together. When travelling, pods sometimes swim abreast in long 'chorus lines', and they are frequently accompanied by Bottlenose Dolphins and other small cetaceans. In some parts of the world, they may also be shadowed by Oceanic Whitetips and other pelagic sharks, although the nature of these associations is poorly understood. Females live almost twice as long as males (up to 63 years compared with 30–40 years); they have their final calf when they are about 40 years old, but often continue to lactate and care for it until it is at least 15 years old (all their previous calves would have been weaned at two to three and a half years old).

Identification

- Medium size
- Strong, low bushy blow
- Jet-black, dark gray or brown color
- Variable gray 'saddle-patch' behind fin
- Stocky but elongated body
- Rounded, bulbous forehead (exaggerated in older males)
- Extremely short or non-existent beak
- Large, broad-based dorsal fin sweeps backward
- Dorsal fin set far forward on body

At a glance

Alternative names: Shortfin Pilot Whale; rarely – Pacific Pilot Whale, Blackfish, Pothead Whale.

Scientific name: *Globicephala macrorhynchus.*

Adult size: 12–23ft (3.6–7.2m); 1.1–3.9 tons (1–3.5 tonnes); males significantly larger than females.

Diet: mainly squid, but will take octopuses and fish when opportunities arise.

Behavior: sometimes lobtails, spyhops and breaches; pods may rest motionless at the surface, allowing boats to approach closely.

Breeding: single calf born year-round (peaks in fall and winter in most northern hemisphere populations), after a gestation period of 15–16 months.

Distribution: deep warm temperate to tropical waters worldwide; some overlap with Long-finned Pilot Whale in extreme northern parts of range in North Atlantic and southern parts of range in southern hemisphere.

World population: no reliable global estimate, but certainly hundreds of thousands.

Best places to look in North America: Hawai'i, Baja California (Gulf of California).

Distribution Map

Surface profile   Spyhopping   Fluking   Lying on side

Long-finned Pilot Whale

female

male

Long-finned Pilot Whales typically live in close-knit family groups of 8–20 individuals, but when several of these combine there can be 100 or more travelling together; superpods of as many as 1,200 have been reported. They are often found in the company of other small cetaceans, too, such as Bottlenose Dolphins and Atlantic White-sided Dolphins. Unfortunately, these tight social bonds can work against them. They will not separate – so, if one member of the pod is forced ashore, the others stay with it – and this partly explains why Long-finned Pilot Whales suffer from more mass strandings than any other cetacean. It also makes them easy targets for whalers. They have been hunted in many parts of their range, from Newfoundland to Scotland and the Falkland Islands, and are still being taken in Greenland and the Faroe Islands. Long-finned and Short-finned Pilot Whales are almost impossible to tell apart at sea but, fortunately, there is relatively little overlap in their range. The main differences are in the length and shape of the flippers, the shape of the skull and the number of teeth.

Identification

- Medium size
- Strong, low bushy blow
- Jet-black or dark-gray/brown color
- Variable gray 'saddle-patch' behind fin
- Stocky but elongated body
- Rounded, bulbous forehead (exaggerated in older males)
- Extremely short or non-existent beak
- Large, broad-based dorsal fin sweeps backward
- Dorsal fin set far forward on body

Surface profile   Spyhopping   Lobtailing   Lying on side

At a glance

Alternative names: Longfin Pilot Whale; rarely – Caaing Whale, Atlantic Pilot Whale, Blackfish, Pothead Whale.

Scientific name: *Globicephala melas.*

Adult size: 12.5–22ft (3.8–6.7m); 1.4–2.5 tons (1.3–2.3 tonnes); males larger than females.

Diet: mainly squid, but will take octopuses and fish when opportunities arise.

Behavior: sometimes lobtails and spyhops, but breaching less common than in Short-finned; pods may rest motionless at the surface, allowing boats to approach closely.

Breeding: single calf born year-round (peaks in spring and summer), after a gestation period of 12–16 months.

Distribution: two distinct populations in deep cold temperate to sub-polar waters: one in the southern hemisphere and the other in the North Atlantic; some overlap in range with Short-finned Pilot Whale.

World population: no reliable global estimate, but possibly as high as 1 million.

Best places to look in North America: The Gully, St Lawrence River & Gulf of St Lawrence.

Distribution Map

Pygmy Killer Whale

Pygmy Killer Whales (and their relatives – Killer Whales, Pilot Whales, False Killer Whales and Melon-headed Whales) actually belong to the dolphin family. They are no bigger than dolphins themselves, but are known to attack dolphins in some parts of the world and, in captivity, have been quite aggressive toward people. They are very similar to Melon-headed Whales, with which they share almost the same habitat and range, and the two species can be difficult to distinguish at sea. The Pygmy Killer has a more rounded head and flippers and a slightly straighter and narrower cape, although these features can only be seen sufficiently clearly when the animals are very close and in calm conditions. Some individuals have a distinctive white 'chin' but, again, this is only visible at close range. Although they are widely distributed in warm waters around the world, typically living in groups of 12–50 individuals, they do not appear to be particularly abundant anywhere. Surprisingly little is known about them and they are rarely encountered on whale-watching trips. A glimpse of a pod, perhaps swimming abreast in a perfectly coordinated 'chorus line', is an unusual and welcome sight.

Identification

- Small size
- Dolphin-like
- Robust, dark-gray to black body
- Darker dorsal cape not as low as in Melon-headed
- Large white or gray patch on belly
- Conical head with no beak
- White, light gray or pinkish 'lips'
- Some individuals have white chin
- Tall, falcate dorsal fin near midpoint of back

Surface profile   Spyhopping   Breaching   Lobtailing

At a glance

Alternative names: rarely – Lesser Killer Whale, Slender Blackfish, Slender Pilot Whale.

Scientific name: *Feresa attenuata.*

Adult size: 6.9–8.5ft (2.1–2.6m); 240–500lb (110–225kg); minimal size difference between sexes.

Diet: squid and various small fish; may also prey opportunistically on other dolphins in some parts of range.

Behavior: aerial behavior quite rare, though may spyhop, breach and lobtail; occasionally bow-rides and wake-rides but normally avoids boats.

Breeding: single calf, otherwise details unknown.

Distribution: deep waters in the sub-tropics and tropics, mainly between *c*. 40°N–*c*. 35°S; rarely occurs close to shore, except around oceanic islands.

World population: unknown.

Best places to look in North America: nowhere for reliable sightings. Occasional sightings in Hawai'i.

Distribution Map

Melon-headed Whale

Despite its wide distribution, the Melon-headed Whale is rarely encountered at sea and is relatively poorly known. The main exception is Hawai'i – a particular hotspot where there is a resident population of some 450 animals around Hawai'i Island and another population of about 8,000 that ranges throughout the archipelago. The Melon-headed Whale was originally thought to be a dolphin, but when scientists studied a large herd that had been caught and killed off Japan, in 1965, it was found to be so different that it deserved its own genus (although it is a member of the dolphin family). Melon-headed Whales are often seen together with Fraser's Dolphins and, to a lesser degree, with other species of dolphin. They often travel at high speed, porpoising out of the water and creating a lot of spray as they surface and rapidly change direction. They are very similar to Pygmy Killer Whales, with which they share almost the same habitat and range, and the two species can be difficult to distinguish at sea. Generally speaking, if a large number of animals is seen together (more than 100) they are more likely to be Melon-headed Whales; they normally travel in tightly packed herds of 100–500, although as many as 2,000 have been seen together.

Identification

- Small size
- Dolphin-like
- Robust, charcoal-gray to dark-gray body
- Conical head with no beak
- Darker dorsal cape dips lower than in Pygmy Killer
- Dark 'mask' on face
- White, light gray or pinkish 'lips'
- Tall, falcate dorsal fin near midpoint of back
- Sickle-shaped, sharply pointed flippers

Surface profile

Leaping

At a glance

Alternative names: rarely – Electra Dolphin, Little Killer Whale, Melonhead Whale, Many-toothed Blackfish.

Scientific name: *Peponocephala electra*.

Adult size: 6.9–9.2ft (2.1–2.8m); 350–600lb (160–275kg); males slightly larger than females.

Diet: squid and various small fish, some crustaceans.

Behavior: may bow-ride, breach and spyhop, and often moves at high speed; will approach boats in some regions, but elsewhere avoids boats and is less demonstrative.

Breeding: single calf born possibly July–August (northern hemisphere), after a gestation period of about 12 months.

Distribution: deep waters in the sub-tropics and tropics, mainly between *c.* 40°N–*c.* 35°S; rarely occurs close to shore, except around oceanic islands.

World population: unknown.

Best places to look in North America: nowhere for reliable sightings. Occasional sightings in Hawai'i.

Distribution Map

False Killer Whale

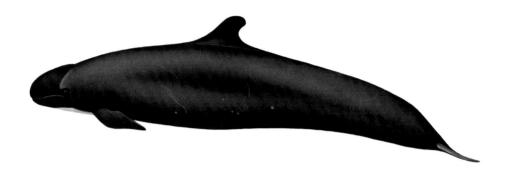

The False Killer Whale can look rather menacing, with its black torpedo-shaped body and rows of sharp teeth. Indeed, it is known to attack groups of small cetaceans and has even been observed attacking Sperm Whales and killing Humpback Whale calves. But this sort of aggression appears to be uncommon and False Killer Whales often interact peacefully with Bottlenose Dolphins and other cetaceans. In many ways, they behave more like dolphins – leaping high into the air, making rapid turns underwater, and even riding the bow waves of passing boats and ships. Despite their name they are, after all, members of the dolphin family. False Killer Whales are extremely social, with most pods containing 10–60 animals (although several hundred have been seen travelling together) including both sexes and all ages. They are often involved in mass strandings; one of the largest recorded involved more than 1,000 animals. Their size distinguishes them from Pygmy Killer Whales and Melon-headed Whales, and they are slimmer and have a more prominent dorsal fin than Pilot Whales (more like the fin of a young Killer Whale).

Identification

- Medium size
- Uniformly dark gray to black color (may be lighter on throat and chest)
- Long, slender body
- Slender, conical head with no discernible beak
- Head all black with no white 'lips'
- Tip of upper jaw slightly overhangs lower jaw
- Prominent, falcate dorsal fin near midpoint of back
- Unique 'elbow' on flippers

Surface profile   Leaping

At a glance

Alternative names: Pseudorca; rarely – False Pilot Whale, Blackfish.

Scientific name: *Pseudorca crassidens*.

Adult size: 14–20ft (4.3–6.1m); 1.2–2.5 tons (1.1–2.2 tonnes); males larger than females.

Diet: mainly squid, but also large fish; also known to attack dolphins and whale calves.

Behavior: will approach boats to investigate, bow-ride or wake-ride; highly acrobatic and often breaches, causing a huge splash for a whale of its size.

Breeding: single calf born year-round, after a gestation period of 11–16 months.

Distribution: widely distributed in tropical, sub-tropical and warm temperate waters worldwide; prefers deep water and normally encountered offshore.

World population: unknown.

Best places to look in North America: Hawai'i.

Distribution Map

Rough-toothed Dolphin

A strange-looking animal, with a long narrow beak that blends into its forehead without a crease, the Rough-toothed Dolphin has a slightly reptilian or primitive appearance. It has been described as the 'ugly duckling' of the dolphin world, but has its own unique beauty. It is named for a series of fine, vertical wrinkles on the enamel cap of each tooth although, of course, these are impossible to see in the wild. In contrast, the light-colored blotches on some individuals (mostly caused by the bites of Cookie-cutter Sharks) and the uniquely sloping forehead can be quite distinctive at sea. Often seen in the company of other dolphins such as Bottlenose, Spotted and Spinner, Rough-toothed Dolphins are gregarious, normally traveling in groups of 10–20 at a time (sometimes 100 or more) that often swim shoulder to shoulder. They have a reputation for swimming slowly, and sometimes appear quite lethargic compared with other dolphins, but they do sometimes bow-ride, wake-ride, spyhop and even perform low breaches. They are also know to 'surf', skimming the water with the tips of their beaks and chins above the surface as they move at high speed.

Identification

- Robust body in front of dorsal fin (slimmer behind)
- Dark gray body with darker, narrow dorsal cape
- White or pinkish blotches (variable)
- Conical head
- Moderately long beak continuous with gently sloping forehead
- May have white or pinkish white 'lips'
- Prominent, falcate dorsal fin near midpoint of back
- Large flippers set far back

Surface profile

Surfing

At a glance

Alternative name: rarely – Slopehead.

Scientific name: *Steno bredanensis*.

Adult size: 6.8–9.2ft (2.1–2.8m); 220–350lb (100–160kg); males slightly larger than females.

Diet: mainly fish and squid.

Behavior: shy of boats in some parts of the world, but occasionally bow-rides elsewhere; some aerial behavior.

Breeding: single calf, otherwise details unknown.

Distribution: mainly deep oceanic waters in warm temperate, sub-tropical and tropical waters worldwide; rarely ranges north of 40°N or south of 35°S; found in many semi-enclosed seas, such as the Gulf of Mexico and the Gulf of California.

World population: no reliable global estimate, but possibly low hundreds of thousands.

Best places to look in North America: Hawai'i, Banderas Bay, Bahia de Petatlán.

Distribution Map

Short-beaked Common Dolphin

In 1994, the Common Dolphin was officially separated into two distinct species: the Short-beaked Common Dolphin (*Delphinus delphis*) and the Long-beaked Common Dolphin (*Delphinus capensis*). It is possible that there are other Common Dolphin species yet to be recognized. All of them have a distinctive hourglass pattern of white, gray, yellow and black on their sides, which forms a dark 'V' shape below the dorsal fin and looks almost like a reflection of the fin itself. But they show many variations within this basic framework and it can be extremely difficult to tell the two species apart (they are often seen in the same vicinity but do not appear to mix). As their names suggest, the most distinctive feature is their beaks: the Short-beaked has a relatively shorter, slightly stubbier beak with more open facial markings than the Long-beaked. It also has a more robust body, a brighter, more contrasting body pattern and a more rounded, bulging melon, and it is more likely to have variable amounts of pale pigment in the center of its dorsal fin. From a distance, a large school of Short-beaked Common Dolphins looks like rough water, as the fast-swimming, boisterous animals whip the ocean's surface into a froth.

Identification

- Slightly robust body (chunkier than Long-beaked)
- Shorter beak than Long-beaked
- More rounded, bulging melon than Long-beaked
- Dark cape with 'V' shape under dorsal fin
- Criss-cross or hourglass pattern on sides
- Tan or yellowish patches on sides
- White underside
- Tall, falcate dorsal fin near midpoint of back
- Brighter, more contrasting color pattern than Long-beaked

Surface profile

Porpoising

At a glance

Alternative names: Common Porpoise; rarely – Criss-cross Dolphin, Saddleback Dolphin, White-bellied Porpoise.

Scientific name: *Delphinus delphis.*

Adult size: 5.2–8.9ft (1.6–2.7m); 155–440lb (70–200kg); males slightly larger than females.

Diet: small fish and squid.

Behavior: fast swimmer and energetic, boisterous acrobat; frequently bow-rides; herd sizes range from about 10–10,000.

Breeding: single calf born mainly in June–September (but variable according to location), after a gestation period of 10–11 months.

Distribution: cool temperate to tropical waters in the Atlantic and Pacific Oceans (no confirmed records from the Indian Ocean); from nearshore waters to far offshore.

World population: no reliable global estimate, but at least low millions (including 370,000 along the US west coast and 30,000 along the US east coast).

Best places to look in North America: California, Eastern Seaboard (New York to Georgia), The Gully, Baja California (Pacific Coast, Los Cabos & Gorda Banks, Gulf of California).

Distribution Map

Long-beaked Common Dolphin

The Long-beaked Common Dolphin is not as well known as its Short-beaked relative. This is partly because it is not as common, but also because, until quite recently, it was considered merely as a type of Short-beaked Common Dolphin rather than a separate species in its own right. There is another variation, with an exceptionally long beak, which was once considered to be a separate species called the Indo-Pacific Common Dolphin (*Delphinus tropicalis*), but this is now believed to be a sub-species of the Long-beaked. All have one feature in common that distinguishes them from other dolphins – a unique criss-cross color pattern on their sides. It is not unusual to see schools of Long-beaked and Short-beaked Common Dolphins in the same general area on the same day, but Long-beaked seem to prefer shallower and warmer water and usually occur closer to shore; however, they are known to range up to 100 miles from the coast. From a distance, a large school of Long-beaked Common Dolphins looks like rough water, as the fast-swimming, boisterous animals whip the ocean's surface into a froth.

Identification

- Slender body (less robust than Short-beaked)
- Longer beak than Short-beaked
- Flatter, less bulging melon than Short-beaked
- Dark cape with 'V' shape under dorsal fin
- Criss-cross or hourglass pattern on sides
- Tan or yellowish patches on sides
- White underside
- Tall, falcate dorsal fin near midpoint of back
- More muted color pattern than Short-beaked

Surface profile   Porpoising

At a glance

Alternative names: Indo-Pacific Common Dolphin, Common Porpoise; rarely – Criss-cross Dolphin, Saddleback Dolphin, White-bellied Porpoise.

Scientific name: *Delphinus capensis.*

Adult size: 6.2–8.5ft (1.9–2.6m); 155–520lb (70–235kg); males slightly larger than females.

Diet: small fish and squid.

Behavior: fast swimmer and energetic, boisterous acrobat; frequently bow-rides; herd sizes range from about 10–10,000.

Breeding: single calf probably born year-round (but may vary according to location), after a gestation period of around 10–11 months.

Distribution: warm temperate to tropical waters in the Atlantic, Pacific and Indian Oceans; more tropical and inshore than Short-beaked.

World population: no reliable global estimate, but believed to be 279,000 along the west coast of the US and Mexico.

Best places to look in North America: California (including Monterey Bay), Baja California (Ojo de Liebre, Magdalena Bay, Pacific Coast, Los Cabos & Gorda Banks, Gulf of California).

Distribution Map

Atlantic Spotted Dolphin

In many ways, the Atlantic Spotted Dolphin resembles the Indo-Pacific Bottlenose Dolphin more closely than it does the Pantropical Spotted Dolphin. It begins life with no spots (immature animals look surprisingly like Bottlenose Dolphins) and spots develop, in both number and size, as the animal ages. But no two Atlantic Spotted Dolphins look alike because, even in adults, the spotting varies greatly from one individual to another and from region to region. Most adults have dark spots on the underside and light spots on the sides and back; in some older animals, the spots are so large and multitudinous that their normal background color is barely visible. Spotting usually decreases from west to east across the Atlantic and sometimes with distance from the mainland. This variation can make identification at sea quite challenging, especially since Atlantic Spotted Dolphins and Bottlenose Dolphins sometimes live in mixed schools and part of the range overlaps with Pantropical Spotted Dolphins (although these tend to have smaller spots). Atlantic Spotted Dolphins typically live in fairly large groups of up to 50 animals offshore, with smaller groups of 5–15 animals in coastal populations.

Identification

- Fairly robust body
- Moderately long stubby beak (often white-tipped)
- Beak separated from melon by distinct crease
- Most adults heavily spotted
- Three-toned color pattern (not always clear)
- Pale diagonal shoulder blaze
- Tall, falcate dorsal fin near midpoint of back
- Variable appearance within herd

Surface profile   Leaping   Spyhopping   Porpoising

At a glance

Alternative names: Spotted Porpoise, Spotter; rarely – Bridled Dolphin.

Scientific name: *Stenella frontalis.*

Adult size: 5.6–7.5ft (1.7–2.3m); 220–315lb (100–143kg); males slightly larger than females.

Diet: wide variety of fish and squid, as well as benthic invertebrates.

Behavior: fast and energetic swimmer and can be very active at the surface; avid bow-rider.

Breeding: single calf, otherwise details poorly known.

Distribution: warm temperate, sub-tropical and tropical waters in the North and South Atlantic, from about 50°N–25°S; coastal and offshore (though mostly over the continental shelf).

World population: unknown.

Best places to look in North America: nowhere for reliable sightings. Occasional sightings in Eastern Seaboard (New York to Georgia), Florida & the Gulf States.

Distribution Map

Pantropical Spotted Dolphin

As their name suggests, adult Pantropical Spotted Dolphins are usually covered in white spots. However, the amount of spotting varies greatly with age as well as within populations and between populations. Newborn calves and some adults are unspotted, but other adults are very heavily spotted. Two sub-species are currently recognized: one living in oceanic tropical waters worldwide and the other mainly in coastal waters of the eastern Pacific (which tends to be larger, more spotted and more robust, and occurs in smaller schools than the offshore animals). Pantropical Spotted Dolphins spend a lot of time in the air and the youngsters, in particular, can make some impressively high vertical leaps. Tuna-fishing operations in the eastern tropical Pacific killed some 3–4.9 million Pantropical Spotted Dolphins (along with large numbers of other dolphin species) from 1959–72. New laws and release techniques have reduced the level of slaughter dramatically, but it has still not been stopped altogether. It is unclear why the dolphins associate with tuna – it might increase foraging efficiency or provide better protection from predators.

Identification

- Slender, elongated body (coastal form more robust)
- Dark gray cape, lighter underside
- Many adults heavily spotted
- Long, narrow beak with white tip and 'lips'
- Beak separated from melon by distinct crease
- Thick, dark stripe from beak to flipper
- Tall, strongly falcate dorsal fin near midpoint of back
- Variable appearance within herd

Surface profile   Leaping   Fluking   Porpoising

At a glance

Alternative names: Spotter, Spotted Dolphin, Spotted Porpoise; rarely – Bridled Dolphin, White-spotted Dolphin.

Scientific name: *Stenella attenuata*.

Adult size: 5.2–8.5ft (1.6–2.6m); max 265lb (120kg); males slightly larger than females.

Diet: mainly fish and squid, some crustaceans.

Behavior: fast and energetic swimmer and can be very active at the surface; avid bow-rider in some areas (although learned to avoid boats in the tuna-fishing areas of the eastern tropical Pacific).

Breeding: single calf born mainly in spring and summer, after a gestation period of 11–12 months.

Distribution: deep sub-tropical and tropical waters worldwide, both inshore and offshore; most abundant near the equator, but occurs from 40°N–40°S.

World population: no reliable global estimate, but perhaps more than 2 million (believed to be one of the most abundant dolphins in the world).

Best places to look in North America: Hawai'i, Banderas Bay, Bahia de Petatlán.

Distribution Map

Spinner Dolphin

One of the most acrobatic of all dolphins, the Spinner was named for its incredibly high spinning leaps. It can spin round on its longitudinal axis as many as seven times before splashing back into the water. Few other cetaceans show so much variation in appearance from one region to another and there are currently four recognized sub-species, differing greatly in body shape, size, color and even behavior. The color pattern in most regions is basically three-toned, albeit with considerable regional variations, consisting of a dark-gray cape, light-gray sides and white underside. Numbers were reduced by more than two-thirds by tuna-fishing in the eastern tropical Pacific (the Spinner was the second-most affected dolphin in this fishery, after the Pantropical Spotted Dolphin). Fortunately, public outrage forced the authorities to introduce new rules and regulations, which include releasing dolphins from the nets when they are captured, and the slaughter has dropped to thousands (rather than hundreds of thousands) of deaths a year. However, the population is still not recovering particularly well.

Identification

- Slender, elongated body
- Three-toned color pattern
- Long, narrow beak often with dark tip
- Dark stripe from eye to flipper
- Gently sloping melon
- Tall, slightly falcate or erect dorsal fin near midpoint of back
- Males may have forward-leaning dorsal fin
- Performs high, spinning leaps

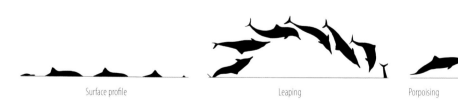

Surface profile   Leaping   Porpoising

At a glance

Alternative names: Long-snouted Spinner Dolphin, Spinner; rarely – Longsnout, Rollover, Long-beaked Dolphin.

Scientific name: *Stenella longirostris.*

Adult size: 4.3–7.9ft (1.3–2.4m); max 130–180lb (60–80kg); males larger than females.

Diet: variety of small fish, squid and crustaceans.

Behavior: fast and energetic swimmer and can be very active at the surface; avid bow-rider in some areas (though learned to avoid boats in the tuna-fishing areas of the eastern tropical Pacific).

Breeding: single calf born late spring to fall (depending on location), after a gestation period of about 10 months.

Distribution: deep sub-tropical and tropical waters worldwide (although sometimes in warm temperate waters as well) both inshore and offshore; most abundant near the equator, but occurs from 40°N–40°S.

World population: no reliable global estimate, but certainly many hundreds of thousands (believed to be one of the most abundant dolphins in the world).

Best places to look in North America: Hawai'i, Bahia de Petatlán.

Distribution Map

Clymene Dolphin

For many years the Clymene Dolphin, or Short-snouted Spinner Dolphin as it is sometimes called, was considered to be one of the many variations of the Long-snouted Spinner. The two animals sometimes associate with one another and, like the Spinner, the Clymene has a three-toned coloration: a dark gray cape, lighter gray sides, and a white underside. Some populations even spin longitudinally when breaching, although not as frequently or as elaborately as Spinners (up to three to four revolutions compared with seven). There is considerable overlap in range between the two species in the Atlantic and, although the Clymene Dolphin is smaller and generally more robust than the Long-snouted Spinner, with a shorter and stockier beak, they can be difficult to tell apart at sea. The Clymene Dolphin was officially classified as a separate species in 1981 and the latest genetic research suggests that it may, after all, be more closely related to the Striped Dolphin. The Clymene (pronounced cly-mee-nee) is a keen bow-rider and will go out of its way to accompany a boat or ship, yet remains one of the least-known oceanic dolphins.

Identification

- Relatively small, fairly robust body
- Three-toned color pattern
- Dark-gray or black cape dips below dorsal fin and above eye
- Long beak often with black tip, lips and 'moustache'
- Distinct crease between beak and melon
- Pale-gray stripe from eye to flipper
- Prominent, slightly falcate or triangular dorsal fin near midpoint of back
- Performs high, spinning leaps

Surface profile   Leaping   Porpoising

At a glance

Alternative names: Short-snouted Spinner Dolphin; rarely – Atlantic Spinner Dolphin, Helmet Dolphin, Senegal Dolphin.

Scientific name: *Stenella clymene.*

Adult size: 5.9–6.6ft (1.8–2m); 165–200lb (75–90kg); males larger than females.

Diet: probably small fish and squid.

Behavior: fast and energetic swimmer and can be very active at the surface; avid bow-rider.

Breeding: single calf, otherwise details poorly known.

Distribution: sub-tropical and tropical waters of the Atlantic Ocean (sometimes also warm temperate), mainly in deep waters offshore and not often seen near shore (except where deep water approaches the coast).

World population: no reliable global estimate.

Best places to look in North America: nowhere for reliable sightings. Occasional sightings in Eastern Seaboard (New York to Georgia).

Distribution Map

Striped Dolphin

The ancient Greeks marvelled at the beauty of Striped Dolphins and painted them in their frescoes several thousand years ago. The various stripes and brush strokes on their bodies, and the bright pink undersides of some individuals, make them look as if they have been hand-painted in real life. Their name comes from the distinctive dark stripes that run down the sides of their bodies. They are highly conspicuous animals, seeming to spend an inordinate amount of their time in the air. Their acrobatic repertoire includes breaches up to 23ft high, belly-flops, back somersaults, and upside-down leaps; they also specialise in a remarkable behavior called 'roto-tailing', which involves whipping their tails in a circle as they perform high-arcing leaps out of the water. They prefer deep water, often feeding close to the seabed, and have been recorded diving to depths of 2,300ft. Herds of 100–500 are quite common and sometimes as many as several thousand are found together. Their distinctive stripes and high-speed swimming – and the fact that they are more easily spooked than other tropical dolphins – prompted fishermen to call them 'Streakers'.

Identification

- Fairly robust body
- Dark gray or blue-gray dorsal cape
- White or pinkish underside
- Dark stripes from eye to flipper and from eye along flank
- Pale brush stroke from head toward dorsal fin
- Dark, prominent, slightly falcate dorsal fin near midpoint of back
- Moderately long beak
- Distinct crease between beak and melon

Surface profile   Leaping

At a glance

Alternative names: Streaker; rarely – Streaker Porpoise, Euphrosyne Dolphin, Whitebelly, Meyen's Dolphin, Gray's Dolphin.

Scientific name: *Stenella coeruleoalba*.

Adult size: 5.9–8.9ft (1.8–2.7m); 200–350lb (90–160kg); males slightly larger than females.

Diet: mainly fish and squid, possibly crustaceans.

Behavior: highly conspicuous and capable of amazing acrobatics; will readily bow-ride in the Atlantic and Indian Oceans (less often in the Pacific).

Breeding: single calf (peak season varies with locality), after a gestation period of about 12–13 months.

Distribution: warm temperate, sub-tropical and tropical waters worldwide (typically between 50°N–40°S); usually encountered offshore, but will venture close to land if water sufficiently deep.

World population: no reliable global estimate, but probably at least 2 million.

Best places to look in North America: nowhere for reliable sightings. Occasional sightings in California, The Gully.

Distribution Map

Common Bottlenose Dolphin

In many ways, the Common Bottlenose Dolphin is the archetypal dolphin. The star of television programs, films and (unfortunately) marine parks around the world, it is the species most people imagine when the word 'dolphin' is mentioned. It can have rather complex coloring, although under many lighting conditions appears to be a uniform and quite featureless gray. There are many geographical variations, differing in size, shape and color, and their taxonomy is still in dispute (even though the Bottlenose Dolphin is one of the best-studied cetaceans in the world). An entirely separate species, called the Indo-Pacific Bottlenose Dolphin, is now recognized in the Pacific and Indian Oceans and it is quite possible that other species will be separated in the future. There are also differences between inshore and offshore populations: inshore forms tend to be smaller and lighter, live in smaller groups and travel much less. In many parts of the world, lone individuals have become 'friendlies', apparently more interested in sharing the company of human swimmers and small boats than others of their own kind; they often remain in the same area for years at a time.

Identification

- Relatively robust body
- Light gray to nearly black coloring
- Lighter underside
- Faint dorsal cape (variable)
- Short to moderate-length stubby beak
- Rounded forehead with marked crease at beak
- Mouthline looks like a 'smile'
- Prominent, falcate dorsal fin near midpoint of back

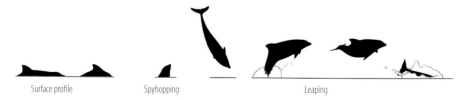

Surface profile   Spyhopping   Leaping

At a glance

Alternative names: Bottle-nosed Dolphin; rarely – Black Porpoise.

Scientific name: *Tursiops truncatus.*

Adult size: 6.2–13.1ft (1.9–4m); 300–1,300lb (135–650kg); males slightly larger than females.

Diet: mainly fish and squid, but wide range of other prey; opportunistic feeder, adapting feeding technique to prey and local conditions.

Behavior: highly active at the surface and frequently lobtails, bow-rides, wake-rides, body surfs and leaps.

Breeding: single calf born year-round (mainly spring and summer), after a gestation period of about 12 months.

Distribution: cool temperate to tropical waters worldwide, mainly coastal and over continental shelves; found in many enclosed seas, including the Gulf of Mexico and Gulf of California, and in bays, lagoons, gulfs, channels and river mouths.

World population: no reliable global estimate, but believed to be at least 600,000.

Best places to look in North America: Hawai'i, California (including Monterey Bay), Eastern Seaboard (New York to Georgia), Florida & the Gulf States, Baja California (breeding lagoons, Pacific Coast, Los Cabos & Gorda Banks, Gulf of California), Revillagigedo Archipelago, Banderas Bay, Bahia de Petatlán, Yucatán Peninsula.

Distribution Map

Risso's Dolphin

female

male

Risso's Dolphins are unmistakable, with their slightly bulging foreheads, tall dorsal fins and distinctly battered appearance. They are the most heavily scarred of all the dolphins. The scratches and scars all over the bodies of older animals are caused mainly by the teeth of other Risso's Dolphins (possibly when they are fighting or playing with each other) but confrontations with squid are also to blame. Young animals can be almost as dark as pilot whales, but their body color tends to lighten with age and, although there is a great deal of variation between individuals, this adds to the scarring to make some older animals almost as white as Belugas; higher-latitude animals tend to be much lighter, too. The dorsal fin, flippers and flukes normally remain darker than the rest of the body. There is a distinctive crease down the center of the forehead (rarely visible and only then at close range) that is unique to this species. Risso's Dolphins tend to avoid overlapping habitats with Cuvier's Beaked Whales and Sperm Whales (which also feed on deep-water squid).

Identification

- Robust body heavily scarred
- Great color variation within school from dark gray to nearly white
- Large, bulbous head with indistinct beak
- Shallow vertical crease on front of melon
- Extremely tall, falcate dorsal fin near midpoint of back
- Long, pointed, recurved flippers
- Flippers, flukes and dorsal fin tend to remain dark

At a glance

Alternative names: Grampus; rarely – Gray Dolphin, Gray Grampus, White-headed Grampus.

Scientific name: *Grampus griseus.*

Adult size: 12.5–13.5ft (3.8–4.1m); 660–1,100lb (300–500kg); minimal size difference between sexes.

Diet: favorite prey is squid, but will also take octopuses and crustaceans.

Behavior: often quite lethargic, but frequently breaches, porpoises and spyhops; will bow-ride but more likely to swim alongside a vessel, or in its wake.

Breeding: single calf born year-round (peak period varies according to location), after a gestation period of 13–14 months.

Distribution: mainly deep warm temperate to tropical waters worldwide, particularly over the continental slope and outer shelf; rarely in water less than 10°C.

World population: no reliable global estimate, but probably more than 500,000.

Best places to look in North America: California (including Monterey Bay).

Distribution Map

Surface profile   Spyhopping   Breaching

White-beaked Dolphin

Strikingly large and robust for a dolphin, the White-beaked Dolphin really does have a white beak (at least, most individuals do: in some, it is ashy gray or even darker). Capable of swimming at considerable speed, sometimes churning the water and creating a 'rooster tail' reminiscent of a Dall's Porpoise, it can be quite acrobatic and will often breach. It frequently bow-rides in some parts of its range, too, but likes speed and tends to lose interest rather quickly if the vessel is travelling too slowly. White-beaked Dolphins share much of their North Atlantic home with Atlantic White-sided Dolphins, but venture farther north into sub-Arctic waters and have one of the most northerly ranges of all the world's dolphins (as far north as Svalbard). The two species are sometimes seen feeding together (White-beaked Dolphins also associate with baleen whales such as Fin Whales and Humpbacks, Long-finned Pilot Whales, Killer Whales, Bottlenose Dolphins and Common Dolphins). Groups of fewer than 30 White-beaked Dolphins are most common, though as many as 1,500 have been seen together on rare occasions.

Identification

- Very robust body
- Complex white, gray and black markings
- Tailstock generally paler
- White blaze on each flank
- Very prominent, falcate dorsal fin near midpoint of back
- Short and thick white, brown or gray beak
- Mostly dark flippers, dorsal fin and flukes
- Often dark or light flecking between eye and flipper

Surface profile

Leaping

Porpoising

At a glance

Alternative names: rarely – White-beaked Porpoise, White-nosed Dolphin, Squid-hound.

Scientific name: *Lagenorhynchus albirostris*.

Adult size: 7.9–10.2ft (2.4–3.1m); 400–770lb (180–350kg); males slightly larger than females.

Diet: mainly small schooling fish, some squid, octopuses and crustaceans.

Behavior: fast, powerful swimmer and sometimes acrobatic; may wake-ride or bow-ride, especially in front of large, fast-moving vessels (although some populations are elusive).

Breeding: single calf born mainly during May–September, after a gestation period of about 11 months.

Distribution: widely distributed in cool temperate to sub-Arctic waters of the northern North Atlantic, even at the polar ice edge; found inshore, offshore and over the continental shelf (mainly in water less than 650ft (200m) deep).

World population: no reliable global estimate, but possibly low hundreds of thousands.

Best places to look in North America: Newfoundland, St Lawrence River & Gulf of St Lawrence.

Distribution Map

Atlantic White-sided Dolphin

Atlantic White-sided Dolphins were well known to early fishermen and whalers in the North Atlantic, and were given names such as 'Springer' or 'Jumper' to reflect their acrobatic antics. At first glance, the striking yellow or tan streak along each side of the body makes this species look superficially similar to a Common Dolphin. But the position of the streak on the tailstock, the lack of an hourglass pattern, and the complex and sharply demarcated pattern of bold gray, white and black on the rest of the body, make it quite distinctive at close range. It often feeds in association with White-beaked Dolphins, Long-finned Pilot Whales, Short-beaked Common Dolphins and even baleen whales such as Fin Whales and Humpbacks. It seems to enjoy playing around large whales and sometimes rides their bow waves. Researchers often call the Atlantic White-sided Dolphin a 'Lag', which is short for the scientific name *Lagenorhynchus*.

Identification

- Robust body with thick tailstock
- Black or dark gray upperside
- Complex patterning of gray, white and yellow or tan along flanks
- White underside
- Short, thick beak
- Thin dark-gray stripe from eye to flipper
- Black or dark-gray dorsal fin, flukes and flippers
- Tall, falcate dorsal fin near midpoint of back

Surface profile

Porpoising

At a glance

Alternative names: Lag, White-side; rarely – Jumper, Springer.

Scientific name: *Lagenorhynchus acutus*.

Adult size: 6.2–9.2ft (1.9–2.8m); 360–520lb (165–235kg); males slightly larger than females.

Diet: fish, squid and crustaceans.

Behavior: fast swimmer and acrobatic (especially in large groups), often breaching and tail-slapping; larger animals (particularly males) will sometimes bow-ride and wake-ride.

Breeding: single calf born mainly during May–September (earlier in the west, later in the east), after a gestation period of about 11 months.

Distribution: cold temperate to sub-Arctic waters of the northern North Atlantic, especially over the outer continental shelf and slope (but anywhere from relatively shallow to oceanic waters).

World population: no reliable global estimate, but over 52,000 along the eastern US.

Best places to look in North America: New England, Newfoundland, The Gully, St Lawrence River & Gulf of St Lawrence.

Distribution Map

Pacific White-sided Dolphin

Pacific White-sided Dolphins are great fun to watch. They often live in large schools containing hundreds or even thousands of individuals, and are so lively and boisterous that their splashes can be seen long before it is possible to see the animals themselves. They leap into the air and spin or turn complete somersaults before splashing back into the water, and often ride the bow waves of passing boats or ships. Seen from above when they are bow-riding, the two narrow stripes down each side look like a pair of braces and are very distinctive. Pacific White-sided Dolphins look remarkably similar to Dusky Dolphins and it was once suggested that the two belong to the same species. However, genetic evidence does not support this idea and there is no overlap in range (the Dusky Dolphin does not occur in North America). Like their Atlantic counterparts, Pacific White-sided Dolphins are gregarious animals and they can often be seen with other cetaceans, especially Risso's Dolphins and Northern Right Whale Dolphins, as well as sea lions and seals. Researchers often call them 'Lags', which is short for the scientific name *Lagenorhynchus*.

Identification

- Robust body
- Black or dark-gray upperside
- Complex patterning of gray and black along flanks
- White lower jaw and underside (demarcated by bold black border)
- Short, thick, black-tipped beak
- Black or dark-gray flukes and flippers
- Large, falcate, broad-based dorsal fin near midpoint of back
- Front of dorsal fin dark gray, rear light gray to white

Surface profile   Porpoising

At a glance

Alternative names: Lag, White-side; rarely – Pacific Striped Dolphin, Hook-finned Porpoise, Jumper, Springer.

Scientific name: *Lagenorhynchus obliquidens.*

Adult size: 7.5–8.2ft (2.3–2.5m); 360–440lb (165–200kg); males slightly larger than females.

Diet: fish and squid.

Behavior: highly acrobatic and playful, often breaching and somersaulting; will readily bow-ride and wake-ride.

Breeding: single calf (peak season usually May–September, but varies with locality), after a gestation period of about 12 months.

Distribution: cool temperate waters of the North Pacific, and some adjacent seas; mainly offshore (or in deep water close to shore); may be seasonal inshore–offshore and north–south movements.

World population: no reliable global estimate, but believed to be approaching 1 million.

Best places to look in North America: Southeast Alaska, San Juan Islands & Puget Sound, Westport & the Olympic Coast, California (including Monterey Bay), Vancouver Island (Johnstone Strait, Salish Sea), Baja California (Pacific coast).

Distribution Map

Fraser's Dolphin

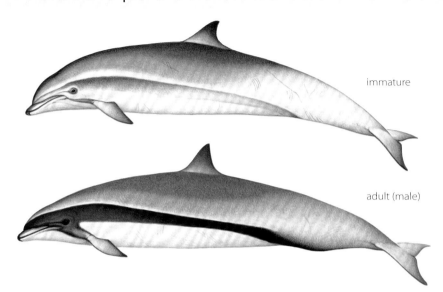

immature

adult (male)

Fraser's Dolphin was not scientifically described until 1956, after cetologist Francis Charles Fraser found a mislabelled skeleton in the British Museum that had been collected 60 years earlier from a beach in Sarawak, Malaysia (it was originally named the Sarawak Dolphin). Western scientists did not know what the animal looked like in real life, or where it lived, until the early 1970s when several complete specimens were stranded in widely separated parts of the world. The species was first seen alive at around the same time. Fraser's Dolphins have been observed on many occasions since then and do not appear to be as rare as was once thought, although they remain poorly known. They are quite variable in appearance, but in some individuals the color pattern is particularly striking: the most distinctive feature is a dark band that runs across the face and all the way along the side of the body of many adults (especially males). Most schools are large, containing 100–500 and as many as several thousand individuals, and they are often associated with other species of warm-water toothed whales and dolphins such as Melon-headed Whales, Short-finned Pilot Whales and Spinner Dolphins.

Identification

- Stocky body
- Blue-gray or gray-brown upperside
- Creamy white or pinkish underside
- Variable bandit 'mask' on some animals (esp males)
- Variable dark lateral stripe (darkest and widest in older males)
- Short but well-defined beak
- Dark stripe from tiny flipper to middle of lower jaw
- Small, triangular or slightly falcate dorsal fin near midpoint of back

At a glance

Alternative names: Fraser's Porpoise; rarely – White-bellied Dolphin, Sarawak Dolphin, Shortsnout Dolphin, Bornean Dolphin.

Scientific name: *Lagenodelphis hosei.*

Adult size: 6.6–8.9ft (2–2.7m); 290–460lb (130–210kg); males slightly larger than females.

Diet: mid-water fish, squid and crustaceans.

Behavior: aggressive fast swimming style, often leaving the water in a burst of spray; will bow-ride in some parts of its range.

Breeding: single calf (peak season varies with locality), after a gestation period of 12–13 months.

Distribution: sub-tropical to tropical waters worldwide, normally between 30°N–30°S; prefers deep offshore waters, but sometimes occurs inshore where deep water approaches the coast.

World population: no reliable global estimate.

Best places to look in North America: nowhere for reliable sightings.

Distribution Map

Surface profile

Porpoising

Northern Right Whale Dolphin

Superficially similar to its southern counterpart (the Southern Right Whale Dolphin) the Northern Right Whale Dolphin is the only dolphin in the North Pacific without a dorsal fin. Its primarily black body color is also distinctive, although it does have a big white patch on its chest that stretches in a white line along the underside of the body to the flukes. The calves of both species are usually dark gray or creamy gray, but they become black and white like their parents when they are about a year old. There is no overlap in range between the two species – they are separated by thousands of miles. Northern Right Whale Dolphins are capable of swimming very fast, making long, low-angled leaps and appearing to bounce across the water – not unlike penguins. But they sometimes surface slowly and keep a low profile, making them difficult to see in anything but the calmest conditions. They are often encountered in the company of other cetaceans, especially Pacific White-sided Dolphins and Risso's Dolphins, and sometimes travel in huge schools of up to 3,000 animals (most schools contain 100–200 animals).

Identification

- Streamlined, slender body
- Predominantly black, with white underside
- No dorsal fin
- White spot under short, slender beak
- Small, predominantly black flippers
- Low-angled leaps give impression of bouncy swimming motion

Surface profile   Porpoising

At a glance

Alternative names: rarely – Pacific Right Whale Porpoise.

Scientific name: *Lissodelphis borealis.*

Adult size: max 10.2ft (3.1m); max 250lb (115kg); males larger than females.

Diet: fish and squid.

Behavior: usually a fast swimmer, creating great surface disturbance, but sometimes swims slowly and unobtrusively; will bow-ride (especially in the company of other dolphins) and sometimes breaches.

Breeding: single calf usually born in July and August, after a gestation period of about 12 months.

Distribution: cool temperate to sub-Arctic waters across the northern North Pacific, mainly in deep offshore waters between about 34–50°N; rarely near land, except in sufficiently deep water.

World population: believed to be 68,000 in the North Pacific (including 20,000 along the coasts of California, Oregon and Washington).

Best places to look in North America: California (including Monterey Bay).

Distribution Map

Dall's Porpoise

Dall's Porpoise is probably the fastest small cetacean and is often seen as a blur when it breaks the surface at high speed. It produces a distinctive V-shaped spray called a 'rooster tail', which is made by a cone of water coming off its head as it rises to breathe and can almost obscure the animal itself. It is very distinctive, with an exceptionally stocky body and striking markings: mostly black but with brilliant white patches on the sides and underside. Young animals are a more muted dark gray and light gray. There are two distinct sub-species: the Dalli-type, which occurs throughout the range and has a relatively smaller area of white on the flanks, and the Truei-type, which migrates between the Pacific coast of Japan and the Sea of Okhotsk and has more white. In the northeastern North Pacific, hybrids between Dall's Porpoises and Harbor Porpoises are relatively common. Unlike most other porpoises, Dall's Porpoises often approach boats and readily bow-ride (although they soon lose interest in vessels travelling too slowly). Thousands of Dall's Porpoises are taken by Japanese fishermen for human consumption and pet food (they are harpooned as they ride the bow waves of catcher boats).

Identification

- Small, exceptionally stocky body
- Sharply demarcated black-and-white markings
- Prominent, broad-based triangular dorsal fin near midpoint of back
- White 'frosting' on upper portion of otherwise black dorsal fin
- Trailing edge of flukes white
- Tiny head in relation to body
- Short, indistinct beak
- Distinctive spray common when surfacing

Surface profile

Porpoising

At a glance

Alternative names: True's Porpoise; rarely – Spray Porpoise, White-flanked Porpoise, White-sided Porpoise.

Scientific name: *Phocoenoides dalli.*

Adult size: 5.6–7.9ft (1.7–2.4m); 300–440lb (135–200kg); males slightly larger than females.

Diet: fish and squid, occasionally crustaceans.

Behavior: often a fast swimmer, creating a great spray of water as it surfaces, but will also move slowly and make little or no disturbance; avid bow-rider, but aerial behavior such as breaching rare.

Breeding: single calf usually born in late spring and summer, after a gestation period of 10–12 months.

Distribution: cool temperate waters of the northern North Pacific and adjacent seas (usually between 30–62°N); mainly offshore and rarely near land, except in sufficiently deep water.

World population: probably over 1.2 million (including 86,000 in Alaska and 100,000 along the west coast of the US).

Best places to look in North America: Southeast Alaska, Northwestern Gulf of Alaska, Aleutian Islands & Pribilof Islands, San Juan Islands & Puget Sound, Westport & the Olympic Coast, California (including Monterey Bay), Vancouver Island (Johnstone Strait, Salish Sea), Baja California (Pacific coast).

Distribution Map

Vaquita

In imminent danger of extinction, the Vaquita is the most endangered marine mammal in the world. Even on official surveys around its home in the northern Gulf of California, western Mexico, this very small porpoise often eludes professional biologists for days or even weeks at a time. Consequently, few scientists have ever seen one alive, and we know little about its life and habits. Most sightings are of pairs or small groups in the western portion of the range, between San Felipe Bay and Rocas Consag. The main threat to Vaquitas is entanglement and drowning in near-invisible gillnets, since at least the late 1940s, and in the past as many as 84 were being drowned every year. Conservation efforts were slow to start, but there has been a determined effort to save the species in recent years, including a temporary ban on the use of gillnets, compensation for fishermen, and efforts to develop alternative fishing gear. Unfortunately, it may be too little too late: there are believed to be as few as 30 Vaquitas left and their future is undoubtedly very bleak indeed.

Identification

- Small, stocky body
- Complex but subtle brownish-gray cape
- Lighter brownish-gray sides, whitish underside
- Tall, falcate, dolphin-like dorsal fin near midpoint of back
- Rounded head with virtually no beak
- Black to dark-gray 'lips' and eye rings
- Dark stripe from corner of beak to flipper

Surface profile   Porpoising

At a glance

Alternative names: Gulf of California Porpoise, Cochito; rarely – Gulf Porpoise, Desert Porpoise.

Scientific name: *Phocoena sinus.*

Adult size: 4.3–4.9ft (1.3–1.5m); 66–120lb (30–55kg); females larger than males.

Diet: fish and squid, occasionally crustaceans.

Behavior: usually avoids boats and ships that are travelling, but will sometimes approach if they are drifting; aerial behavior such as breaching is very rare.

Breeding: single calf usually born in March or April, after a gestation period of 10–11 months.

Distribution: most restricted distribution of any marine cetacean, surviving only in the murky, shallow waters at the extreme northern end of the Gulf of California, western Mexico, near the Colorado River Estuary.

World population: approximately 30.

Best places to look in North America: very rarely seen in restricted range in extreme northern Gulf of California.

Distribution Map

Harbor Porpoise

The Harbor Porpoise is commonly seen along the coasts of many countries in the northern hemisphere. However, it often drowns in fishing nets and, consequently, some populations have been severely reduced or they have disappeared altogether. It can be difficult to observe closely and is generally wary of boats – a brief glimpse of its dark back and low, triangular dorsal fin is all this undemonstrative little cetacean usually shows of itself. It is also easy to miss, because the slightest swell or wave action can shield it from view. When it rises to breathe, the lasting impression is of a slow, forward-rolling motion, as if the dorsal fin is mounted on a revolving wheel lifted briefly above the surface and then withdrawn. While some whale watchers find it a frustrating animal to observe, most come to enjoy the familiar sneezing sound of its invisible blow; this gives the Harbor Porpoise one of its alternative names, the Puffing Pig. It is believed to be one of the shortest-lived cetaceans, with an average lifespan of only 10–12 years. In the northeastern North Pacific, hybrids between Dall's Porpoises and Harbor Porpoises are relatively common.

Identification

- Small size and robust body
- Nondescript coloring (dark above, light below)
- Low, broad-based triangular dorsal fin near midpoint of back
- Small, conical head with indistinct beak
- One or more dark stripes from mouth to flipper
- Slow, forward-rolling motion on surfacing
- Usually shy and undemonstrative
- Usually alone or in small groups

Surface profile

At a glance

Alternative names: Common Porpoise; rarely – Puffing Pig, Puffer, Herring Hog.

Scientific name: *Phocoena phocoena.*

Adult size: 4.3–6.6ft (1.3–2m); 110–165lb (50–75kg); females slightly larger than males.

Diet: fish and squid.

Behavior: slow swimming behavior very distinctive, surfacing with a gentle roll; generally uninterested in boats, or actively avoids them; very rarely breaches.

Breeding: single calf born mainly April–August, after a gestation period of 10–11 months.

Distribution: cool, shallow temperate to sub-Arctic coastal waters of the northern hemisphere, including bays, estuaries and harbors; rarely in water deeper than 650ft (200m).

World population: no reliable global estimate, but possibly around 700,000.

Best places to look in North America: Southeast Alaska, Northwestern Gulf of Alaska, Aleutian Islands & Pribilof Islands, San Juan Islands & Puget Sound, Westport & the Olympic Coast, California (including Monterey Bay), Vancouver Island (Johnstone Strait, Salish Sea, west coast), Bay of Fundy, Newfoundland, St Lawrence River & Gulf of St Lawrence.

Distribution Map

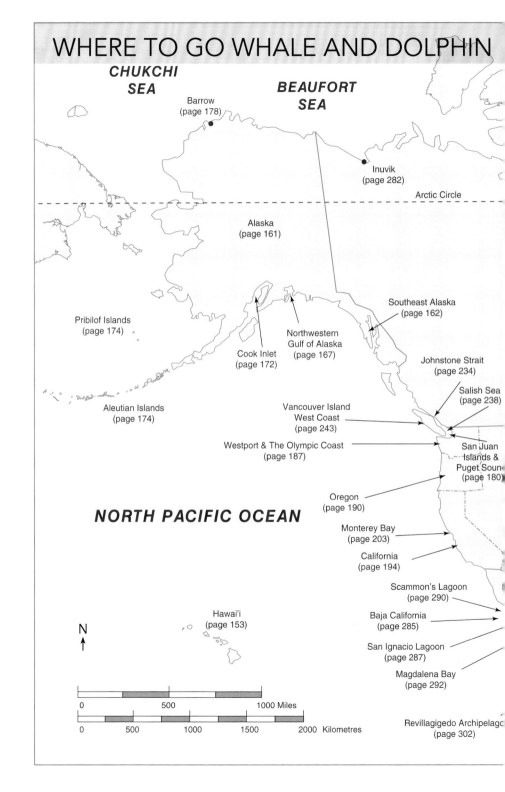

CHUKCHI SEA

Barrow
(page 178)

BEAUFORT SEA

Inuvik
(page 282)

Arctic Circle

Alaska
(page 161)

Pribilof Islands
(page 174)

Southeast Alaska
(page 162)

Northwestern
Gulf of Alaska
(page 167)

Cook Inlet
(page 172)

Johnstone Strait
(page 234)

Salish Sea
(page 238)

Aleutian Islands
(page 174)

Vancouver Island
West Coast
(page 243)

Westport & The Olympic Coast
(page 187)

San Juan
Islands &
Puget Sound
(page 180)

Oregon
(page 190)

NORTH PACIFIC OCEAN

Monterey Bay
(page 203)

California
(page 194)

Scammon's Lagoon
(page 290)

Hawai'i
(page 153)

Baja California
(page 285)

N

San Ignacio Lagoon
(page 287)

Magdalena Bay
(page 292)

0   500   1000 Miles

0   500   1000   1500   2000 Kilometres

Revillagigedo Archipelago
(page 302)

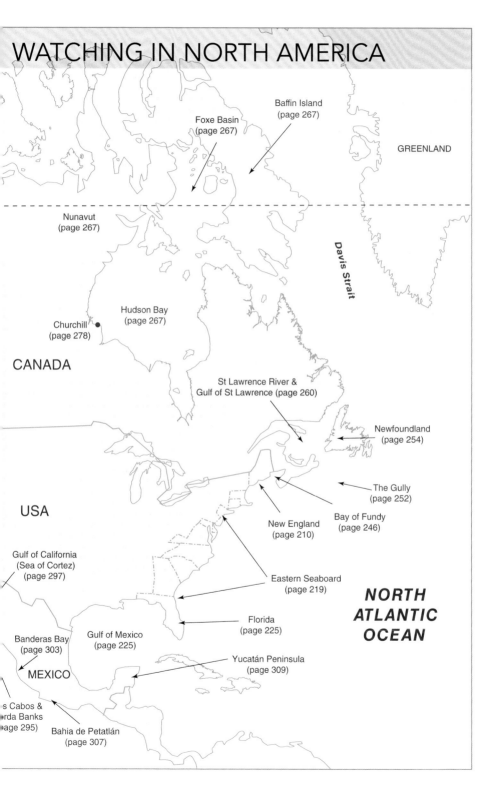

WATCHING IN NORTH AMERICA

Baffin Island
(page 267)

Foxe Basin
(page 267)

GREENLAND

Nunavut
(page 267)

Davis Strait

Hudson Bay
(page 267)

Churchill
(page 278)

CANADA

St Lawrence River &
Gulf of St Lawrence (page 260)

Newfoundland
(page 254)

The Gully
(page 252)

USA

New England
(page 210)

Bay of Fundy
(page 246)

Gulf of California
(Sea of Cortez)
(page 297)

Eastern Seaboard
(page 219)

NORTH
ATLANTIC
OCEAN

Florida
(page 225)

Banderas Bay
(page 303)

Gulf of Mexico
(page 225)

Yucatán Peninsula
(page 309)

MEXICO

s Cabos &
rda Banks
age 295)

Bahia de Petatlán
(page 307)

UNITED STATES OF AMERICA

Whale watching in the United States began in 1955, when fisherman Chuck Chamberlin charged tourists US$1 for a ride in his boat to see migrating Gray Whales off the coast of San Diego. Now it has the largest whale-watching industry in the world, with more than 5 million whale watchers joining commercial trips every year.

It can boast an unparalleled number and variety of whale- and dolphin-watching opportunities. There are major hotspots on both the Atlantic and Pacific coasts, and it is home to some world-renowned whale-watching destinations such as Hawai'i, Southeast Alaska, the San Juan Islands, Monterey Bay and Cape Cod. Depending on where you go, it is possible to join research groups studying Humpback Whales, kayak with Killer Whales, mingle with literally thousands of Northern Right Whale Dolphins, observe migrating Gray Whales, and much more.

Land-based whale watching is particularly popular along much of the west coast, with dozens of sign-posted whale-watch lookouts and many other good vantage points. Gray Whales and Killer Whales, in particular, can be seen surprisingly close to shore, but with binoculars or a telescope it is possible to spot a couple of dozen other species farther out to sea. There is even an official Whale Trail: a collection of whale-focused museums, parks and viewpoints in California, Oregon and Washington where there is a reasonably good chance of seeing whales, dolphins or porpoises.

Along the east coast, it is possible to watch Bottlenose Dolphins in Florida, you might spot a North Atlantic Right Whale among the myriad other whales feeding in the Gulf of Maine, and there are even trips to see Humpback Whales from New York City (they have been known to fluke in front of the Manhattan skyline).

A Humpback Whale breaches within sight and sound of New York City.

UNITED STATES: WEST COAST

Hawai'i

Hawai'i is one of the longest and most isolated archipelagos in the world. Some 2,600 miles from California, it consists of eight main islands (in size order: Hawai'i, Maui, O'ahu, Kaua'i, Moloka'i, Lana'i, Ni'ihau and Kaho'olawe), several atolls and 124 islets. Forming a broad 2,000-mile arc in the mid-Pacific, the archipelago ends almost at the international dateline, with a small speck in the ocean called Kure Atoll. Seven of the islands are permanently inhabited – Kaho'olawe is not – with a total human population of about 1.4 million.

For the purposes of whale watching, there are five main regions: Hawai'i Island; the central group or '4-island region' (consisting of Maui, Kaho'olawe, Lana'i and Moloka'i); O'ahu; Kaua'i/Ni'ihau; and the distant

Overview

Main species: Humpback Whale, Short-finned Pilot Whale, False Killer Whale, Rough-toothed Dolphin, Spinner Dolphin, Pantropical Spotted Dolphin, Common Bottlenose Dolphin.

Occasional species: Cuvier's Beaked Whale, Blainville's Beaked Whale, Melon-headed Whale, Pygmy Killer Whale, Dwarf Sperm Whale.

Other wildlife highlights: Hawaiian Monk Seal, Laysan Albatross, Black-footed Albatross, Wedge-tailed Shearwarer, White-tailed Tropicbird, Red-tailed Tropicbird, Fairy Tern, Sooty Tern, Black Noddy, Brown Booby, Red-footed Booby, Masked Booby, Great Frigatebird, Green Turtle, Hawksbill Turtle, Manta Ray.

Main locations: whale watching: Lahaina, Ma'alaea, Olowulu, Wailuku, Makena, Ka'anapali, Kihei (Maui); Kawaihae, Waikoloa, Honokohau Harbor, Hilo, Hapuna Beach, Kailua-Kona, Waimea (Hawai'i); Port Allen, Po'ipu, Ele'ele, Kukui'ula, Princeville, Hanalei (Kaua'i); Waikiki, Ko Olina, Wai'anae, Nanakuli, Hale'iwa, Kapolei, Honolulu (O'ahu); Kaunakakai (Moloka'i); dolphin watching: Lahaina, Ma'alaea, Wailuku, Ka'anapali (Maui); Waikoloa, Kailua-Kona, Kawaihae, Honokohau (Hawai'i); Port Allen, Po'ipu (Kaua'i); Ko Olina, Hale'iwa, Wai'anae, Honolulu, Kane'ohe,

Nanakuli (O'ahu); snorkelling with dolphins from many locations on Hawai'i, Maui, O'ahu, Kaua'i, Moloka'i.

Types of tours: 1.5-hour to two-day trips; multi-day research programs; multi-day expedition cruises; kayaking tours; excellent land-based whale watching (including walking tours).

When to go: early December–late April for Humpback Whales (some tours late November–mid-May, peak densities February–March); dolphins and other whale species year-round.

Regulations and guidelines: National Marine Sanctuary regulations; NOAA Guidelines for Viewing Marine Mammals; US Federal Regulations prohibit unauthorized approaches to Humpback Whales within 300ft (90m) on the water, or below 1,000ft (300m) in the air (researchers flying yellow flags with permit numbers from their boats can approach closer); Dolphin SMART voluntary guidelines and proposed regulations for swimming with dolphins; National Marine Fisheries Service regulations; Marine Mammal Protection Act (1972).

Wildlife species are listed systematically (not in order of abundance) and frequency of sightings varies with location and season.

and uninhabited Northwestern Hawaiian Islands, which include Midway Atoll.

They are all the visible tips of a chain of gigantic submerged volcanoes, and this helps to explain why they are such a magnet for whales and dolphins. Sitting out in the open ocean, they provide two critical habitats: shallow banks that encircle and, in some cases, connect the islands (important for breeding Humpback Whales, as well as Spinner Dolphins, Pantropical Spotted Dolphins and Bottlenose Dolphins); and deep water close to shore, in channels between the main groups of islands and an ocean floor that, in places, plummets to a depth of more than 16,400ft (important for a wide variety of toothed whales, from Rough-toothed Dolphins to Short-finned Pilot Whales). With such an abundance and diversity of species, it is not surprising that Hawai'i is one of the most popular whale-watching destinations in the world.

The main attraction is Humpback Whales. There are estimated to be more than 21,000 Humpbacks in the North Pacific and roughly half of them – at least 10,000– breed in Hawai'i every winter. Indeed, it would be difficult to visit Hawai'i at this time of year and not see a Humpback Whale. You just have to look out to sea – particularly in a hotspot such as along the west coast of Maui – and, sooner rather than later, you will see one. Humpbacks are part of daily life here and the locals are accustomed to seeing whales while commuting to work, driving the kids to school or eating in waterfront restaurants. The tourists, meanwhile, rarely take them in their stride – a unique feature of Hawai'i is the 'whale-jams', when dozens of cars hit the brakes or suddenly swerve off the highways to watch whales close to shore.

While whale-watching trips focus on Humpbacks during the winter, there are year-round dolphin-watching trips that focus on Spinner Dolphins, with regular sightings of Bottlenose and Pantropical Spotted Dolphins (and, off Kona, Short-finned Pilot Whales), and less frequent sightings of a variety of other species.

Altogether, no fewer than 25 cetacean species have been recorded in the Aloha State. Some of these have been observed just once or a handful of times, others are seen frequently but only in particular locations, while quite a few are encountered regularly on whale-watching trips throughout the archipelago. What you are likely to see depends on where you are: the relatively shallow waters between islands in the 4-island region, for example, has the greatest abundance of Humpbacks but the least diversity of other species, while the deep waters off the north and west coasts of Hawai'i Island have less abundance of Humpbacks but the greatest diversity (all 18 species of toothed whales recorded in Hawai'i have been seen here). The Kona coast of Hawai'i Island is a hotspot for sightings of lesser-known species.

There are many ways of watching whales and dolphins in Hawai'i: aboard everything from sports-fishing boats and catamarans to glass-bottomed boats and yachts, by joining research programs, from the shore, underwater, or even as part of a sunset cruise with cocktails. Some trips last for less than two hours, others go for as long as two days. Most take place on the sheltered, leeward sides of the islands: the prevailing trade winds come from the east and northeast.

Humpback Whales

Humpbacks are the only commonly seen baleen whales in Hawai'i, but they are here in force every winter. When they first arrive, usually some time in September or

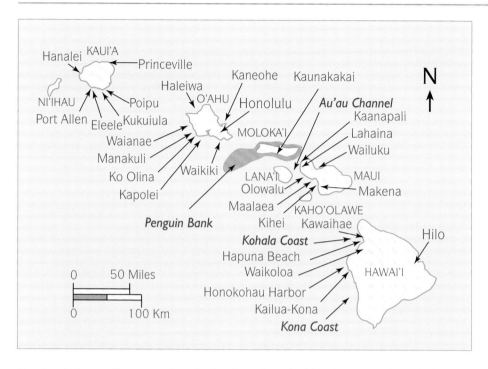

Hanalei KAUI'A
Princeville
Haleiwa
Kaneohe   Kaunakakai
NI'IHAU
Poipu
O'AHU
Honolulu
Au'au Channel
Port Allen Eleele Kukuiula
Kaanapali
Waianae
MOLOKA'I
Lahaina
Manakuli
Wailuku
Ko Olina   Waikiki
LANA'I
MAUI
Kapolei
Olowalu
Makena
Maalaea
KAHO'OLAWE
Penguin Bank
Kihei   Kawaihae
Kohala Coast
Hilo
Hapuna Beach
Waikoloa
HAWAI'I
0   50 Miles
Honokohau Harbor
0   100 Km
Kailua-Kona
Kona Coast

N ↑

October, it is actually reported in the local news: they are back! Most come all the way from their summer feeding grounds in the Aleutian Islands, Southeast Alaska, the Gulf of Alaska and British Columbia, having migrated about 2,800 miles across the open ocean to get here. Some stay until as late as June (though sightings before November or after May are rare).

They are in Hawai'i to mate and raise their calves in the warm water over the archipelago's relatively shallow banks, typically in depths of less than 650ft. Generally, the greater the extent of the shallow banks the more abundant the whales: the highest densities occur in the central group, especially in the 9 mile-wide Au'au Channel – between Maui and Lana'i – the most shallow and protected channel in the Hawaiian Islands. The name means 'to

take a bath', referring to the Au'au's bath-like conditions. Females with calves (which are most common during February and March and are the last to depart in April or soon after) tend to prefer this channel, though they can be seen almost anywhere in the archipelago. Another hotspot is Penguin Bank, to the southwest of Moloka'i. Humpbacks are also plentiful (though less concentrated) off the Kona coast of Hawai'i Island, off O'ahu, and around Kaua'i and Ni'ihau; in all these areas, densities are increasing substantially year by year.

As well as in these top locations, they are found throughout the main islands of the archipelago and regularly cross the deep inter-island channels to move between them. They have recently been documented in the Northwestern Hawaiian Islands, although it is likely they have been there all along (there is even some suggestion that this may be one of the 'missing' Humpback Whale breeding grounds).

A delightful feature of whale watching in Hawai'i is the opportunity to hear live concerts of male Humpback Whales singing underwater. They can be heard pretty much anywhere, at any time of the day or night during the winter. The captain simply turns off the boat's engine, drops a hydrophone overboard, and everyone can listen to the most wonderful mixture of jazz, bebop, blues, heavy metal, classical and reggae all rolled into one – an extraordinary collection of moans, groans, snores, roars, squeaks and whistles in a continuous acoustic extravaganza. Sometimes, on a quiet day, it is so loud that Humpback Whale song can be heard emanating from above the surface.

Alternatively, if you are a strong swimmer, try venturing out into the ocean – take a friend and check on currents and other potential dangers first – until you are just past the surf breaks. Then take a deep breath, dive down to the bottom, clear your ears, and listen to the whales sing. Incidentally, although many snorkelling tours during whale season emphasize the possibility of seeing whales in their marketing material, it is illegal to swim with them (except under a scientific research permit).

In 1992, US Congress created the Hawaiian Islands Humpback Whale National Marine Sanctuary. Located from the shore to the 100-fathom line, it is comprised of five separate areas abutting six of the main islands, and includes most of the whales' critical habitat. In reality, Humpback Whales are protected outside the sanctuary as much as inside, but the designation is significant symbolically and reflects the importance attributed to protecting them.

Whaling history

The first whaling ship to enter Hawaiian waters was the *Balaena*, out of New Bedford, Massachusetts. It anchored in Kealakekua Bay, on the Kona coast of the island of Hawai'i, in 1818, and promptly killed a large Sperm Whale. This was unusual because American whalers concentrated on richer Sperm Whale grounds elsewhere in the North Pacific. But word of the safe anchorage (and Hawaiian hospitality) spread quickly and soon the whole Yankee Pacific whaling fleet was coming into Lahaina and Honolulu, in particular, every winter to rest and recuperate. Hawai'i, centrally located between the rich Sperm Whale grounds off Japan and the American west coast, developed into a major staging area. No fewer than 736 whaling ships stopped in Hawaiian ports in the record year of 1846. The whaling industry was the mainstay of the island economy for about 40 years altogether, and Lahaina remained a favorite location throughout this era, with clashes between whalers and missionaries making for a colorful history. There are at least 18 documented wrecks of whaling vessels in and around the state.

Yet Hawai'i may be the only place in the North Pacific with a healthy population of whales where there is no history of large-scale commercial whaling. The whalers who came here were so focused on Sperm Whales – which they hunted during the summer – that they made no mention of Humpback Whales in their ships' logs. So why didn't they hunt them? The most likely explanation is that there was not, after all, a healthy population of whales in the archipelago during that period.

It is just possible that Hawaiians simply paid little attention to the whales for many centuries, but it seems more likely that

Humpbacks are relative newcomers to their islands. There are records of them dating from the mid-1800s onwards, and for two or three decades there were some efforts to hunt them from shore-based whaling stations manned mainly by inexperienced native Hawaiians. But relatively few were taken and the small number of Humpbacks around were probably driven away from populated areas, so the emphasis of large-scale commercial whaling was still firmly on the Sperm Whales.

It may have taken several generations before the Humpback Whales ventured back. From the late 1930s through to the early 1950s, their re-appearance in Hawaiian waters began to be reported in local newspapers: they were apparently a novel sight at that time and attracted much attention.

Meanwhile, however, during this period (and well into the 1960s) there was intensive exploitation of Humpback Whales on their summer feeding grounds. They were hunted ruthlessly, in one of the greatest massacres of mammals in human history and at least some of those killed probably included individuals that wintered in Hawai'i. Precise figures are not known but, between 1905–65, commercial whalers are believed to have killed about 28,000 in the eastern North Pacific. Humpback Whales received official protection in 1966 but, by then, there were so few left that the whalers had already stopped trying to find them. Rough estimates suggest that there may have been only 1,600 survivors left in this population.

But there is a positive side to this story of annihilation. The first back-of-the-envelope estimates of Humpback numbers in Hawaiian waters suggested a population of low to mid-hundreds in the 1970s; and the population has continued to grow ever since. Current estimates suggest at least 10,000, with an average increase of 5.5–6 per cent every year, and the population around Hawai'i was removed from the endangered species list in 2016.

Humpback Whales are part of daily life during the winter in Hawai'i.

Spinner Dolphins

Most dolphin-watching trips in Hawai'i – which are year-round and marketed independently of whale-watching trips – focus on Spinner Dolphins. They are found throughout the archipelago, spending most of the day in shallow bays and coves close to shore, then moving out into the open ocean to feed at night. This predictability, and proximity to shore, makes the Spinner one of the most easily encountered cetaceans in Hawaiian waters.

During the day, from sunrise until late afternoon, the dolphins are resting, caring for their young, reproducing and hiding from large sharks and other predators. As dusk approaches, they become more active and this is when they tend to perform most of the spectacular spinning leaps for which they are so well known.

Many trips offer the opportunity to snorkel with the dolphins, and underwater visibility is usually excellent. Some operators have been taking people to swim with them for decades, and take their responsibilities seriously. But the number of trips has grown dramatically in recent years – and some operators have been ignoring voluntary guidelines already in place – so the activity has become increasingly controversial. The problem is that in-water encounters are during a critical time for the dolphins, when they are particularly susceptible to disturbance, and the pressure on them is huge. There is some concern that too much disturbance may be forcing them to change locations which, apart from the obvious disruption, may mean risking higher levels of predation.

In late 2016, a formal proposal was made to prohibit swimming closer than 50 yards (46 metres) to Spinner Dolphins (the same distance ruling would also apply to boats) and this would be implemented within two nautical miles from shore around the main Hawaiian Islands, and in designated waters between Maui, Lana'i and Kaho'olawe. There may also be a ban on dolphin swimming at certain times of the day (6.00 a.m. to 3.00 p.m.) within certain essential daytime resting places.

Other species

Many other species can be seen around Hawai'i. In the shallow waters where Humpback Whales gather, Bottlenose and Pantropical Spotted Dolphins are abundant and False Killer Whales regularly pass through. Humpback tours usually include sightings of Bottlenose Dolphins, which often hang around the whales (the Humpbacks sometimes become irritated with such constant companionship, and researchers have seen them waving their tails at the dolphins, trying to discourage them and drive them away). Pantropical Spotted Dolphins may be the most abundant cetaceans in Hawai'i, and account for more than one-fifth of all sightings on research surveys here. Hotspots include the west coast of Hawai'i Island, between Maui and Lana'i, and off the southwest coast of O'ahu, but they can be seen almost anywhere.

Some of the more unusual species are attracted to the deep water very close to shore. Hawai'i is probably the best place in North America to see some of the lesser-known members of the dolphin family, for example. Rough-toothed Dolphins are year-round residents and, while they prefer deep oceanic waters with depths of 3,300ft or more, in Hawai'i they are found relatively close to shore. There is a known population around Kaua'i/Ni'ihau and another of about 300 animals off the west coast of Hawai'i Island. Altogether, there are estimated

Hawai'i is one of the best places in the world to see Spinner Dolphins.

to be 72,000 Rough-toothed Dolphins in Hawaiian waters – more than any other cetacean. There are very occasional sightings of Risso's and Striped Dolphins, but they are considered rare around Hawai'i, and Fraser's Dolphins have been recorded once or twice.

Short-finned Pilot Whales are found throughout the archipelago, and are seen regularly on whale-watching trips (Long-finned Pilot Whales do not occur in the North Pacific); they are particularly common off the west coast of Hawai'i Island and the west coast of Lana'i. False Killer Whales are seen fairly frequently, too, with three recognized populations: offshore, in the Northwestern Hawaiian Islands, and around the main islands between Kaua'i and Hawai'i Island. In the late 1980s, there were about 500 False Killer Whales around the main islands, but the population has declined to about 150–200 today and is now endangered – no one knows why. They are sometimes seen close to shore, feeding on Mahi Mahi and Yellowfin Tuna.

There is a sizeable population of several thousand Melon-headed Whales that ranges over a wide area between the islands and offshore. A smaller resident population in the Kohala area, off the northwest coast of Hawai'i Island, is estimated to have about 450 individuals. Large groups of 200 or more are sometimes encountered. Pygmy Killer Whales are rarer and less well known, but they are seen from time to time and there are small resident populations off O'ahu, over Penguin Bank and off the Kona coast of Hawai'i Island. Killer Whales are extremely rare and, while they do appear in Hawai'i from time to time, the chances of seeing them are slim; a pod of Killer Whales did once kill a juvenile Humpback Whale here, but most attacks take place on the colder feeding grounds.

Sperm Whales are quite plentiful in the open ocean far offshore, as part of a broadly ranging population that extends across much of the central tropical Pacific, but are rarely seen on whale-watching trips close to the islands. Most sightings have been off Hawai'i Island, or in the deepwater channel between Kaua'i and Ni'ihau, and they are known to occur around some of the Northwestern Hawaiian Islands. Sightings on research vessels range from 3–20 miles from shore, with an average of 12 miles.

There is a small resident population of Dwarf Sperm Whales off the west coast of Hawai'i Island, with most sightings relatively close to shore in water 1,600–3,300ft deep. There may be other populations elsewhere in the archipelago, but there is too little information to confirm. Even less is known about Pygmy Sperm Whales in Hawai'i, but they are seen from time to time.

Three species of beaked whales – Blainville's, Cuvier's and Longman's – have been recorded in Hawai'i. None of these are seen frequently, even by researchers, who encounter beaked whales roughly once every five days of survey effort. However, there is a small resident population of Cuvier's Beaked Whales; most sightings are off Hawai'i Island, but they are rarely seen elsewhere. There is also a small resident population of Blainville's Beaked Whales and, while they have been encountered in deep waters off most of the main Hawaiian Islands, there is a relatively well-known population off the west coast of Hawai'i Island. They are frequently close to shore, particularly in water 1,600–5,000ft deep. Longman's Beaked Whales – among the rarest and least known of all the world's cetaceans – have been recorded but they are very rarely seen.

Other rare sightings over the years have included six species of baleen whale: North Pacific Right Whale, Blue Whale, Fin Whale, Sei Whale, Bryde's Whale and Minke Whale.

Land-based Whale Watching

Humpback Whales can be seen quite easily from most good vantage points around the islands – even from many oceanside hotel rooms and coastal roads. The stretch of Highway 30 on Maui between Ma'alaea and Lahaina is particularly good (though it can also be one of the windiest and most crowded drives on the island).

Other well-known hotspots include: Makapu'u Lighthouse, Hanauma Bay, Diamond Head Scenic Lookout and Halona Blowhole (O'ahu); Papawai Point and Sanctuary Visitor Center (Maui); Kawaihae, Lapakahi State Historical Park and Kapaa Beach Park (Hawai'i); and Makahuena Point, Kilauea Point National Wildlife Refuge and Kapa'a Overlook (Kaua'i).

The Maui Whale Festival is held in February every year.

At least 10,000 Humpback Whales breed in Hawai'i every winter.

ALASKA

Alaska is one of the best-known whale-watching destinations in the United States, with Humpback Whales, Gray Whales and Killer Whales in particular drawing more than half a million whale watchers every year.

Many head for the famed Inside Passage, in Southeast Alaska, where Humpbacks famously feed throughout the summer. This is the place to see bubble-netting – a remarkable behavior in which the whales join ranks to build enormous fishing nets with bubbles – and it has a wide variety of other cetaceans, too. It is also one of the best places in the world for Killer Whale watching, with significant numbers of both residents and transients. The Gulf of Alaska is another prime territory where, alongside the ubiquitous Humpbacks, there are several other summer visitors and a variety of species passing through.

Humpback numbers have increased dramatically in recent years and even Blue Whales are slowly returning to Alaskan waters, after decades of intensive hunting.

Every spring, Gray Whales migrate past the outer coast on their way to their summer feeding grounds in the Bering, Chukchi and Beaufort Seas, and some remain in the state year-round. There are Belugas here, too, with five major stocks: Cook Inlet, Bristol Bay, eastern Bering Sea (Norton Sound), eastern Chukchi Sea and the Beaufort Sea. Along the way, you can encounter anything from Fin Whales and Minke Whales to Pacific White-sided Dolphins and Dall's Porpoises.

The offerings in Alaska are diverse: half-day trips from hubs such as Juneau and Gustavus, a wide variety of small-group nature cruises on live-aboard yachts combining whales with glaciers and other wildlife, multi-day kayaking expeditions and some excellent land-based whale watching. There are so many whales in certain hotspots, particularly in the Southeast, that even massive cruise ships have been known to stop to allow passengers to watch the animals feeding around their vessels.

Alaska is home to significant numbers of both resident and transient Killer Whales.

Southeast Alaska

Southeast Alaska is the state's whale-watching hub. It is a wild place where you can sense what the world might have been like before Europeans arrived: deep fjords filled with fish and plankton, steep mountains, ancient forests, icebergs, glaciers, and a host of wildlife from Brown Bears to Bald Eagles.

Known simply as 'Southeast' or the 'Panhandle' to local residents, this narrow strip of coastline is almost entirely surrounded by Canada's British Columbia. It stretches 530 miles from the southern end of Prince of Wales Island in the south, to Icy Bay in the north, and averages 124 miles from east to west. It embraces more than 1,000 islands – including six that are over 1,000 square miles in area – and myriad sounds, straits, canals, narrows, passages and channels. Known for its wildness, the entire region – covering an area roughly the size of Maine – is home to fewer than 75,000 people. And nearly half of those live in the state capital of Juneau.

Perhaps its most famous feature is the Inside Passage, a protected waterway of convoluted passages between islands that begins in Puget Sound, Washington State, passes through British Columbia and ends at the northern end of Southeast Alaska. Connecting the main port communities along the way, it has been an important travel corridor for centuries and, even today, is a critical route for Alaska Marine Highway ferries (which often pass whales) and is popular with cruise ships.

The main attractions for whale watchers are Humpback Whales and Killer Whales, with a supporting cast that includes Minke

Overview

Main species: Humpback Whale, Gray Whale, Minke Whale, Killer Whale, Pacific White-sided Dolphin, Dall's Porpoise, Harbor Porpoise.

Occasional species: Fin Whale.

Other wildlife highlights: Brown Bear, Black Bear, Wolf, Wolverine, Moose, Sitka Black-tailed Deer, Mountain Goat, Sea Otter, River Otter, Steller Sea Lion, Harbor Seal, Bald Eagle, Pelagic Cormorant, Sandhill Crane, Common Loon, Red-throated Loon, Arctic Tern, Black-legged Kittiwake, Tufted Puffin, Rhinoceros Auklet, Pigeon Guillemot, Marbled Murrelet, Harlequin Duck, Barrow's Goldeneye, Surf Scoter, White-winged Scoter, Surfbird.

Main locations: Ketchikan, Wrangell, Petersburg, Sitka, Juneau/Auke Bay, Haines, Skagway, Hoonah, Gustavus; long-range live-aboard trips from Ketchikan, Wrangell, Petersburg, Sitka, Juneau and British Columbia (Prince Rupert).

Types of tours: 3-hour to full-day trips; multi-day boat-based nature cruises; multi-day kayaking tours; wilderness lodges and camps, US Forest Service cabins.

When to go: May–September (peak period for Humpback Whales mid-June to early September; fall in Sitka Sound and Seymour Canal).

Regulations and guidelines: NOAA Guidelines for Viewing Marine Mammals (including Humpback Whale Approach Regulations); Whale SENSE program; US Federal Regulations; Marine Mammal Protection Act (1972).

Wildlife species are listed systematically (not in order of abundance) and frequency of sightings varies with location and season.

Whales, Pacific White-sided Dolphins and Dall's Porpoises. During the summer the waters here boil with life and there are so many whales in key hotspots that sightings are guaranteed (if you are unlucky you get a second trip free or, in some cases, a complete refund).

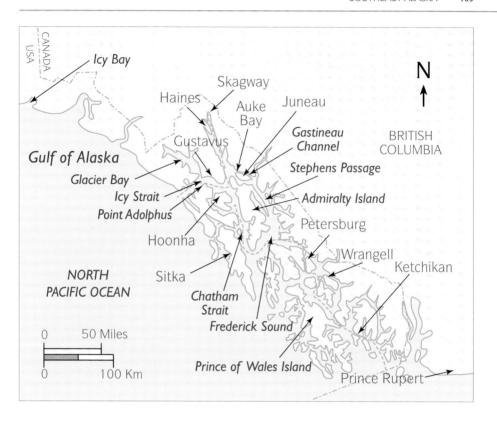

There are more than 45 operators offering a variety of trips. Most are in the whale-watching hubs of Juneau (including Auke Bay and the downtown area), and Gustavus, on Icy Strait. But there are a few farther south around Petersburg, Sitka and Ketchikan, and these three communities are where many multi-day nature cruises begin, with whales (and bears) the star attractions.

Whale-watching vessels in Southeast Alaska include everything from one-person kayaks to cruise ships, with a variety of dedicated whale-watch boats, yachts, catamarans and converted fishing boats in between. Many are quite small, with a

capacity of 6–15 passengers, and there is a sizeable (50–100 passenger) mini-cruise ship fleet.

Summer cruise ships are popular in the Inside Passage. Some actively advertise the chance of seeing Humpback Whales and Killer Whales, in particular, and customers frequently demand that ships stop for them. Clearly, they are too large and unmaneuverable to approach closely and attempting to do so is frowned upon by local experts. However, many local whale-watch operators are geared up for cruise ship passengers, picking them up at the ferry terminals and marinas and taking them on more intimate half-day tours.

Humpback Whales

Humpbacks are the most commonly seen whales on whale watching trips in Southeast Alaska. Altogether, more than 4,000 of them frequent the region during the foraging season. They spend every summer feeding on small schooling fish and krill in the protected waters here, then migrate 2,800 miles to their winter breeding grounds in Hawai'i. There are always a few exceptions to this rule: some remain in Alaska for most of the winter, and a small number migrate instead to Mexico to breed.

They are found throughout the region, with particular concentrations in Glacier Bay, western Icy Strait, Sitka Sound, Tebonkof Bay and western Prince of Wales Island. However, the top spots are undoubtedly in Stephens Passage and Frederick Sound, where vast pastures of krill attract literally hundreds of Humpbacks. Local hotspots are found around Keku Strait, The Brothers, Cape Fanshaw and Five Finger Lighthouse, which frequently provide intimate views of echelon feeding, lateral lunging, flick feeding, bubble-netting, breaching, flipper slapping and lobtailing. At night, the sound of spouts, breaches and trumpets drift into secluded anchorages and lull passengers on live-aboard whale watching boats to sleep.

Glacier Bay is one of the best known areas and provides an outstandingly spectacular backdrop. Humpbacks were first reported in the Bay in 1899 and they are now some of the best-known whales in the world. Numbers are usually quite low in April and May, typically rise in mid-June, peak in July and August, and begin to decline again in late September. Icy Strait - the primary channel for water flowing between the open North Pacific and the northern Inside Passage – is another major draw. Point Adolphus, on the southern shore of the Strait opposite Gustavus, is especially well known for its abundant Humpbacks.

Between 1973 and 2014, no fewer than 740 different individuals were identified by researchers in Glacier Bay and Icy Strait. The current population is estimated to be more than 300 whales and is increasing by year by year. Two of these individuals have been known to researchers for longer than any other whales in the world – since 1972 and 1973 respectively.

Humpbacks are frequently seen from a number of communities in Southeast Alaska. In Petersburg, for example, the best place is Outlook Park, about 2 miles east of town, where there is a covered viewing area and fixed binoculars; peak sightings are usually during July and August. Similarly, it is sometimes possible to see them right in front of Juneau, and from the main dock in Gustavus. In some communities, increasing numbers of Humpbacks have actually become a nuisance, by dining on a windfall of salmon fingerlings released at fish hatcheries.

Sitka is notable because, in the fall and early winter, it seems to be a 'last stop' for many migrating Humpback Whales. They are still plentiful here long after they have left the rest of Southeast Alaska. A good place to see them is from aptly-named Whale Park, an unlikely city park with covered viewing shelters, fixed binoculars and interpretive signs. The Sitka Whalefest, which celebrated its twentieth anniversary in 2016, is an annual festival celebrating this late-season abundance; it takes place in early November. Seymour Canal, on Admiralty Island, also hosts impressive numbers of krill-feeding Humpbacks during the fall and early winter.

For a few short weeks in mid-summer, when huge schools of Herring and large numbers of whales converge, it is possible

A cooperative group of Humpback Whales bubble-netting.

to see one of the most spectacular animal behaviors on the planet – bubble-netting – in which Humpback Whales construct enormous circular fishing nets with bubbles. It is a team effort – there can be just a few or more than 20 whales working together – and each individual appears to have a different role and favored position. One whale is the bubble blower, creating the ring of bubbles that will act as a net to contain the fish. Another is the caller, using a loud, haunting and rather melancholic feeding call to scare the Herring upwards from the deep (these feeding calls have recently been heard in northern British Columbia, as the culture spreads). The school is frightened into a tighter shoal within the confines of the bubble net and becomes trapped against the surface. Meanwhile, the other whales in the group use their bodies to corral the fish into the net (the white undersides of their flippers may be used as 'flashers' to scare the Herring in the right direction). When everything is ready, all the whales rapidly swim up from underneath, with their mouths wide open, and engulf the concentrated prey.

Not all Humpbacks participate in this cooperative behavior. Most bubble-netters come from a core community consisting of just three dozen whales. There is an average group size of eight individuals, but membership appears to be fluid and there are often visitors who join only for a day or two. Altogether, about half the whales in northern Southeast Alaska have been observed in bubble-netting cooperatives at one time or another.

It is very exciting to observe. Whale watchers first hear the loud feeding calls emanating from the deep, then they glimpse the bubbles breaking the surface and, seconds later, the whales explode high out of the water with their cavernous mouths agape and the wriggling, silvery fish leaping for their lives. Some Humpback Whale groups may feed like this for 12 hours or more, completing a bubble-net as often as every four minutes.

Bubble-netting can be seen almost anywhere in Southeast Alaska (and, to a much lesser degree, in a few other parts of the world). There are no hard and fast rules but, in recent years, there have been several key areas and seasons: late June to mid-July around Juneau; and late July to late September (peaking from mid-August to early September) in northern and central Chatham Strait, particularly between Iyoukeen Cove and Tenakee Inlet. It typically occurs quite close to shore.

Traditionally, Frederick Sound has a good reputation for bubble-netters, but it is hit and miss and they can be plentiful or scarce, depending on the abundance of Herring. The north shores of Kuprenof and Kuiu islands have hosted the most bubble-netting pods in the past.

Killer Whales

Killer Whales are a welcome bonus on trips that focus on Humpback Whales. It is possible to see both residents, which are here to feed on salmon, and transients (Bigg's), which come to feed on seals, sea lions, porpoises, dolphins and whales. Intriguingly, there is very little predation by transient Killer Whales on Humpbacks in Southeast Alaska, despite the large numbers of females with calves throughout the region every summer.

Three different resident Killer Whale stocks are known in the area. The most familiar to whale watchers in Southeast Alaska belong to the Southern Alaska Resident stock, consisting of more than 700 individuals, which ranges from Southeast Alaska to the Shumagin Islands in the Aleutians. The Northern Resident stock, consisting of about 290 individuals, ranges from Washington State through parts of Southeast Alaska; and the Southern Resident stock, currently consisting of 78 individuals, occurs mainly in the waters of Washington State and southern British Columbia, but very occasionally appears in Southeast Alaska and beyond. Resident Killer Whales are most concentrated in the western end of Frederick Sound and from there north along Chatham Strait (including Peril Strait, Tenakee Inlet and Freshwater Bay), in Icy Strait around the entrance to Glacier Bay, and in Favorite Bay (north of Juneau).

Most transient Killer Whales seen in the protected waters of Southeast Alaska belong to the West Coast Transient stock, with about 300 members, which travel between Southeast Alaska, British Columbia and Washington State (and possibly as far down the west coast as California). Another stock called the Gulf of Alaska Transients, which consists of several hundred individuals ranging over a wide area from the Bering Sea and the Aleutian Islands through the Gulf of Alaska, is also sometimes seen in Southeast Alaska. Transients can be found anywhere from open straits and near tidewater glaciers to inshore waters and bays throughout the year, with an increase in sightings from July to September.

Other Whales

Minke Whales are the (distant) second most often seen baleen whales in Southeast Alaska; they are believed to be migratory, occurring here mainly during the spring and summer, with many in western Icy Strait in particular. Fin Whales were common in these protected waters prior to commercial whaling, and have not really returned since, but are seen occasionally along the outer coast, especially in Dixon Entrance. Most of the eastern North Pacific population of Gray Whales migrate around the Gulf of Alaska twice every year on their way between their breeding grounds in Baja California, Mexico, and their feeding grounds in the Bering, Chukchi and Beaufort seas. The majority travel along the outer coast, but they are sometimes seen in the south during April and May, as far 'inside' as Ketchikan. A small number remain to feed most summers in Sitka Sound (and they can be seen here on migration, though the main route is about 20 miles offshore).

Dall's and Harbor Porpoises abound in Southeast Alaska (Dall's are seen more often simply because of their more boisterous behavior) and Pacific White-sided Dolphins are frequently found in small to large schools along both the outer coast and in the Inside Passage and surrounding waterways.

A transient Killer Whale spyhopping.

Northwestern Gulf of Alaska

The Gulf of Alaska is a gigantic semi-enclosed basin along the US state's south coast. Stretching all the way from the Alaska Peninsula in the west to the Alexander Archipelago in the east, it has a surface area of roughly 590,000 square miles (its southern boundary with the open North Pacific is not strictly defined).

The coast is deeply indented by fjords and other inlets, including Glacier Bay, the waterways of the Inside Passage and Cook Inlet (see pages 162 and 172), Prince William Sound and Resurrection Bay (a huge indentation in Kenai Fjords National Park). Many of these are important feeding grounds for a variety of whales – particularly Humpbacks and Killer Whales – and, while there are relatively few dedicated whale-watch operators in this area, there are some good opportunities and, of course, the backdrop is spectacular.

Humpback Whales are widely distributed in this corner of the North Pacific during summer, inhabiting coastal waters and inland waterways from Southeast Alaska north to the Gulf of Alaska and west along the Aleutian Islands into the Bering Sea. It is estimated that every summer there are 3,000–5,000 in the Gulf of Alaska alone.

The coastal waters of Prince William Sound and the Kenai Fjords are used by two distinct stocks of transient Killer Whales: the so-called Gulf of Alaska Transients (which consists of several hundred individuals that travel throughout the Gulf and as far west as the Shumagin Islands in the Aleutians and as far south as the outside waters of Southeast

Overview

Main species: Gray Whale, Humpback Whale, Fin Whale, Minke Whale, Killer Whale, Dall's Porpoise, Harbor Porpoise.

Occasional species: Sei Whale, Sperm Whale, Pacific White-sided Dolphin.

Other wildlife highlights: Brown Bear, Black Bear, Moose, Caribou, Mountain Goat, Sitka Black-tailed Deer, Sea Otter, River Otter, Steller Sea Lion, Harbor Seal, Bald Eagle, Northern Harrier, Tufted Puffin, Horned Puffin, Rhinoceros Auklet, Kittlitz's Auklet, Pigeon Guillemot, Marbled Murrelet, Black-legged Kittiwake, Glaucous-winged Gull, Surf Scoter, Harlequin Duck.

Main locations: Seward (Kenai Fjords National Park); Whittier, Valdez (Prince William Sound); Kodiak (Kodiak Island); bus–boat trips from Anchorage; see separate section for Cook Inlet.

Types of tours: half-day to full-day boat tours; multi-day expedition cruises; kayaking tours; wilderness lodges; land-based whale watching.

When to go: early March–early September.

Regulations and guidelines: guidelines for Observing Marine Mammals in Kenai Fjords (developed by the Kenai Fjords Tour Vessel Operators Association and the North Gulf Oceanic Society); NOAA Guidelines for Viewing Marine Mammals (including Humpback Whale Approach Regulations); Whale SENSE program; US Federal Regulations; Marine Mammal Protection Act (1972).

Wildlife species are listed systematically (not in order of abundance) and frequency of sightings varies with location and season.

Alaska and British Columbia) and the AT1 or Chugach Transients (a much smaller group which spends most of its time in and around Prince William Sound and the Kenai Fjords region). The AT1s are more commonly encountered well inside fjords and bays. A third stock, the West Coast Transients, travel

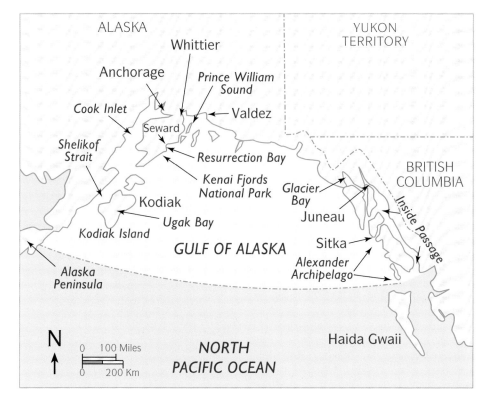

between Southeast Alaska and Washington State (possibly as far as California). There are also resident Killer Whales in the Gulf of Alaska, belonging to the Southern Alaska Resident population. This large population, consisting of more than 700 individuals, ranges from Southeast Alaska to the Shumagin Islands in the Aleutians.

Gray Whales migrate around the Gulf of Alaska twice every year on their way between their breeding grounds in Baja California, Mexico, and their feeding grounds in the Bering, Chukchi and Beaufort seas. Rather than taking a shortcut directly across the Gulf – which would save them two to three days' travel time – they prefer to take the longer way round, hugging the coast. Some remain in feeding locations along the Gulf and Kodiak Island throughout the summer.

There is a population of about 235 Sperm Whales, all male, that regularly feed in the Gulf of Alaska (they were once also common in Southeast Alaska). Some remain in the Gulf year-round, others travel as far afield as the Gulf of California, Mexico. They are staging a comeback after years of intensive whaling, but are rarely seen on whale-watching trips, because they spend most of their time far offshore along the edge of the continental shelf. About 10 of these whales – dubbed the 'Bad Boys' – have learned to take Sablefish off commercial longline fishing gear in the Gulf. The whales are able to work out, by the different sounds the fishing boats make, when the fish are being pulled up. The problem was first reported in the 1970s, but has grown so bad (costing hundreds of thousands of dollars each year) that the fishermen are talking about abandoning their traditional hooks and lines in favor of baited traps, to protect their catch from the whales.

After decades of intensive whaling, and an absence of many years, Blue Whales are slowly starting to reappear in the Gulf of Alaska. Researchers first saw one or two more than a decade ago, then as many as five in one day, and it seems they may be re-establishing a traditional migration pattern. At least some of the individuals identified in the Gulf are known from a long-established summer feeding ground farther south, off the coast of California, and there seems to have been a northward shift in their distribution. But studies of Blue Whale vocalizations suggest that others may come from Russia and Japan to spend their summers in the Gulf, too. Unfortunately, like the Sperm Whales, Alaska's Blue Whales are mostly in open water and rarely seen on whale-watching trips.

There are believed to be no more than 30–50 North Pacific Right Whales in the eastern North Pacific, and they are very rarely seen outside a small area in the southeastern Bering Sea (where they have been observed most summers since 1996). However, there have been a small number of sightings (and acoustic recordings) in offshore areas of the Gulf of Alaska and near Kodiak Island. Historically, during the whaling era, a large zone to the east and southeast of Kodiak Island was clearly a critical habitat, but it is unknown whether this area remains important.

Kenai Fjords National Park

Kenai Fjords National Park is a 1,047-square-mile wonderland of ice fields, towering glaciers, dense Sitka Spruce and Mountain Hemlock forests, and abundant wildlife. If it were possible to distill the essence of coastal Alaska into one place – this would be it. Yet it is only 130 miles south of Anchorage.

The nearest town is Seward, just outside the park boundary, which is the main departure point for whale-watching trips (and large cruise ships). Many of the tours are guided by National Park Rangers and have on-board hydrophones; most combine whales with glaciers and other local attractions, although some are dedicated to whale watching.

A Humpback Whale blows and flukes close to the Alaskan shore.

Kenai Fjords and its surrounding waterways are a haven for whales during the summer. Depending on where you go – and when in the season – half-day, full-day and multi-day cruises frequently encounter Humpback Whales, Gray Whales, Killer Whales and Dall's Porpoises, with occasional sightings of other species.

Humpback Whales are the main focus and are present from mid-April to November (when most of them migrate to their winter breeding grounds, in Hawai'i). They are found throughout the region, though Resurrection Bay is particularly good and the Chiswell Islands, outside Aialik Bay, is another hotspot.

Resident and transient Killer Whales are also seen frequently (though not as often as the Humpbacks), while offshore Killer Whales visit occasionally. Aggregations of resident Killer Whales appear in Resurrection Bay in early summer (from mid-May until the end of June), when King Salmon congregate along the shoreline of the Aialik Peninsula. There are dedicated whale-watching tours, from mid-May to mid-June, to see them in the waters relatively close to Seward.

Other cruises head out to Resurrection Bay from the end of March to mid-May, to witness the annual return of the Gray Whales. They are nearing the end of their long migration from their breeding grounds in Baja California, Mexico, and have nearly arrived at their main summer feeding grounds in the Bering, Chukchi and Beaufort seas.

Fin Whales are encountered from time to time, with two peaks in sightings: May and August. The area between the end of the Resurrection Peninsula and Cheval Island, and nearby Agnes Cove, tend to be the best areas. Minke Whales are sometimes seen in bays and shallow coastal waters during the summer; in the park itself, Pilot Rock is a known hotspot.

Pacific White-sided Dolphins were rarely seen in the Kenai Fjords area until recently, but they have been appearing more frequently in recent years. Meanwhile, Dall's Porpoises can be encountered almost anywhere, and frequently bow-ride in front of the whale-watching boats. Particularly good places include the mouth of Resurrection Bay, in front of Bear Glacier, on the crossing to Aialik Bay and within the first part of Aialik Bay.

Prince William Sound

Prince William Sound, to the northeast of Kenai Fjords National Park, is renowned for its spectacular coastal scenery and for having the densest concentration of tidewater glaciers in the world. A vast area of about 15,000 square miles, largely protected from the full force of the weather in the Gulf of Alaska, it is also well known for its whales. Most boat trips are not dedicated to whales, however, but combine glaciers with wildlife. The Sound is very good for Dall's Porpoises; resident Killer Whales can be anywhere, though are particularly common in the southwest (in Montague Strait and Hinchinbrook Channel); and tours often see Humpback Whales, Minke Whales and other species. Some Humpbacks remain in the area all winter.

Prince William Sound is where the Exxon Valdez oil tanker famously struck Bligh Reef, on 24 March 1989, and spilled at least 11 million gallons of crude oil over the next few days. The oil eventually contaminated 1292 miles of coastline and covered 10,800 square miles of ocean. Among the known casualties were 22 Killer Whales (including nine AT1 or Chugach Transients), 3,000 Sea Otters, 300 Harbor Seals, 250 Bald Eagles and no fewer than 250,000 seabirds.

Fin Whales are sometimes encountered in Kenai Fjords National Park.

Kodiak Island

Kodiak Island is the largest island in an archipelago in the northwestern Gulf of Alaska, separated from Katmai National Park on the mainland by Shelikof Strait. The second largest island in the US – only the Big Island of Hawai'i is bigger – it is most famous for being home to 3,500 of the largest Brown Bears in the world.

But it is also ideally located for whale watching. Gray Whales are the first to arrive in force, mainly from mid-March, as they migrate past on their way to the Arctic. Females with calves normally show up in mid-May and keep coming until the end of June. People on Kodiak are lucky to have nearly the entire Eastern Pacific Gray Whale population pass by their island home on their journey north – many of them very close to shore. They tend to migrate along the south and east coasts (Cape Chiniak and Narrow Cape are favorite viewing spots) and very few are seen on the other side in Shelikof Strait. Some even stay around Kodiak and feed until it is time to migrate south again, while a few may remain year-round. These 'residents' are seen most frequently, and in greatest numbers, near the entrance to Ugak Bay (with a peak

from September to November and lowest numbers from June to August), but their distribution extends to roughly 60 miles east-southeast of Ugak.

During the summer, from June to November, there are Humpback Whales, Fin Whales, Minke Whales and Killer Whales, with occasional sightings of Sei Whales and other species. The area between the northern end of Kodiak and the Barren Islands, at the entrance to Cook Inlet, can be particularly good for Humpbacks and they are sometimes seen bubble-netting here, particularly during June and July. Marmot Bay, in the northeast of the island, is particularly good for resident Killer Whales. Belugas from the Cook Inlet population (see page 172) have been seen during spring and summer in Shelikof Strait, between Kodiak Island and the Alaska Peninsula, but they are very rare.

Several Kodiak operators offer whale watching alongside bear watching and other wildlife viewing. It is also possible to spot whales from many clifftops and other vantage points – they sometimes swim directly underneath the cliffs along Chiniak Highway, for example, where it is possible to look straight down on them.

Cook Inlet

Cook Inlet is a large tidal estuary flowing into the Gulf of Alaska, extending 220 miles from Anchorage to the Barren Islands, just north of Kodiak Island. Some 9 miles wide at the head and 81 miles at the mouth, it is a very dynamic inlet, with large tides, strong currents and seasonal sea ice cover.

It is the home of a well-known population of Belugas, which are present year-round. This is the most isolated and genetically distinct of Alaska's five Beluga populations, and has been separated from the other four by the geographical barrier of the Alaska Peninsula for over 10,000 years.

There were about 1,300 Belugas in Cook Inlet in 1979, but by the late 1990s numbers had declined precipitously. The most recent aerial survey, in 2014, counted 340 survivors, and numbers are still declining by 0.4% each year. It is unclear exactly what is happening – why numbers are dropping so rapidly – but over-harvesting was certainly a major factor (though no subsistence hunting has been allowed since 2006). Also, Cook Inlet is the most populated and the fastest-growing watershed in Alaska, so the Belugas face a wide range of other possible threats from declining prey abundance and interactions with fisheries, to noise pollution and disturbance; global warming, and its impact on ice cover, may also be an issue. There are strenuous efforts, by a coalition of local and national conservation groups, concerned citizens and scientists, to ensure their survival and boost their recovery.

During spring, summer and fall the whales can be found in shallow, coastal waters (such as tidal flats and river mouths)

Overview

Main species: Beluga.

Occasional species: Humpback Whale, Fin Whale, Minke Whale, Killer Whale, Dall's Porpoise, Harbor Porpoise.

Other wildlife highlights: Sea Otter, Harbor Seal, Steller Sea Lion, Tundra Swan, Steller's Eider, Bonaparte's Gull, Mew Gull, Glaucous-winged Gull, Tufted Puffin, Horned Puffin, Kittlitz's Murrelet, Red-faced Cormorant.

Main locations: boat tours: Homer; land-based whale watching: Turnagain Arm, Knik Arm, 49th Street Brewery (Anchorage).

Types of tours: half-day to full-day nature tours; land-based whale watching.

When to go: May–September (best mid-July to end of August).

Regulations and guidelines: NOAA Guidelines for Viewing Marine Mammals; Whale SENSE program; US Federal Regulations; Marine Mammal Protection Act (1972).

Wildlife species are listed systematically (not in order of abundance) and frequency of sightings varies with location and season.

in the upper inlet, particularly in Turnagain Arm and Knik Arm, on either side of Anchorage. During late fall and winter, it was presumed that they move farther south to Kachemak Bay, near Homer, and the Barren Islands, at mouth of the inlet near Kodiak Island, to avoid heavy ice. However, recent aerial surveys and satellite-tagging studies indicate that many now remain in the upper inlet all winter.

There are no dedicated whale-watching trips here, although there are boat tours and water-taxis from Homer that include whale watching in Cook Inlet as well as Kachemak Bay and the Gulf of Alaska. However, the

Cook Inlet Belugas are a popular roadside attraction for summer tourists and there are a number of good vantage points to see them from the shore. Aptly named Beluga Point, a rocky outpost about 6 miles south of Anchorage (on the Seward Highway) and jutting out into Turnagain Arm, is particularly good. The best time is from mid-July to the end of August, and there are interpretive signs, spotting scopes and Beluga sculptures in the extensive viewing area. However, the whales can readily be observed from other lookouts along Turnagain Arm. Alternative hotspots include the Beluga River and, sometimes, at the mouth of the Kenai River, halfway along Cook Inlet (they sometimes travel as much as 5 miles upstream on incoming high tides). Or take binoculars to the rooftop patio of the 49th Street Brewery in downtown Anchorage. This offers a commanding view of where Knik Arm connects with Upper Cook Inlet.

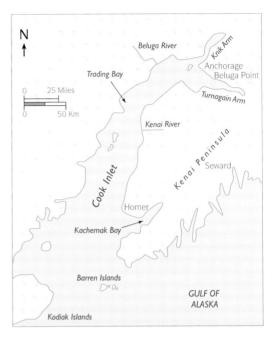

Both resident and transient (Bigg's) Killer Whales have been observed in Cook Inlet. Residents enter to feed on salmon, while transients – which are more regular visitors – enter to hunt Belugas. The transients tend to arrive at the beginning of August, and will readily swim into the upper inlet; they have also been observed attacking immature Humpback Whales in the mouth of the inlet. Harbor Porpoises are fairly common in Upper Cook Inlet, chasing salmon along with the Belugas. Other whales and dolphins are sometimes seen in and around the mouth of Cook Inlet, but are rare farther 'inland'.

Beluga numbers in Cook Inlet are declining.

Aleutian Islands & Pribilof Islands

The Aleutian Islands is a chain of small islands that separates the North Pacific from the Bering Sea. The archipelago extends in an arc southwest, then northwest, for about 1,100 miles from the tip of the Alaska Peninsula toward Russia's Kamchatka Peninsula. A renowned wildlife paradise, it consists of 14 large islands, some 55 smaller islands and innumerable islets.

As many as 10 million seabirds of 26 different species breed here and there are huge stocks of fish (Dutch Harbor is home to one of the largest commercial fishing ports in the country). It also has some of the country's foggiest, windiest and rainiest weather.

At least 26 species of marine mammals visit the Aleutian Islands, particularly during summer. These include three species of beaked whale, which are known to occur but are rarely seen. There are Baird's Beaked Whales and Cuvier's Beaked Whales but, more importantly, strandings records suggest that the archipelago is right in the heart of the range of Stejneger's Beaked Whale.

Unalaska Island

Unalaska is one of the largest islands in the Aleutians. It is also the name of the main town, which has a population of nearly 5,000, and is split between Unalaska Island and neighboring Amaknak Island. Many people refer to the part of town on Amaknak as Dutch Harbor, or simply 'Dutch', though technically this is incorrect (it is the name of a body of water and home to the Port of Dutch Harbor).

Overview

Main species: Gray Whale, Humpback Whale, Fin Whale, Minke Whale, Killer Whale, Dall's Porpoise, Harbor Porpoise.

Occasional species: North Pacific Right Whale, Sei Whale, Sperm Whale, Pacific White-sided Dolphin.

Other wildlife highlights: Red Fox, Arctic Fox, Reindeer, Pribilof Island Shrew, Sea Otter, Northern Fur Seal, Steller Sea Lion, Harbor Seal, Bald Eagle, Red-faced Cormorant, Tufted Puffin, Horned Puffin, Whiskered Auklet, Crested Auklet, Marbled Murrelet, Thick-billed Murre, Short-tailed Shearwater, Short-tailed Albatross, Black-legged Kittiwake, Red-legged Kittiwake, Tundra Swan, Steller's Eider, Black Oystercatcher, Leatherback Turtle.

Main locations: Unalaska Island, Unimak Pass, Pribilof Islands.

Types of tours: half-day to full-day tours; multi-day expeditions; kayaking tours; land-based whale watching.

When to go: late May to early September; mid-November to late December for migrating Gray Whales through Unimak Pass.

Regulations and guidelines: NOAA Guidelines for Viewing Marine Mammals; Whale SENSE program; US Federal Regulations; Marine Mammal Protection Act (1972).

Wildlife species are listed systematically (not in order of abundance) and frequency of sightings varies with location and season.

There is great potential for whale watching here, though it is currently mostly land based. There are occasional boat trips to see Humpback Whales in Unalaska Bay, however, and it is sometimes possible to arrange longer trips to places like Cape Cheerful and beyond to Chelan Bank, where sightings include Humpback Whales,

Gray Whale calves are frequently hunted by Killer Whales in Unimak Pass.

Minke Whales, Killer Whales and Pacific White-sided Dolphins.

Good places for watching whales from the shore include the 'S-curves' of Airport Beach Road, looking out toward Hog Island from Dutch Harbor, which is well known locally as a great place to watch feeding Humpbacks and other species. There can also be good whale watching from the top of Mount Ballyhoo, a 1,634-ft mountain on Amaknak, with spectacular views across Unalaska Bay. Humpbacks gather to feed in the protected waters of Captains Bay, farther south, too. July and August are generally the best months.

The twice-monthly Alaska Marine Highway ferry between Dutch Harbor/Unalaska and Homer can be good for whale watching. Running from May to September, it makes a number of stops along the way and takes about 3–3.5 days each way.

Unimak Pass

Unimak Pass is a wide channel on the west side of desolate and volcano-shrouded Unimak Island. There are many corridors between islands in the Aleutian chain, but this is the first substantial passage west of the Alaska Peninsula that whales can use to swim between the North Pacific and the Bering Sea. Measuring 11.5 miles across at its narrowest point, and 30 miles at its widest, it was once described as 'standing room only' for whales.

At the end of their summer feeding season in the Arctic, Gray Whales start moving south. Those in the farthest reaches of the Beaufort or East Siberian seas turn southward first, as early as mid-August, and others follow a little later. They converge in the Chukchi Sea, then move into the Bering Sea, and ultimately nearly all of them leave the Bering Sea through Unimak Pass. Some

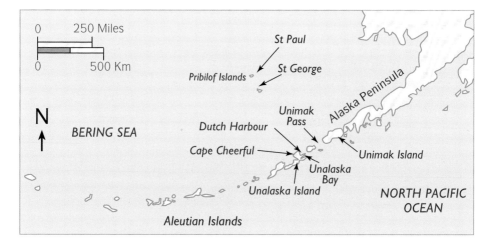

pass through as early as October, others as late as January, but 90 per cent exit between mid-November and late December.

It is the same orderly arrangement on the way back. They leave their winter breeding lagoons, about 4,100 miles away in Baja California, Mexico, hug the west coast of North America on their way north and file through Unimak Pass into the Bering Sea. Most of them pass through in late April, May or June (the peak is the end of May and early June). This is a major hotspot for Killer Whale predation, like Monterey Bay farther south, and significant numbers of transient (Bigg's) Killer Whales are in the area at this time of year, hunting Gray Whale calves. Attacks are normally by groups of three to four Killer Whales, which attempt to drown the calves; they quickly give up if the calves are aggressively defended by their mothers, or if they manage to escape into water less than about ten feet deep.

The whales are sometimes counted by researchers from Cape Sarichef, a promontory on the northwestern corner of Unimak Island. As many as 50 whales per hour have been recorded passing by here, many of them swimming past this point within 1,500ft of shore. Other large whales also use Unimak as the gateway to the Bering Sea, including Humpbacks, Fin Whales and even, on occasion, North Pacific Right Whales.

New Whale Species from the Aleutian Islands

A new species of beaked whale, closely related to Baird's Beaked Whale, has been identified with the help of a handful of specimens found in Alaska. Although no scientist has ever seen one of these whales alive, recent DNA studies on eight specimens (three from Japan and five from the Bering Sea and eastern Aleutian Islands) confirm that it is sufficiently different to be granted species status.

Amazingly, the skeleton of one of these specimens was found hanging in the gymnasium of Unalaska High School. The new species has yet to be officially accepted, but the researchers have proposed two possible common names: Black Baird's Beaked Whale or Dwarf Baird's Beaked Whale. The Japanese call it Karasu, or the Raven.

Pribilof Islands

The fabled 'Fur Seal Islands' of the Bering Sea lie near the shelf break, 240 miles north of the Aleutian Islands. Best known for their vast colonies of about 3 million seabirds – including three-quarters of the world's Red-legged Kittiwakes and North America's largest murre colony – it is also home to almost three-quarters of the world's Northern Fur Seals (900,000 animals altogether). There are two main islands, St Paul and St George, and three islets (Otter Island, Sea Lion Rock and Walrus Island).

Relatively little is known about cetaceans around the Pribilofs, though there has been some research work. There are no dedicated whale-watching trips, but there are multi-day packages focusing on birds or general natural history. Whale watching from shore can be good, too, with regular sightings of half a dozen different species during the summer. Considerable numbers of transient (Bigg's) Killer Whales visit to feed on Northern Fur Seals, particularly around the two main islands; they bring their calves to hunt fur seals straight from the beaches. Humpback Whales, Fin Whales, Minke Whales and Dall's Porpoises are also fairly frequent. Gray Whales from both the eastern and western North Pacific populations are known to feed in the area (at least one has been satellite tagged all the way from Russia's Sakhalin Island). There are also occasional sightings of Blue Whales, Bowhead Whales and even North Pacific Right Whales. And one of the specimens of the recently discovered new species of Baird's Beaked Whale was found on a beach on St George Island.

Professor Reid Brewer measures a new species of beaked whale in the Aleutian Islands.

Barrow

There are significant populations of whales in Alaska's Far North, but currently very limited opportunities for watching them. There are a few dedicated bird-watching tours to Nome – one of North America's legendary birding destinations – that see whales from time to time, but that is about it.

There is potential in a few other locations. Sightings of 1,000 or more Belugas were commonly reported in Kotzebue Sound, for example, between 1960 and 1981. Since then sightings have been much less frequent, and usually of considerably smaller groups, but they are still around in small numbers. Meanwhile, there are many more Killer Whales in the area than there used to be. Gambell, on the northern tip of St Lawrence Island, and just 36 miles from Russia, is another potential whale-watching destination. It is not the easiest place to get to, but Gray Whales and Bowhead Whales often pass very close to the point during spring and summer.

Barrow

The northernmost community in the US, Barrow is located on the Chukchi Sea coast, near the border with the Beaufort Sea. It was traditionally known as Utqiagvik and, indeed, local residents recently voted for its name to be changed back to the original. Some 320 miles north of the Arctic Circle, it has a population of about 4,400 (of which 61 per cent are Iñupiat Eskimo).

Gray Whales and Belugas are occasionally seen from shore during the summer, and Killer Whales pass by from time to time. Possible places to watch for them are the bluffs just south of the village

Overview

Main species: Bowhead Whale, Gray Whale, Beluga.

Other wildlife highlights: Polar Bear, Arctic Fox, Caribou, Walrus, Ringed Seal, Bearded Seal, Snowy Owl, Peregrine, Gyrfalcon, Ross's Gull, Glaucous Gull, Sabine's Gull, Ivory Gull, Black Guillemot, Tundra Swan, King Eider, Steller's Eider, Spectacled Eider, Common Eider.

Main locations: Barrow.

Types of tours: land-based whale watching.

When to go: late April–October.

Regulations and guidelines: off-road driving on local tundra requires local land-use permit and only by charter.

Wildlife species are listed systematically (not in order of abundance) and frequency of sightings varies with location and season.

and Point Barrow, or Nuvuk, a headland about 9 miles northeast of town that is famous for being the northernmost point in the United States. It is possible to get there by four-wheel drive charter.

But Barrow is better known for its Bowhead Whales, which migrate past the community every spring and fall (although they are rarely seen from shore). There are two peak periods: when they are travelling from the Bering Sea to the southeastern Beaufort Sea, from March to June, and when they are heading back, from September to November.

The Iñupiat have hunted Bowhead Whales for generations. Thanks to profits from the North Slope oil fields, modern-day Barrow now has many modern amenities (light is supplied by electricity instead of seal oil, for example, and dogsleds have mostly been replaced by snowmobiles) but subsistence hunting is still important. The spring whale hunt tends to take place in April and May; the end of this whaling season is celebrated during the Nalukataq Whaling Festival, usually held around the summer solstice in the third week of June. The fall hunt takes place in early October, before the onset of winter (the sun disappears below the horizon in mid-November and is not seen again until mid-January). As ice conditions have changed, with global warming, the primary hunting season has also changed, from spring to fall. If you visit during this period, it is quite possible that you will see a Bowhead Whale being brought onto the beach and butchered. The whalers use traditional *umiaqs* (boats made with Bearded Seal skin), but nowadays their hand-held harpoons are armed with small incendiary devices that detonate inside the whale.

The International Whaling Commission approved a catch limit for 2013–18 of up to 336 Bowhead Whales – the population is currently about 17,000 animals – to be shared between Alaska (306) and Chukotka, in Russia (30), with no more than 67 strikes in any one year. Eleven Alaskan communities share 306 and each has an annual quota of whales, ranging from just 1 to Barrow's 25.

Polar Bears are seen in the Barrow area mainly from October to June, when the sea

ice is closer to shore, but they are particularly common immediately after the fall whaling season, when they often feed on the whale remains at Point Barrow.

Bowhead Whales migrate past Barrow every spring and fall.

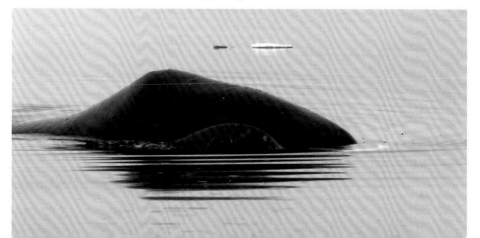

WASHINGTON

San Juan Islands & Puget Sound

More than 500,000 people go whale watching around the San Juan Islands and in the Salish Sea every year, making it one of the world's top whale-watching destinations. Southern Resident Killer Whales – a famous community currently comprising 78 different individuals – are undoubtedly the star attraction, but transient (Bigg's) Killer Whales are also regular visitors and a variety of other cetaceans, from Humpback Whales to Dall's Porpoises, are seen on many trips.

The San Juan Islands are in the northern reaches of Puget Sound, sandwiched between the Strait of Georgia and the Strait of Juan de Fuca. They are remnants of a mountain range that once connected Vancouver Island to the Washington State

Overview

Main species: Humpback Whale, Minke Whale, Killer Whale, Pacific White-sided Dolphin, Dall's Porpoise, Harbor Porpoise.

Occasional species: Gray Whale, Fin Whale.

Other wildlife highlights: Black Bear, Steller Sea Lion, Northern Fur Seal, California Sea Lion, Northern Elephant Seal, Harbor Seal, River Otter, Sea Otter, Bald Eagle, Rhinoceros Auklet, Tufted Puffin, Pigeon Guillemot, Marbled Murrelet, Pacific Loon, Surf Scoter, Bonaparte's Gull, Glaucous-winged Gull.

Main locations: boat trips: Friday Harbor, Roche Harbor (San Juan Island); Deer Harbor, Orcas, Eastsound (Orcas Island); Anacortes (Fidalgo Island); Lopez Island, Lummi Island, Whidbey Island (Langley); Bellingham, Everett, Edmonds, Port Townsend, Port Angeles, Seattle (boat tours and floatplane-boat/bus-boat packages to other locations); land-based: Lime Kiln Point State Park/Whale Watch Park, San Juan Island National Historical Park, Land Bank Westside Scenic Preserve, Eagle Point, Cattle Point Lighthouse (San Juan Island); Langley, Coupeville (Whidbey Island); Alki Point, Seattle Aquarium (Seattle); Point Robinson Lighthouse (Vashon Island); Port Defiance, Dosewallips State Park, Port Townsend, Freshwater Bay, Salt Creek County Park, Sekiu Overlook, Shipwreck Point, Neah Bay; the Whale Trail (Washington State to California).

Types of tours: one-hour to full-day tours; multi-day packages; multi-day kayaking tours; land-based whale watching.

When to go: April–October (peak period May to September for Southern Resident Killer Whales); some tours also operate from March–November.

Regulations and guidelines: Best Practice Guidelines developed by Pacific Whale Watch Association; Be Whale Wise Marine Wildlife Guidelines endorsed by Fisheries and Oceans Canada and BC Parks; US Federal Regulations (with additional state laws regulating behavior near Southern Resident Killer Whales); Washington State Vessel Law; Soundwatch Boater Education Program; Straitwatch; Kayakers Code of Conduct; Marine Mammal Protection Act (1972); different regulations apply in Canadian waters.

Wildlife species are listed systematically (not in order of abundance) and frequency of sightings varies with location and season.

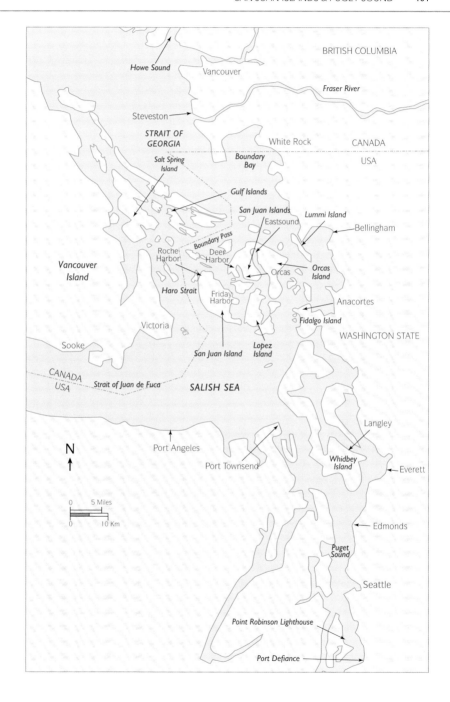

BRITISH COLUMBIA

Howe Sound

Vancouver

Fraser River

Steveston

STRAIT OF
GEORGIA

White Rock   CANADA

Salt Spring
Island

Boundary
Bay

USA

Gulf Islands

San Juan Islands   Lummi Island

Eastsound

Bellingham

Roche
Harbor

Boundary Pass

Deer
Harbor

Orcas
Island

Vancouver
Island

Orcas

Haro Strait

Friday
Harbor

Anacortes

Fidalgo Island

WASHINGTON STATE

Victoria

Sooke

San Juan Island

Lopez
Island

CANADA
USA   Strait of Juan de Fuca   SALISH SEA

Langley

N

Whidbey
Island

Everett

Port Angeles

Port Townsend

0   5 Miles

0   10 Km

Edmonds

Puget
Sound

Seattle

Point Robinson Lighthouse

Port Defiance

mainland (strictly speaking, they form part of a much larger archipelago that includes Canada's Gulf Islands). The San Juan Islands themselves consist of no fewer than 172 named islands and reefs (some only visible at low tide) and is fondly referred to as the 'Banana Belt' (it lies in the rain shadow of the Olympic Mountains and enjoys an average of 250 days of sunshine every year). There are three large islands – San Juan, Orcas and Lopez – all of which are accessible by passenger ferry; Shaw Island, which is considerably smaller, is also reachable by ferry. Killer Whales are frequently seen on the San Juan Island Washington State Ferries routes (with occasional sightings of Minke Whales, Pacific White-sided Dolphins, Dall's Porpoises and Harbor Porpoises). Seattle is about 100 miles to the south.

The archipelago lies in the heart of a much wider whale-watching area called the Salish Sea, which is a large, biologically rich, semi-enclosed sea shared between the southwestern portion of the Canadian province of British Columbia and the northwestern portion of the US state of Washington. Also known as the Emerald Sea, due to its color and nutrient content, this intricate network of coastal waterways includes the Strait of Juan de Fuca, Haro Strait, the Strait of Georgia, Puget Sound and all their connecting channels and adjoining waters.

The Canada–US border runs right through the middle of the whale-watching area, but whale-watch boats can move freely back and forth across the border wherever the whales happen to be at the time (though they are not allowed to land passengers outside their own country).

Best of all, from a whale-watching point of view, the Salish Sea is readily accessible from many towns and cities, including Seattle, Vancouver and Victoria. Throughout the summer and fall, there are a great many tours leaving on and off all day every day from many ports in the region (with the largest number on the US side leaving from Friday Harbor, on San Juan Island). The Pacific Whale Watch Association – which is committed to research, education and responsible wildlife viewing in the region – has no fewer than 35 member companies operating about 100 vessels in the Salish Sea, departing from 20 different ports in Washington State and British Columbia.

There was one occasion in Haro Strait when no fewer than 107 commercial and recreational boats were observed following the same small pod of Killer Whales. That was exceptional, and it was at the height of the expansion of the whale-watching industry, but there is no doubt that it can get crowded and the number of vessels is the only downside to whale watching in the Salish Sea. The commercial whale-watch operators are mostly very careful in the way they maneuver around the whales, and they follow local regulations and guidelines to the letter, but private boaters are often either oblivious or not so responsible.

Fortunately, there are strenuous efforts to prevent vessel disturbance to Killer Whales and other marine wildlife in the region, such as through the Soundwatch Boater Education Program (created by The Whale Museum, in Friday Harbor, San Juan Island). This puts staff and volunteers on the water every day during summer to educate recreational boaters on the least intrusive ways to watch whales in the wild and to monitor all vessel activity near the whales. The Washington Department of Fish & Wildlife and the National Oceanic Atmospheric Administration also have patrol vessels monitoring the conduct of all

Killer Whales swim past whale watchers on Stuart Island, in the San Juan Islands.

boats around the Southern Residents during peak season. One of the aims is to spread the fleet out to different groups of whales, to minimize disturbance. Federal Regulations for all Killer Whales require that boaters stay 200 yards (183 meters) away and keep the path of the whales clear for 400 yards (366 meters) (with no waiting in their path).

Southern Resident Killer Whales

The Salish Sea is the core summer and fall range of a famous community of Killer Whales called the Southern Residents. This is the smallest of the three resident Killer Whale communities in the Northeast Pacific, currently with 78 individuals in three pods: J-pod (24 members), K-pod (19 members) and L-pod (35 members). Northern Resident Killer Whales very occasionally appear this far south (they normally spend their summers off northeastern Vancouver Island) but they are seen no more than once every few years, on average.

Southern Residents congregate in the Salish Sea to intercept salmon – particularly Chinook, which is their favorite – as the fish funnel into the narrow waterways on their way to spawning rivers. Their favorite area tends to be off the western side of San Juan

Island, but they forage as far as Swiftsure Bank on the west coast (roughly between the northern end of the Strait of Juan de Fuca and Tofino), and as far as the Fraser River on the mainland (the Fraser River being where most of the salmon go to spawn).

Increasingly, J-pod tends to remain in the same inshore waters for much of the winter, too, but the other two pods spend more time offshore during the colder months and travel as far south as Monterey, in California, and as far north as Haida Gwaii (formerly the Queen Charlotte Islands).

The Southern Resident Killer Whales have been studied intensively since 1976 and every individual is known to researchers (and, of course, to the best whale-watch operators). There are many well-known whales among them. The first to be named was Ruffles, or J1, who was the icon of the Southern Residents for three decades, thanks to his exceptionally tall and wavy dorsal fin. There are claims that Ruffles was the most photographed Killer Whale in the world (sadly, he died in November 2010, aged about 60 – his death was reported in newspapers and on TV news bulletins worldwide). Ruffles was once actually captured to be sold and put on display in captivity but, in a twist of fate, was set free because he was too big.

Other members of the Southern Residents were not so lucky: Lolita, or Tokitae as she used to be known, was captured near Seattle in Penn Cove, Puget Sound, in 1970, when about four years old. She still lives in Miami Seaquarium and is the last survivor of 45 members of the Southern Resident community that were captured and sold for display in marine parks between 1965 and 1977. Lolita's 89-year-old mother, Ocean Sun, or L25, still swims freely in the Salish Sea with the rest of the family.

There are many other characters among the Southern Residents: Deadhead, named in honor of the rock band The Grateful Dead's lead singer, Jerry Garcia; Slick, who recently gave birth to her sixth young calf (who would have died without the help of Aunt Alki); Princess Angeline, who was one of three females in J-pod, all of whom were pregnant at the same time (they were affectionately known as 'The Pregnancy Club'); and many more.

Granny

But the real superstar has to be Granny, or J2, who was probably Ruffles's mother and was the oldest known Killer Whale in the world. It is estimated that she celebrated her 105th birthday in 2016. Still the matriarch leader of J-pod, she led her family group of no fewer than five generations (she outlived her children, but spent every day with her remaining grandchildren, great-grandchildren and great-great-grandchildren) and was a fount of knowledge on all the best feeding, resting and socializing spots in the Salish Sea. She travelled up to 100 miles every day, and even breached. Sadly, she went missing in October 2016 and is now considered deceased.

Transient (Bigg's) Killer Whales

As their name suggests, transient (Bigg's) Killer Whales are indeed 'transient'. They may be seen one day and then move on to an entirely different area the next, or they may be seen several times before disappearing for weeks or even months. Similarly, some family groups of transients are rare visitors to the area, while others come and go many times throughout the year.

However, it is becoming more and more common to see them in the central Salish Sea and Puget Sound. Local experts are even joking that some of the transients are almost becoming 'resident transients' – it's been dubbed the 'transient invasion'. The reason is probably a boom in the local seal and sea lion populations – which means plenty of food – although they also hunt porpoises in the area and, in April 2016, were observed attacking two adult Gray Whales in Puget Sound.

Many whale-watching boats have on-board hydrophones, to listen to the Killer Whales vocalizing underwater. Transient (Bigg's) Killer Whales are generally silent while they are foraging (because their mammalian prey can hear them), but they do vocalize after a successful hunt. The residents, on the other hand, can be highly vocal and make a variety of whistles, squeaks, screams, squawks and other sounds. Each pod has its own unique dialect and the best operators can tell one from another just by listening to them (you can listen to the hydrophone feeds – live – on OrcaSound.net).

Other cetaceans in the Salish Sea

Humpback Whales were once common in the Salish Sea but, between 1905 and 1925, more than 5,500 were killed by commercial whalers in the region. By 1925, they were so scarce that the whaling stations shut down operations and catcher boats moved on to Alaska and California.

But after being absent for nearly a century, Humpback Whales began to return to the Salish Sea in the 1990s. Researchers have recorded a steady increase in numbers since then: each year has record sightings, and then it is topped the following year. It has been called the 'Humpback comeback'. Nowadays, they are seen in every month of the year and nearly every day during the peak period from May to November. There are no official estimates, but it is possible that as many as 15–25 different Humpbacks are present on some days. The Strait of Juan de Fuca is a particular hotspot.

One of the first recognizable individuals to return was a female called 'Big Mama' (or, more officially, BCY0324). She was first photo-identified in 1997 and has returned every year since 2003. In fact, since 2003, she has come back with no fewer than six different calves (she returned with her sixth in 2016). Big Mama used to feed mainly southwest of Victoria, but seems to have expanded her range in recent years into the Strait of Georgia.

Minke Whales are most often seen from late spring to fall, with peak sightings in July and August. They are most frequent around the Gulf Islands, particularly in Boundary Pass and Haro Strait, but can also be seen in the Strait of Juan de Fuca and elsewhere; they like to forage off Hein Bank and Salmon Bank, at the bottom of Haro Strait/East Entrance to Juan de Fuca. In winter, they probably move to warmer waters farther south to breed and, while sightings have been recorded in the Salish Sea in all months of the year, there are relatively few for December to February. During summer, there are records of the same individuals returning year after year – one particular Minke Whale has been sighted in the Salish Sea over a period of more than 20 years. Interestingly, they have even been seen playing with resident Killer Whales in Haro Strait on several occasions – suggesting that they can distinguish between the harmless fish-eating residents and the potentially dangerous mammal-eating transients (which occasionally hunt Minke Whales).

Gray Whales are much more sporadic. On their way north, while migrating between their breeding grounds in Baja California,

The 'Humpback comeback' – Humpback Whales are returning to the Salish Sea.

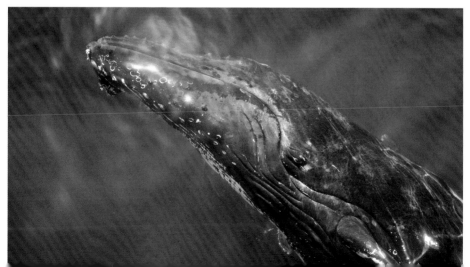

There is some great land-based whale watching in the San Juan Islands.

Mexico, and their Arctic feeding grounds in the Bering, Chuckchi and Beaufort seas, a few individuals wander into the Salish Sea region. Some are seen, most years, in Boundary Bay, south of Vancouver, for example, especially early in the season. There is also a core group of about 10–15 Gray Whales that takes a little detour into Puget Sound and around Whidbey and Camano Islands to forage there for a few months, typically from February until May or June. Sightings in other parts of the Salish Sea are sparse.

For much of the past century, Pacific White-sided Dolphins were rarely encountered in British Columbia's inside coastal passages, but that seems to be changing. Since the early 1980s they have been appearing with increasing regularity. Nowadays, they are seen increasingly often in the Salish Sea, typically in pods of 50–150 (sometimes more than 300), with particular hotspots including the southern Strait of Georgia and Howe Sound, near Vancouver. The increase in sightings in the past 10 years, in particular, has been nothing short of remarkable.

The only other species seen regularly in the Salish Sea are Dall's Porpoises and Harbor Porpoises. However, others do turn up from time to time: Fin Whales, for example, have been recorded but are extremely rare, with only 10 confirmed sightings since 1930 (intriguingly, four of which have been recent – in 2013, 2015 and 2016, when there were two). And a pod of Short-beaked Common Dolphins appeared in Juan de Fuca in June 2016.

Land-based whale watching

There is some good land-based whale watching, mainly centered around Killer Whales and particularly overlooking Haro Strait. The most frequently visited location is Lime Kiln Point State Park (dubbed Whale Watch Park), on the west side of San Juan Island, which welcomes a quarter of a million people every year. It offers frequent views of Killer Whales and Minke Whales, with occasional sightings of Gray Whales, Pacific White-sided Dolphins and Dall's Porpoises.

There are a number of other well-known sites on San Juan Island and on the mainland overlooking Rosario Strait and the Strait of Juan de Fuca. Sites around Seattle, and in northern Puget Sound, are sometimes rewarded with sightings of Gray Whales, Killer Whales, Dall's Porpoises and Harbor Porpoises.

Westport & the Olympic Coast

While 95 per cent of the whale watching in Washington State is focused on the San Juan Islands and the Salish Sea, there is a long history of whale watching from Westport, a small town facing the open Pacific.

Dedicated trips are predominantly on charter boats that undertake fishing tours at other times of the year. During March, April and May, they sometimes go to see the Gray Whales that migrate past Westport en route to their summer feeding grounds in the Arctic. The whales also pass by on their return journey to their breeding grounds in Baja California, Mexico, of course, but the southerly migration tends to be faster and farther offshore and is not so conducive to whale watching.

Westport is located on a peninsula on the south side of the entrance to Grays Harbor. Most trips head a few miles offshore but, if you are lucky, there could be Gray Whales right inside Grays Harbor. (Despite the coincidence, this large semi-enclosed estuarine bay is not named after the whales, but after Captain Robert Gray, who discovered it during a fur-trading expedition in 1792.)

At the height of the season, there have been as many as 40 Gray Whales passing Westport every hour. They are often very curious and may approach whale-watching boats closely.

There are also some excellent pelagic bird-watching trips, from April to October, and these nearly always encounter a good number of whales, dolphins and porpoises. The full-day trips usually head for Grays

Overview

Main species: Gray Whale, Humpback Whale, Pacific White-sided Dolphin, Dall's Porpoise, Harbor Porpoise.

Occasional species: Fin Whale, Minke Whale, Sperm Whale, Killer Whale, Risso's Dolphin, Northern Right Whale Dolphin.

Other wildlife highlights: Steller Sea Lion, California Sea Lion, Northern Fur Seal, Harbor Seal, Sea Otter, Bald Eagle, Black-footed Albatross, Short-tailed Shearwater, Pink-footed Shearwater, Flesh-footed Shearwater, Buller's Shearwater, Leach's Storm Petrel, Fork-tailed Storm Petrel, South Polar Skua, Thayer's Gull, Sabine's Gull, Glaucous-winged Gull, Black-legged Kittiwake, Red-necked Phalarope, Red Phalarope, Pigeon Guillemot, Cassin's Auklet, Rhinoceros Auklet, Tufted Puffin, Pacific Loon, Red-throated Loon, Harlequin Duck, Surf Scoter, Blue Shark, Ocean Sunfish.

Main locations: boat trips: Westport; land-based: Lewis & Clark Interpretive Center, North Head Lighthouse, Westport Observation Tower, North Jetty (Ocean Shores), La Push, Kalaloch, Cape Flattery; Whale Trail (Washington State to California).

Types of tours: two- to three-hour tours nearshore; nine- to ten-hour pelagic birding tours; land-based whale watching.

When to go: early March to late May for migrating Gray Whales; April–October for pelagic trips; early March to October for land-based whale watching (limited opportunities year-round).

Regulations and guidelines: Best Practice Guidelines developed by Pacific Whale Watch Association; US Federal Regulations; Washington State Vessel Law; Marine Mammal Protection Act (1972).

Wildlife species are listed systematically (not in order of abundance) and frequency of sightings varies with location and season.

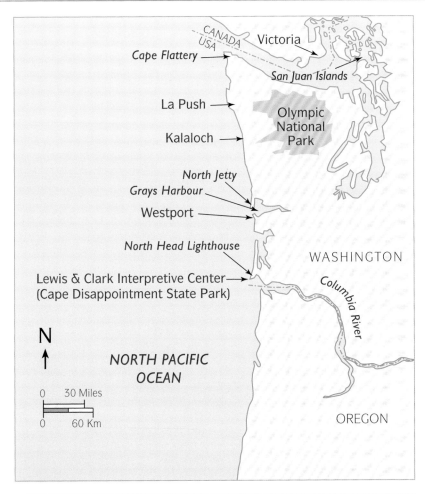

Humpback Whale blows off the coast of Washington.

Gray Whales are often seen close to shore in parts of Washington's Olympic Coast.

Canyon, a submarine canyon some 40 miles due west from the mouth of Grays Harbor, which is right on the edge of the continental shelf and rich in marine life. While the trips focus on seabirds – with the chance of seeing a remarkable variety of species – they nearly always encounter Humpback Whales, Pacific White-sided Dolphins, Dall's Porpoises and Harbor Porpoises, while Gray Whales, Killer Whales, Risso's Dolphins, Northern Right Whale Dolphins and other species are seen from time to time.

There is some land-based whale watching along Washington's Pacific coast, though there are relatively few vantage points high enough to allow a good look at passing whales. Hotspots include: Lewis & Clark Interpretive Center (which stands on the high cliffs in Cape Disappointment State Park) and nearby North Head Lighthouse; Westport Observation Tower (particularly if juvenile whales have entered Grays Harbor); and the rocks on the North Jetty, at the southern end of Ocean Shores (on the peninsula directly opposite Westport).

Farther north, along the Olympic Coast, La Push is also popular, and the Quileute Nation hosts an annual 'Welcoming of the Whales Ceremony' here, in April. Gray Whales are commonly seen, and there are occasional sightings of Humpback Whales, Minke Whales, Killer Whales, Pacific White-sided Dolphins, Dall's Porpoises and Harbor Porpoises.

The Olympic Coast National Marine Sanctuary, which stretches from Cape Flattery, in the north, to the Copalis River, about 160 miles to the south, can also be good for cetaceans. Designated in 1994 to protect the diversity of marine mammals and seabirds, as well as the rich fishing grounds, and various historical and cultural sites, the sanctuary extends 25–50 miles seaward. It includes much of the continental shelf and several major submarine canyons. Altogether, no fewer than 24 species of whales, dolphins and porpoises have been recorded along this wild and largely undeveloped coastline. From vantage points on shore, the most commonly seen are Gray Whales, but it is also possible to see Humpback Whales, Killer Whales, Pacific White-sided Dolphins, Dall's Porpoises and Harbor Porpoises with some regularity.

Oregon

Whales, dolphins and porpoises are visible along the Oregon coast year-round, and no fewer than 27 species have been recorded at one time or another.

But the focus of whale watching here is Gray Whales – there are boat trips to see them and some outstandingly good shore-based whale watching – and all other species are considered a bonus. There are a dozen species or more farther offshore (typically at least 10 miles from the coast), but there are few trips long enough to venture far enough to find them. Many of the trips here, which are mostly on sports-fishing boats, last for no more than an hour. Yet the potential for pelagic trips, weather permitting, is substantial, with the promise of anything from Blue Whales to rare beaked whales.

Migrating Gray Whales

Almost the entire world population of 18–21,000 Gray Whales migrates along the Oregon coast every winter between their feeding grounds in the Bering, Chukchi and Beaufort seas and their breeding grounds in Baja California, Mexico – and then migrates back again every spring. The Gray Whales here are so plentiful and easy to find that, at peak times (mainly during the second half of December), it is possible to see 30 or more passing every hour.

The two seasons are quite different. On their northerly migration, the whales tend to be slower and closer to shore, often less than half a mile from the best vantage points. They begin to appear off Oregon in early March, increase to a peak from the end of March to mid-April, then decline in numbers from mid-May to early June.

Overview

Main species: Gray Whale.

Occasional species: Blue Whale, Fin Whale, Humpback Whale, Minke Whale, Sperm Whale, Killer Whale, Short-finned Pilot Whale, Pacific White-sided Dolphin, Short-beaked Common Dolphin, Common Bottlenose Dolphin, Dall's Porpoise, Harbor Porpoise.

Other wildlife highlights: Elk, California Sea Lion, Steller Sea Lion, Northern Fur Seal, Harbor Seal, Bald Eagle, Peregrine, Tufted Puffin, Common Murre, Pigeon Guillemot, Marbled Murrelet, Cassin's Auklet, Bonaparte's Gull, Heerman's Gull, Mew Gull, Thayer's Gull, Sabine's Gull, Black Oystercatcher, Bufflehead, Leatherback Turtle, Green Turtle, Loggerhead Turtle.

Main locations: boat tours: Garibaldi, Tillamook, Lincoln City, Depoe Bay, Newport, South Beach, Winchester Bay, Coos Bay, Charleston, Brookings; bus-boat packages from Portland; aerial whale watching: Astoria, Tillamook, Florence, North Bend, Bandon.

Types of tours: one- to two-hour tours; aerial whale watching; excellent land-based whale watching.

When to go: year-round (most trips March–October); Gray Whales rarely seen mid-November to mid-December or mid-January to early March.

Regulations and guidelines: NOAA Guidelines for Viewing Marine Mammals; US Federal Regulations; Marine Mammal Protection Act (1972).

Wildlife species are listed systematically (not in order of abundance) and frequency of sightings varies with location and season.

Mothers with calves tend to be the last to appear, usually in May. On their southerly migration, from mid-December to early February (with a peak during the end of December and early January) they are faster and farther offshore: typically about 5 miles away, though still often within sight of land. There is some overlap: the majority of whales swimming north often pass stragglers still heading south. But the bottom line is that the northerly migration tends to be better for whale watching – and the weather is more amenable at this time of year, too.

Summer resident Gray Whales

For the majority of these whales, Oregon serves solely as a migration corridor. But since the early 1970s a significant number of them have been choosing not to migrate all the way to the Arctic: they are present in Oregon throughout the summer (mainly from late May to mid-November, with a peak in late August and early September). Researchers have identified some 200 'summer residents' between northern California and southeastern Alaska, forming what is known as the 'Pacific Coast Feeding Group'. Nearly a third of these whales tend to stay in Oregon – and, of these, about 40 hang out along the short stretch of coast between Lincoln City and Newport. Around Depoe Bay, for example, 5–15 different whales are typically seen most days. Many are known by name to researchers and whale-watch operators: the most famous, and easily the most recognizable, is 'Scarback', who has a large scar on her back, believed to have been caused by an explosive harpoon some time in the mid- to late 1980s. Another one, 'Eagle Eye', was born in 1992 and has been seen repeatedly every summer since.

Remarkably, the 'friendly' behavior seen among Gray Whales in their breeding lagoons in Baja California is becoming increasingly common outside Mexico and they are beginning to seek out interactions with boaters in other areas, including Oregon. This is particularly the case with

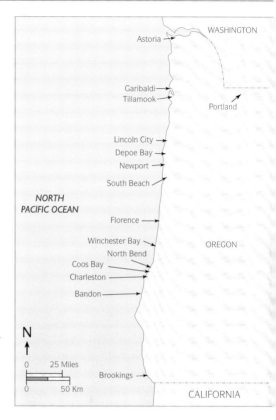

the summer residents. While thrilling for the whale watchers, there is concern that, away from the safety of the lagoons, such behavior carries risks to the whales, which may be inadvertently injured by boat propellers or entangled in fishing gear. It is illegal to touch them in US waters.

Other species

Humpback Whales are being seen more frequently in Oregon, especially along the north coast. They are summer visitors and mostly in deeper waters offshore but, in recent years, have been feeding in a few hotspots within sight of land. They tend to be closest to shore during El Niño years,

Pelagic birdwatching trips often encounter Humpback Whales.

when the water is warmer and perhaps they have trouble finding suitable prey.

Male Sperm Whales are occasionally encountered, from March to November, during pelagic birding trips that venture into deeper waters farther offshore. The same is true for Pacific White-sided Dolphins and Dall's Porpoises. Oregon is at the northern extreme of the range for Bottlenose Dolphins, but they are occasionally seen during the summer (again, usually offshore).

Seeing Killer Whales off the Oregon coast is a rare treat. But there is often at least one pod of transients around in late April and May – just in time to intercept Gray Whale calves, travelling with their mothers to their feeding grounds in the north. Killer Whales can be seen unpredictably anywhere, but the coast between Depoe Bay and Newport is a particular hotspot and, several times in recent years, they have entered Yaquina Bay in Newport to hunt Harbor Seals and California Sea Lions.

The 'Whale-watching Capital of the Oregon Coast'

Whale-watch operators in Oregon are at the mercy of the weather – perhaps more so than in many other parts of the continent.

But Depoe Bay has a slight geographical advantage – it is one of very few locations with the potential for whale watching within the protection of a bay – and so it bills itself as 'The Whale-watching Capital of the Oregon Coast'. True enough, most operators are in Depoe Bay (or Newport, 12 miles to the south) and it is not unusual for them to find one of the summer resident Gray Whales within minutes of leaving the harbor.

The excellent Whale Watching Center in Depoe Bay sits on a huge sea wall that runs the length of the downtown area, and is a great location for spotting whales. Many claim that this is the best spot for land-based whale watching in the entire state. It certainly seems to be a magnet for Gray Whales, which frequently come in very close to the wall, and you can even watch them from the warm and rain-free indoors.

Land-based whale watching

Land-based whale watching in Oregon is really popular and there are numerous accessible headlands and nationally acclaimed lookouts up and down the coast. It makes whale watching here a more contemplative experience than in some other parts of the world.

For more than 30 years, the 'Whale Watching Spoken Here' program has been placing volunteers at 24 of the best whale-watching sites along the Oregon coast (with a few more in southern Washington and northern California) during official 'Whale Watch Weeks'. There are two official weeks timed to coincide with peak Gray Whale migration times and key holiday periods: one between Christmas and New Year, and the other during the last week of March. It is not unusual to have 1,500–2,000 Gray Whale sightings up and down the coast during one of these special weeks.

From north to south, the 24 Whale Watching Spoken Here sites (generally the best locations along the coast to spot whales) are: Ecola State Park, Neahkahnie Mountain Historic Marker Turnout on Highway 101, Cape Meares State Scenic Viewpoint, Cape Lookout State Park (with a 2.5-mile hike to the site), Cape Kiwanda, Inn at Spanish Head in Lincoln City (Lobby on the tenth floor), Boiler Bay State Scenic Viewpoint, The Whale Watching Center/Depoe Bay Sea Wall, Rocky Creek State Scenic Viewpoint, Cape Foulweather, Devil's Punchbowl State Natural Area, Yaquina Head Outstanding Natural Area, Don Davis City Park, Cape Perpetua Interpretive Center, Cook's Chasm Turnout, Sea Lion Caves Turnout (large Highway 101 turnout south of the tunnel), Umpqua Lighthouse (near Umpqua Lighthouse State Park), Shore Acres State Park, Face Rock Wayside State Scenic Viewpoint, Battle Rock Wayfinding Point (Port Orford), Cape Ferrelo and Harris Beach State Park. But almost any headland off Highway 101 will do.

Aerial whale watching

Half a dozen air charter companies also offer aerial whale watching from runways along the Oregon coast. Most of these tours are not scheduled, but on demand. Federal regulations require pilots to maintain an altitude of 1,000ft or higher over whales, so you are not close, but it can be a wonderful opportunity to see the entire animals swimming just beneath or on the surface.

Almost the entire world population of Gray Whales migrates along the Oregon coast.

California

California has the longest established whale-watching industry in the world. It all began in San Diego: formal land-based whale watching started here in 1950, when an old army gun station became the first public whale-watching lookout; and formal boat-based whale watching started in 1955, when fisherman Chuck Chamberlin charged tourists US$1 to see Gray Whales migrating along the coast.

Gray Whales have traditionally been the main focus of whale watching in California and, for animals 'just passing through', they get the most extraordinary attention. There are more than 75 whale-watch operators up and down the coast, many offering money-back guarantees if you do not get to see one. Most are in central and southern California, where a greater number and variety of whales are seen, though there

Overview

Main species: Gray Whale, Blue Whale, Fin Whale, Humpback Whale, Minke Whale, Killer Whale, Pacific White-sided Dolphin, Northern Right Whale Dolphin, Risso's Dolphin, Short-beaked Common Dolphin, Long-beaked Common Dolphin, Common Bottlenose Dolphin, Dall's Porpoise, Harbor Porpoise.

Occasional species: Sei Whale, Bryde's Whale, Sperm Whale, Short-finned Pilot Whale, Striped Dolphin.

Other wildlife highlights: Sea Otter, Northern Elephant Seal, Harbor Seal, Northern Fur Seal, Steller Sea Lion, California Sea Lion, Black-footed Albatross, Pink-footed Shearwater, Buller's Shearwater, Sooty Shearwater, Black-vented Shearwater, Ashy Storm Petrel, Black Storm Petrel, Least Storm Petrel, Sabine's Gull, Tufted Puffin, Pigeon Guillemot, Rhinoceros Auklet, Surf Scoter, Leatherback Turtle, Great White Shark, Thresher Shark, Ocean Sunfish.

Main locations: boat trips: Crescent City, Fort Bragg, Mendocino, Sausalito, San Francisco, Berkeley, Half Moon Bay, Morro Bay, Avila Beach, Santa Barbara, Ventura, Oxnard, Malibu, Marina del Ray, Redondo Beach, San Pedro, Long Beach, Huntingdon Beach, Balboa, Newport Beach, Laguna Beach, Dana Point, Oceanside, San Diego; see page 203 for Monterey Bay (Monterey, Moss Landing, Santa Cruz); aerial whale watching: Santa Barbara, Oxnard; land-based whale watching: Cabrillo National Monument (San Diego), Pigeon Point Lighthouse (south of Half Moon Bay), San Simeon and Montaña de Oro State Park (between Monterey and Santa Barbara), Point Vicente Interpretive Center and Rancho Palos Verdes (south of Los Angeles), Point Reyes National Seashore, Bodega Head and Sonoma Coast State Park (north of San Francisco), and many more.

Types of tours: two-hour to full-day boat trips; multi-day expedition cruises; kayaking tours; aerial whale watching; land-based whale watching.

When to go: year-round; mid-December–May (sometimes June) for migrating Gray Whales; Blue Whales May–January (mainly July–September); Humpback Whales May–November; Killer Whales year-round, mainly December–May (peak April–May).

Regulations and guidelines: NOAA Guidelines for Viewing Marine Mammals; US Federal Regulations; National Marine Sanctuaries Act; regulations within specific National Marine Sanctuaries; Marine Mammal Protection Act (1972).

Wildlife species are listed systematically (not in order of abundance) and frequency of sightings varies with location and season.

More than 75 whale-watch operators offer trips to see Gray Whales in California.

are some good opportunities and a few operators in the north.

But there are many other cetaceans off the Golden State's coast. It is one of the best places in the world for reliable sightings of Blue Whales, in particular, it has a healthy and growing summer population of Humpback Whales, there are huge schools of dolphins, and longer trips that venture farther offshore can be rewarded with a wonderful variety of other species. As well as the regulars (Pacific White-sided Dolphin, Northern Rightwhale Dolphin, Risso's Dolphin, Short-beaked Common Dolphin, Long-beaked Common Dolphin and Common Bottlenose Dolphin) it is also worth looking out for Striped Dolphins. In the past, there have been a few straggler Striped Dolphins among Short-beaked Common Dolphin schools – mainly offshore – and, as the climate warms, they are becoming increasingly common.

These days, many operators offer short winter Gray Whale-watching trips and longer, more varied offshore trips in the summer. Between them, they have recorded nearly 30 different whales, dolphins and porpoises altogether.

Migrating Gray Whales

Almost the entire world population of 18–21,000 Gray Whales migrates along the California coast twice every year, between their feeding grounds in the Bering, Chukchi and Beaufort seas and their breeding grounds in Baja California, Mexico.

On their southerly migration, which generally passes California from late December to early February (with a peak in late January) the whales tend to be swimming faster and farther offshore, typically about 5 miles away (though still often within sight of land). On their northerly migration, they begin to appear off California in early February, increase to a peak in mid-March, then decline in numbers from mid-April to late May. Mothers with calves tend to be the last to appear, usually in late April and early May. Heading north, they are slower and closer to shore, often less than half a mile from the best vantage points (mothers with calves are sometimes just a few yards offshore, presumably to avoid Killer Whales). Therefore, with one major exception – San Diego (see page 201) – the northerly migration tends to be better for whale watching.

In case you wonder why they do not always seem to be going in the same direction, there is some overlap: the mainstream of whales swimming north often passes stragglers still heading south.

Summer resident Gray Whales

For the majority of these Gray Whales, California serves solely as a migration corridor. But since the early 1970s a significant number of them have been choosing not to migrate all the way to the Arctic: they remain along the west coast of North America throughout the summer (mainly from late May to mid-November, with a peak in late August and early September). Researchers have identified some 200 so-called 'summer residents' between northern California and southeastern Alaska, forming what is known as the 'Pacific Coast Feeding Group'. A small number of these individuals spend at least part of the summer feeding in northern California, roughly from Eureka to the Oregon border.

Blue Whales

Central and southern California are among the best places in the world to see Blue Whales. The population that feeds off the coast here is by far the largest and healthiest of all Blue Whale populations – and the only one that has shown significant signs of recovery since commercial whaling

officially stopped in 1966. It is estimated that 2,500 Blue Whales spend the summer and early fall along the west coast of the US and Canada, from southern California to the Gulf of Alaska (out of a total world population that could be as low as 10,000) and many of these are in California.

Their primary feeding grounds are around Cordell Bank, in the Greater Farallones Marine Sanctuary, in the Southern Californian Bight and in Monterey Bay National Marine Sanctuary (see page 203). But they can be seen anywhere along the coast.

Sightings are mainly between May and November, though, in southern California at least, they can be around until as late as January. In recent years, they have been seen increasingly frequently – even quite close to shore.

Beaked Whales

Little is known about beaked whales in California, but at least eight species are known to occur here – Baird's, Cuvier's, Hubbs', Blainville's, Gingko-toothed, Perrin's, Pygmy and Stejneger's – and there is a lot of suitable habitat. They are rarely seen on whale-watching trips, because sightings require good conditions and a particularly keen eye and, of course, they are difficult to distinguish from one another. But they are encountered from time to time. Cuvier's Beaked Whales are the most common, particularly in southern California, but there have been a significant number of Baird's Beaked Whale sightings over the years, too. The best chances are on offshore trips over deep water, especially where there are steep underwater geological structures such as submarine canyons, seamounts and along the edge of the continental shelf.

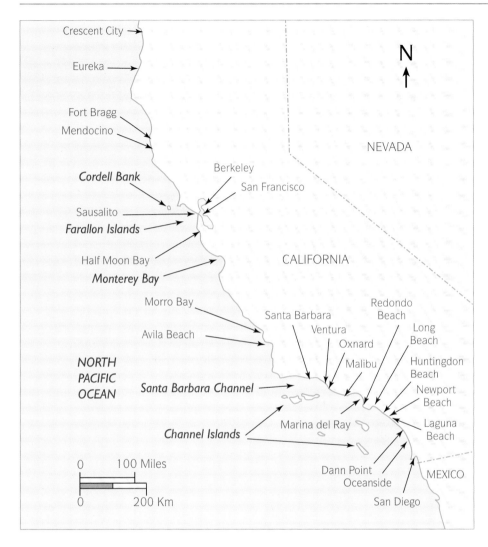

Crescent City →

Eureka →

Fort Bragg
Mendocino

Cordell Bank

Berkeley
San Francisco

Sausalito
Farallon Islands

Half Moon Bay
Monterey Bay

Morro Bay

Avila Beach

NEVADA

CALIFORNIA

Santa Barbara
Ventura
Oxnard

Redondo
Beach
Long
Beach

*NORTH
PACIFIC
OCEAN*

Santa Barbara Channel

Channel Islands

Marina del Ray

Malibu

Huntingdon
Beach
Newport
Beach
Laguna
Beach

0   100 Miles

0   200 Km

Dann Point
Oceanside

San Diego

MEXICO

N
↑

Cordell Bank National Marine Sanctuary

The Cordell Bank National Marine Sanctuary was established in 1989 to protect the extraordinary marine ecosystem around an offshore seamount called Cordell Bank, which sits right on the edge of the continental shelf. In 2015, the sanctuary was expanded to include Bodega Canyon, a prominent seafloor feature that drops to a depth of more than a mile, as well as other important marine areas. With its southernmost boundary about 50 miles northwest of San Francisco, unlike its two nearest neighbours (Monterey Bay National

If you want to see Risso's Dolphins go to California.

Marine Sanctuary and the Gulf of Farallones National Marine Sanctuary) it is entirely offshore – 7 miles from the California coast at its nearest point. It covers an area of 1,274 square miles.

A wide variety of cetaceans occur in the sanctuary. Pacific White-sided Dolphins are the most frequently seen, but many others can be considered common during late spring, summer and fall: Blue Whales, Humpback Whales, Northern Right Whale Dolphins and Dall's Porpoises among them. Gray Whales pass through the eastern sector on migration, while Minke Whales, Killer Whales, Risso's Dolphins, Striped Dolphins and Harbor Porpoises are sometimes encountered. This can also be a good area for beaked whales (though they are rarely seen on whale-watching trips).

San Francisco and the Greater Farallones National Marine Sanctuary

Whales occasionally venture right into San Francisco Bay. It is not unusual to see Gray Whales from the Golden Gate Bridge and Humpback Whales have even been observed lunge-feeding around Alcatraz. Indeed, in 2016, there were so many whales within sight of the city that operators were running short trips to see them right inside the bay.

But generally the whales here stay farther offshore than they do in southern California. There are three- to four-hour trips during the winter, to see the Gray Whales on migration from the end of November to early June, with sightings peaking during January and March. But there are also opportunities in the summer for full-day trips looking for a variety of other species around the Farallon Islands, about 28 miles west of the city.

Close to the edge of the continental shelf, the Farallones are home to a quarter of all breeding seabirds in California (300,000 birds altogether), as well as five species of seals, sea lions and fur seals. Consisting of two main islands and various islets and sea stacks, they first came to international attention for their Great White Sharks. These top predators are attracted to the archipelago by their large seal and sea lion populations; researchers, who have been studying them since 1987, sometimes log as many as 80 shark attacks in a single season (mostly from September to December).

On 4 October 1997, a whale-watching trip from San Francisco witnessed the most extraordinary event – a Great White Shark being killed by a pod of Killer Whales. One of the Killer Whales actually appeared next to the boat with the large Great White held firmly in its mouth. Perhaps not surprisingly, no Great White Sharks were seen in the Farallons for the rest of the season.

These barren and windswept islands are uninhabited and off-limits to people – other than researchers and wardens – though wildlife-viewing boats are allowed to approach with care. But it is the waters around them that are of most interest to whale watchers. No fewer than 28 cetacean species have been recorded in this area, and it is not impossible to see half a dozen on a single trip.

Blue Whales and Humpback Whales are the main focus of whale watching here. Indeed, this is one of the best places in the world to see Blue Whales (which are most common from July to October); Humpback Whales are around from May to November, though sightings tend to be more frequent later in the season. Gray Whales migrating north are often seen early in the season (rarely later than early June, which is when females with calves, and late stragglers, pass this stretch of coast). Less frequent sightings include Fin Whales, Bryde's Whales and Minke Whales, while Sperm Whales are sometimes seen from December to May. Killer Whales are a rare treat at any time of year, though they are seen more frequently in the spring, when they are patrolling for Gray Whale calves. Smaller cetaceans here in the summer include regular sightings of Harbor Porpoises in inshore waters (it is sometimes possible to see mothers with calves), and fairly frequent sightings of Pacific White-sided Dolphins, Long-beaked Common Dolphins, Short-beaked Common Dolphins, Risso's Dolphins and Dall's Porpoises.

The Farallon Islands lie in the heart of the Gulf of Farallones National Marine Sanctuary, which was established in 1981 and includes 3,295 square miles of open ocean and coastal waters as well as bays and estuaries. It is contiguous with Cordell Bank National Marine Sanctuary, to the north, and Monterey Bay National Marine Sanctuary, to the south.

California hosts the world's largest population of Blue Whales.

Santa Barbara Channel and the Channel Islands National Marine Sanctuary

The Santa Barbara Channel and the Channel Islands are in a nationally recognized area of incredible biological diversity and richness known as the Southern California Bight. Stretching more than 370 miles from Point Conception in the north to the border with Mexico in the south (in theory, it continues to Punta Banda, in Baja California Norte), this large indentation in the southern California coastline is a dynamic region with a swirling mass of water and upwellings that are a magnet for whales, dolphins and porpoises.

Among its many claims to fame, the Bight regularly has the highest seasonal concentration of Blue Whales anywhere on the planet. But a host of other species occur here in considerable numbers, with nearly 30 species recorded altogether.

The Santa Barbara Channel, northwest of Los Angeles, stretches about 80 miles from Point Conception in the north to Point Mugu in the south. Within striking distance of several major towns and cities along the coast – including Santa Barbara, Ventura and Oxnard – it averages 28 miles across, filling the gap between the mainland and the Channel Islands. It is about 2,000ft deep at its deepest point and sits right between two oceanic zones, where the cold, nutrient-rich California Current sweeping in from the north meets the warm Davidson Countercurrent from the south.

The rugged Channel Islands consist of eight islands, stretching 160 miles from San Miguel in the north to San Clemente in the south, some 12–71 miles off the California coast. The archipelago consists of two main groups: the Santa Barbara group, to the north, which is separated from the mainland by the Santa Barbara Channel;

and the Santa Catalina group, to the south, which is separated from the mainland by the San Pedro Channel. Santa Catalina Island is the only one with a significant human population, although there are several hundred people on military bases on San Clemente Island and San Nicolas. The Channel Islands National Marine Sanctuary was designated in 1980 and spans 1,467 square miles of ocean surrounding the five northern Channel Islands: San Miguel, Santa Rosa, Santa Cruz, Anacapa (actually, a group of three small islets) and, separately, Santa Barbara Island.

Blue Whales are particularly common in the Santa Barbara Channel and around the northern Channel Islands. Several hundred of them visit here each summer to feed and, on a good day, there can be as many as 100 in a 25 miles by 6 miles area. The western end of the channel is particularly good, though it does vary from year to year. They are present between June and January, with reliable sightings mainly between June and early September.

Fin Whales are also common in the Bight, especially in the southern and central sectors, and are present year-round, though they are generally farther offshore than the Blue Whales. The Santa Barbara Channel is a particularly interesting place to watch Gray Whales, as they file through on migration. Late season mother-calf pairs are often very close to shore, literally hugging the kelp line in an effort to avoid detection by predatory Killer Whales. Late winter and early spring is when Killer Whales are most likely to be seen, but they are being encountered more and more frequently year-round.

Other species regularly encountered in the area include: Humpback Whale, Fin Whale, Minke Whale, Pacific White-sided Dolphin, Long-beaked Common Dolphin,

Short-beaked Common Dolphin, Northern Right Whale Dolphin, Risso's Dolphin and Dall's Porpoise. Huge pods of dolphins – sometimes literally thousands of Long-beaked Common Dolphins, for example – are a familiar sight. Bottlenose Dolphins are frequently seen closer to shore, as the whale-watch trips leave harbor and head out to sea. Cuvier's Beaked Whales are also known in this area – the southern San Nicolas Basin, off the west side of San Clemente Island, is a recognized hotspot – but they are rarely seen on whale-watching trips.

Many of the whale-watching trips have Channel Islands Naturalist Corps volunteers on board. This is a program, run by the Channel Islands National Park and the Channel Islands National Marine Sanctuary, in which trained volunteers educate passengers about the whales and other wildlife.

San Diego

Whale watching in San Diego has two seasons: from mid-December to the end of May, focusing on migrating Gray Whales; and from mid-June to mid-October (and sometimes as late as December), focusing on Blue Whales and a variety of other species.

As far as the Gray Whales are concerned, San Diego is unique. Unlike farther north – where the situation is reversed – the whales swim closer to shore during the southern migration and farther out during the northern migration. So in the beginning of the season, the southbound whales are often no more than half a mile from shore. Toward the end of the season, the northbound whales are farther away and whale-watching trips often have to venture 9–12 miles out to sea. Trips later in the season often encounter mothers with their calves.

Bottlenose Dolphins are frequently seen as whale-watch boats head out to sea.

A variety of other species can be seen during any of these trips, but especially on the longer Blue Whale trips during summer. As well as the Blues, these include Humpback Whales, Fin Whales and Minke Whales, large numbers of dolphins (Pacific White-sided, Long-beaked and Short-beaked Common, Bottlenose and Risso's), Dall's Porpoises, and occasionally Sperm Whales, Killer Whales and sometimes Short-finned Pilot Whales. Bryde's Whales are becoming increasingly common, as climate change warms the waters off California, and there have even been sightings of False Killer Whales in recent years.

Many of the whale-watching tours from San Diego venture across the border into Mexican waters, and some visit Baja California's Coronado Islands. This group of four small islands, 15–19 miles from the entrance to San Diego Bay and just 8 miles off the coast of Tijuana, is a wildlife refuge known for its Harbor Seals, California Sea Lions, Northern Elephant Seals and large numbers of birds. It is also a popular area for whale watching.

Land-based whale watching

Watching whales from suitable vantage points on shore is very popular in California. There are dozens of recognized lookouts up and down the coast and, indeed, any elevated stopping-off point along the coast roads – especially in central and southern California – is worth a look. As many as 40 Gray Whales pass these vantage points every hour during peak migration times, and several other species are seen from time to time.

The most famous location is Cabrillo National Monument, at the top of Point Loma Peninsula, just west of San Diego. There is an extensive visitor center, with rangers on hand to help spot whales, as well as binoculars and telescopes, and a steady stream of Gray Whales migrating past. The Whale Watch and Kelp Forest Overlook and Old Point Loma Lighthouse offer the best viewing. The ideal time to see them is on their southerly migration (so they will be swimming from right to left as you look out to sea) from late December to late February (with a peak during mid-January). Some swim very close to the shore but most are beyond the kelp beds, about half a mile out. Expect them to be moving at a steady speed of 4–5 knots, or about 5 miles per hour. Later in the spring, when the whales are migrating north, they are generally too far out in the ocean to see from Cabrillo National Monument.

Other particularly popular spots include: Pigeon Point Lighthouse, south of Half Moon Bay; San Simeon and Montaña de Oro State Park, between Monterey and Santa Barbara; Point Vicente Interpretive Center and Rancho Palos Verdes, south of Los Angeles; and Point Reyes National Seashore, Bodega Head and Sonoma Coast State Park, north of San Francisco.

There are many annual whale festivals in California, including some that have been running for more than 40 years. Most are held between January and April. They include: Monterey, San Pedro, San Diego, Rancho Palos Verdes, Dana Point, Point Cabrillo, Mendocino, Oxnard, Gualala, Malibu, Little River and Fort Bragg.

Monterey Bay

Monterey Bay is one of the premier whale-watching destinations in North America. Covering an area of 450 square miles, it is one of the most fertile marine environments in the world and supports one of the highest diversities of marine mammals.

No fewer than 28 cetacean species have been documented in and around the Bay altogether: 11 are seen regularly, six turn up from time to time, and a further 11 have been recorded at least once. There are also five species of seals, fur seals and sea lions (as well as occasional sightings of Guadalupe Fur Seals). And this is one of the best places anywhere in the North Pacific to observe Sea Otters, which can be seen close to shore year-round – even from some of the local restaurants.

Whale watching in Monterey Bay is year-round, though there are two main seasons: late spring, summer and fall for Blue Whales, Humpback Whales, Killer Whales and several species of dolphins (in particular, it is a hotspot for Northern Right Whale Dolphins in fall); and winter and early spring for Gray Whales, Killer Whales and dolphins. There are a variety of tours on offer, ranging from short trips

Overview

Main species: Gray Whale, Blue Whale, Humpback Whale, Killer Whale, Pacific White-sided Dolphin, Long-beaked Common Dolphin, Common Bottlenose Dolphin, Northern Right Whale Dolphin, Risso's Dolphin, Dall's Porpoise, Harbor Porpoise.

Occasional species: Fin Whale, Minke Whale, Sperm Whale, Baird's Beaked Whale, Cuvier's Beaked Whale, Short-beaked Common Dolphin.

Other wildlife highlights: Sea Otter, Northern Elephant Seal, Harbor Seal, Northern Fur Seal, Steller Sea Lion, California Sea Lion, Black-footed Albatross, Laysan Albatross, Sooty Shearwater, Pink-footed Shearwater, Buller's Shearwater, Black-vented Shearwater, Flesh-footed Shearwater, Black Storm Petrel, Fork-tailed Storm Petrel, Ashy Storm Petrel, Cassin's Auklet, Rhinoceros Auklet, Pigeon Guillemot, Xantus's Murrelet, Scripp's Murrelet, Guadalupe Murrelet, Red Phalarope, Red-necked Phalarope, Bonaparte's Gull, Glaucous Gull, Glaucous-winged Gull, Sabine's Gull, Leatherback Turtle, Great White Shark, Blue Shark, Ocean Sunfish, Monarch Butterfly.

Main locations: Monterey, Moss Landing, Santa Cruz; land-based whale watching: Pigeon Point Lighthouse (north of Año Nuevo), Davenport (Santa Cruz), Point Pinos (Pacific Grove), Point Lobos, Point Sur Lighthouse (Carmel), many overlooks on Highway 1.

Types of tours: three- to 12-hour boat trips; land-based whale watching.

When to go: year-round; Gray Whales December–May; Blue Whales best May–October; Humpback Whales best late April to early November; Killer Whales year-round, with peaks April–May (coinciding with the arrival of Gray Whale calves) and August–November; dolphins and porpoises year-round (Northern Right Whale Dolphins best September–October).

Regulations and guidelines: NOAA Guidelines for Viewing Marine Mammals; US Federal Regulations; National Marine Sanctuaries Act; Marine Mammal Protection Act (1972).

Wildlife species are listed systematically (not in order of abundance) and frequency of sightings varies with location and season.

in relatively nearshore waters to much longer pelagic trips, seeking more unusual species farther out over the deeper waters of the Bay. The standard of whale watching here is generally high and several of the operators are assisting with research, by photographing and recording all the individually recognizable Blue Whales, Humpbacks and Killer Whales they encounter.

Monterey Bay Submarine Canyon

The centerpiece of Monterey Bay is a huge underwater chasm, called the Monterey Bay Submarine Canyon, which cuts the Bay nearly in half. It is the largest and deepest submarine canyon off the Pacific coast of North America, and one of the longest in the world.

Basically a steep-sided valley, cut into the continental shelf, it has three main tributaries at its upper reaches in the Bay: Soquel Canyon, to the north; the main Monterey Canyon, in the center; and Carmel Canyon, to the south. Numerous smaller (though nonetheless significant) canyons cut into the continental shelf and slope in and around Monterey Bay, including Pioneer, Ascension, Año Nuevo and Cabrillo, to the north; and Sur, Partington, Lucia, Mill Creek, Villa and La Cruz, to the south.

There are several features that make the main Canyon so notable: it begins remarkably close to the shore, it is exceptionally deep and it is unusually long.

Its head is just a few hundred yards from Moss Landing, an historic fishing village about 16 miles north of Monterey. The Canyon is only 60ft deep at this point, but from here it deepens and widens as it extends west into the Bay and out into the wider North Pacific. It is this proximity to shore – quite unusual for a submarine

canyon – that makes deep-water whales and other wildlife so readily accessible.

The Canyon drops to a maximum depth of no less than 2 miles (from the ocean surface to the seabed) and the distance from the rim of the Canyon to the bottom – in other words, the maximum height of the canyon walls – is an impressive 1 mile. This makes it slightly deeper than the Grand Canyon. The maximum rim-to-rim width is 7.5 miles, which is about the same as the Grand Canyon.

With a total length of 60 miles, it is roughly twice as long as the average for most submarine canyons. But if you include the so-called 'submarine fan' (the underwater version of an alluvial fan or sediment deposit) its influence extends to 290 miles.

Monterey Bay National Marine Sanctuary

Monterey Bay falls within the Monterey Bay National Marine Sanctuary, which was established in 1992 to protect the special marine wildlife and wild places of central California (the Bay itself comprises less than 7 per cent of the sanctuary). It stretches along one quarter of California's coast, from just north of the Golden Gate Bridge in San Francisco, to Cambria, 100 miles south of Monterey, and extends seaward to an average of 30 miles offshore. It does not include any areas of dry land. Covering an area of 6,094 square miles – making it roughly the size of Connecticut – it is the largest of the 13 national marine sanctuaries in the US.

The sanctuary is contiguous in the north with the Greater Farallones National Marine Sanctuary and the Cordell Bank National Marine Sanctuary, and, in 2009, was extended to include Davidson Seamount (80 miles southwest of Monterey). The sanctuary protects one of the world's

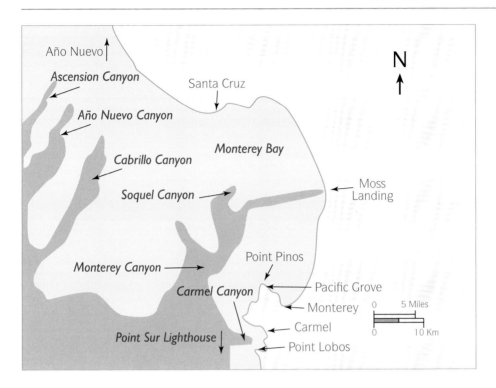

most diverse marine ecosystems. As well as all the marine mammals, it is home to more than 180 species of seabirds and shorebirds, at least 525 species of fish and the largest kelp forests in the country. There are bans on oil and gas exploration, waste dumping, disturbing the wildlife and other potentially damaging activities, but commercial and sports fishing is still permitted within its boundaries.

Blue Whales

Blue Whales spend the summer and fall feeding along the coasts of northern Mexico and California, and, when the krill is abundant, go right into Monterey Bay. They can be seen any time from early May to late November, but the main period is June to October (during times of the highest krill abundance) and numbers traditionally peak in July and August.

This particular population of Blue Whales – which feeds off the coast of California every summer – is one of the few that seems to be doing well after decades of intensive whaling. There are estimated to be 2,500 along the west coast of North America altogether, and they may even be approaching pre-exploitation numbers.

Until a little over a decade ago Blue Whales appeared in the Bay every year like clockwork. But in recent years, with changing oceanic conditions, they have become more variable and difficult to predict. There were relatively few from 2003–09, lots in 2010–11 and few again in 2013–15. The so-called 'Warm Water Blob' (a patch of unusually warm surface water in a vast area of the northeastern Pacific) was largely to blame. Warm water means fewer nutrients and one consequence of that is less krill. However, the Blob began to break up in fall 2015 and, sure enough, the Blue Whales were back in Monterey Bay with a vengeance in 2016. In May, particularly, there were so many – more than 50 in a 0.3-mile radius for several weeks – it was like Blue Whale rush hour.

Blue Whales leave the Monterey Bay region in late fall and migrate south. It is still unclear exactly where they go to mate and calve, but recent evidence suggests that this happens far off the coast of Costa Rica.

Humpback Whales

Humpback Whales are the commonest large whales to be seen in Monterey Bay. They are here to feed on Anchovies, Sardines and krill, arriving from their breeding grounds in Mexico and Central America as early as March and many staying until December (a few juveniles are even around throughout the winter). The peak period is from late April to early November.

They are frequently found along the edges of the Canyon, where their prey tends to concentrate. Since 2013, there have been huge masses of Anchovies concentrated here, remarkably close to the shore, which have been attracting more than 200 Humpback Whales in the largest and most spectacular whale-feeding event ever seen in the Bay. Unfortunately, purse-seine fishing boats took out all the Anchovies, and the Humpbacks dispersed.

In recent years, there have been more 'friendly' encounters with Humpbacks, entirely initiated by the whales. Certain curious individuals will circle whale-watching boats – sometimes for several hours at a time – and rub up against them,

spyhop right next to them and roll on one side to look at their human admirers. It may be that the latest generation of whales has never known whaling and is therefore less fearful of people and boats.

Gray Whales

Almost the entire eastern North Pacific population of Gray Whales passes across, or swims around, Monterey Bay twice every year on migration between their winter breeding grounds in Baja California, Mexico, and their summer feeding grounds in the Arctic.

They are in the vicinity of the Bay from December–May: migrating south from December to mid-February (with peak numbers in mid-January) and north from mid-February–May (with peak numbers in mid-March). Most adults and juveniles have passed by on their way north by mid-April, but mothers with their calves are a little later and pass during the latter half of April and May. They are most susceptible to Killer Whale attacks during this period. Most of these whales prefer to avoid the deep submarine canyon in the middle of the Bay – where transient Killer Whales patrol for calves – and sensibly hug the shoreline instead. Some 90 per cent of mothers and calves travel within 200 yards of land and it is not unusual to see them in very shallow water, or in amongst the kelp beds, as they 'tiptoe' their way around the Bay. Those that risk taking the shortcut across the middle are vulnerable to attack and whale-watching boats sometimes witness these prolonged hunts – a memorable, if rather grim, experience.

Other baleen whales

Minke Whales are present in Monterey Bay year-round, though they are more frequently seen in summer and fall, and are

A Blue Whale dives close to shore in Monterey Bay.

uncommon in winter. Since they tend to live alone and prefer nearshore waters (where they feed on juvenile Rockfish over rocky bottoms) they are easily overlooked. But they can often be seen from shore, especially in southern Monterey Bay and along the Big Sur coastline.

Fin Whales are also present year-round, though they are only seen occasionally (2016 was an exceptional year, with unusually large numbers – sometimes 20–30 at a time – feeding on a mass of Anchovies close to shore throughout the summer). They tend to be farther offshore and are usually encountered from late April–November. Sei Whales are seen offshore from time to time, though not with any regularity, and Bryde's Whales have been recorded rarely.

In the past 40 years, North Pacific Right Whales have been observed in and around the Bay in 1986, 1987 and 1998; there was also a sighting at Piedras Blancas, farther down the coast, in 1995. Sightings of this species are exceptional and should always be reported: there are believed to be only 30–50 of them in the eastern North Pacific altogether.

Killer Whales

Killer Whales occur in Monterey Bay year-round. They are seen on many whale-watch trips, though sightings are by no means daily – roughly once a week is the annual average. They do not stay in the same area for long (otherwise their prey would move away) but there are two peak periods with the most frequent sightings: January–May and September–November. The best time is undoubtedly mid-April to mid-May, when they are in the Bay to hunt Gray Whale calves and are seen much more frequently (often several times a week).

Three ecotypes occur here – transients (or Bigg's), residents and offshores. The transients are by far the most common and, over the years, more than 200 different individuals have been identified in the Bay. They are wanderers, regularly travelling between southern California and Washington, and sometimes as far north as Alaska, but some groups have a home range centered around Monterey Bay and they are seen more often than the others. These groups are sighted repeatedly within the same year and over subsequent years.

Killer Whales are a major attraction in Monterey Bay.

The transients are in Monterey Bay to hunt marine mammals: Gray Whale calves, in particular, but also Minke Whales, Pacific White-sided Dolphins, Dall's Porpoises, Northern Elephant Seals, California Sea Lions, Harbor Seals and other species. This is the only readily accessible place in the world where Killer Whales can predictably be observed feeding on baleen whales and, as the number of Gray Whale calves born each year has increased, more Killer Whales have learnt that Monterey Bay is a prime area to hunt them.

Resident Killer Whales, normally found farther north in Washington State and British Columbia, particularly around the San Juan Islands, were first observed in Monterey Bay in January 2000. Since then they have been seen on quite a few occasions, always in winter. It is believed that they are being forced to expand their range in search of food, due to drastic declines in the numbers of Chinook Salmon, their preferred prey, so sightings may increase in the coming years.

Offshore Killer Whales are poorly known and particularly unpredictable. They are mostly seen during the winter, in large groups of 20–100 animals, and are believed to be feeding on fish, squid and sharks (they were once observed catching a Blue Shark in Monterey Bay). There are not many of them – the total population is believed to be about 350–500 animals – and they are known to wander from southern California to the Bering Sea in Alaska, so it is not surprising that sightings are scarce.

Dolphins and porpoises

Several dolphin species can be seen in the Bay year-round. The commonest are Pacific White-sided, Risso's, Long-beaked Common and Northern Right Whale dolphins. They are often in large, mixed-species groups, with hundreds or even thousands travelling together.

Monterey Bay is probably the best place in the world to see Northern Right Whale Dolphins. In most parts of their range in the North Pacific they are pelagic, in deep waters far offshore, but thanks to the submarine canyon they are often much closer to shore in Monterey Bay. They are present year-round but are seen on many more whale-watching trips in the late summer and fall (the peak period is September–October).

Pacific White-sided Dolphins are probably the most abundant cetaceans along the central and northern California coast and are great fun to watch, often leaping high into the air and performing acrobatic flips and somersaults. Monterey Bay – especially along the Canyon edge – is a particular hotspot, where they feed on small schooling fish and squid year-round.

Risso's Dolphins are also present year-round – and the most frequently seen dolphins in the Bay – feeding mainly on squid in deeper waters over the Canyon.

They are usually in small groups of 10–30 dolphins (though as many as 2,500 or more have been recorded) and are frequently found in mixed-species herds with Pacific White-sided Dolphins and Northern Right Whale Dolphins.

Both species of common dolphin occur in the Bay. Long-beaked Common Dolphins are more abundant, and are seen more frequently due to their preference for nearshore waters. They are most common from late summer to the end of winter, when schools containing several thousand individuals are not unusual. Short-beaked Common Dolphins tend to be seen farther offshore, mainly on pelagic trips, from August–October.

Bottlenose Dolphins were not really known in Monterey Bay until after a major El Niño event in the early 1980s, but nowadays small groups of them are a common sight within half a mile of shore. They are often just beyond the waves, or even surfing in the breakers, and can be spotted year-round from almost any beach in Monterey Bay.

Dall's Porpoises and Harbor Porpoises are both year-round inhabitants, too. Dall's are closely associated with the Canyon edges, while Harbor Porpoises are more commonly seen over shallow sandy bottoms of the Monterey Bay shelf.

Beaked whales

Research using hydrophones on Smooth Ridge, an underwater mountain about 19 miles from shore, suggests that Baird's Beaked Whales and Cuvier's Beaked Whales are both common in the outer reaches of the Bay. They are occasionally seen on longer whale-watching trips that venture farther offshore in the deepest waters of the Canyon, especially during the fall. Baird's are the most frequent, but Cuvier's are also encountered from time to time.

In the past 40 years, there have been isolated records of stranded Stejneger's Beaked Whale, Hubbs' Beaked Whale, Perrin's Beaked Whale, Pygmy Beaked Whale, Rough-toothed Dolphin and Pygmy Sperm Whale.

Other toothed whales

Mature bull Sperm Whales are sometimes seen along the walls and main body of the Canyon during late summer and fall (from August–November), particularly on the longer pelagic trips. Other sightings have included Short-finned Pilot Whales and False Killer Whales, both of which are extremely rare.

Monterey Bay is probably the best place in the world to see Northern Right Whale Dolphins.

UNITED STATES: EAST COAST

New England

New England is one of the most popular whale-watching destinations in the world, with as many as 1 million people joining boat trips to see Humpbacks, Fin Whales, Minke Whales, Atlantic White-sided Dolphins and several other species every year. There are operators up and down the coast – many of whom have been running whale-watching trips for 35–40 years – and there is a strong link with local research organizations. Many trips feature professional marine biologists, who do much of their fieldwork on board.

Whale watching here takes place in the Gulf of Maine, a vast swathe of sea that extends from the Bay of Fundy in Canada south to Cape Cod in the US (the Gulf of Maine is jointly shared by the two countries). Encompassing both Cape Cod Bay and Massachusetts Bay, this is one of the most productive marine regions in the world.

From above the surface the Gulf appears to be exposed to the Northeast Atlantic, but underwater is an entirely different story: it is largely separated from the open sea by two shallow submarine banks that create a barrier at the entrance. The biggest is Georges Bank, mostly in US waters in the southeast, which is slightly larger than Massachusetts (it measures 150 miles by 75 miles). Extending like a giant thumb off the outstretched arm of Cape Cod, its depth ranges from 13–295ft. The much smaller Browns Bank (and Germany Bank, in Canada), lies off the southwestern tip of Nova Scotia. This means that, effectively, the Gulf of Maine is relatively enclosed. There

Overview

Main species: Humpback Whale, Fin Whale, Minke Whale, Atlantic White-sided Dolphin.

Occasional species: North Atlantic Right Whale, Blue Whale, Sei Whale, Long-finned Pilot Whale, Risso's Dolphin, Short-beaked Common Dolphin, White-beaked Dolphin, Common Bottlenose Dolphin, Harbor Porpoise.

Other wildlife highlights: Gray Seal, Harbor Seal, Roseate Tern, Northern Gannet, Black-legged Kittiwake, Greater Shearwater, Sooty Shearwater, Manx Shearwater, Cory's Shearwater, Parasitic Jaeger, Wilson's Storm Petrel, Leach's Storm Petrel, Atlantic Puffin, Red-necked Phalarope, Red Phalarope, Basking Shark, Blue Shark, Ocean Sunfish, Atlantic Bluefin Tuna.

Main locations: Bar Harbor, Portland, Kennebunkport, Boothbay Harbor (Maine); Portsmouth, Rye, Hampton Beach, Seabrook Beach (New Hampshire); Newburyport, Gloucester, Boston, Plymouth, Barnstable, Hyannis, Provincetown, Nantucket (Massachusetts); Narragansett (Rhode Island); trips from Eastport and Lubec (northern Maine) go into Bay of Fundy (see page 246).

Types of tours: three-hour to full-day tours.

When to go: April–October (fewer trips early and late in the season); Humpback Whales May–October (best July–August); North Atlantic Right Whales February–June (best in April); some species present year-round.

Regulations and guidelines: NOAA Whale Watching Guidelines Northeast Region including Stellwagen Bank; WhaleSENSE voluntary program; US Federal Regulations; National Marine Sanctuaries Act; Marine Mammal Protection Act (1972).

Wildlife species are listed systematically (not in order of abundance) and frequency of sightings varies with location and season.

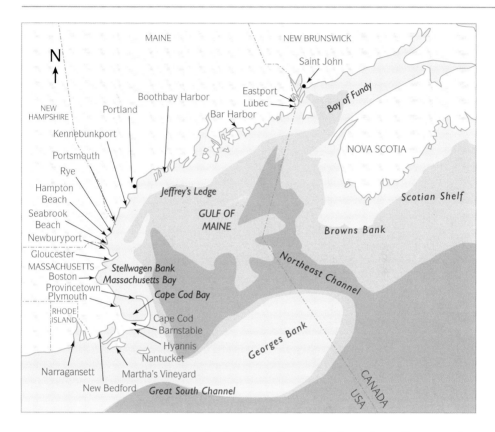

are two major deep-water channels that allow most of the water to enter and exit from the Gulf: the Great South Channel, on the US side, and the Northeast Channel in Canada. Water still flows continuously over the submarine banks, of course, and this contributes to the complex water movements inside.

The seafloor topography of deep basins and shallow banks within the Gulf, combined with powerful tides and currents, is ultimately what attracts the whales. Various submerged banks, plateaus and ledges – great underwater 'islands' of sand and gravel that were formed during the last Ice Age by the retreat of the Laurentide Ice Sheet – rise from the seafloor to within 70ft of the surface. One of these, Stellwagen Bank, is among the best places in the world for whale watching, accounting for as much as 80 per cent of all whale watching in New England. Upwelling around Stellwagen, and neighboring underwater features, brings a rich soup of nutrients to the surface, which nourishes a highly productive ecosystem. It makes the Gulf of Maine what can best be described as a giant underwater restaurant.

Most whale watching is from Massachusetts, the state nearest to Stellwagen. During peak periods in July and August, operators in Provincetown, Boston, Gloucester and other ports in the southern

Gulf each make up to 12 trips a day to the bank, and neighboring Jeffrey's Ledge, typically lasting 3–4 hours a time. The vessels tend to be quite large – 100–400 passengers is normal – and it is not unusual for them to see dozens of whales per trip. There are fewer operators and whale watchers farther north, in New Hampshire and Maine, and the vessels tend to be smaller. But they offer similar-length trips and see similar species. There are also natural history boat trips from Nantucket, about 30 miles south of Cape Cod, which feature seals and seabirds as well as whales, or are more focused on whaling history; they sometimes offer longer whale-watching trips, though they have to travel some distance to the best viewing areas.

There are limited opportunities for whale watching in the southern states of New England (Rhode Island and Connecticut), which are too far to reach Stellwagen easily. But Fin Whales and Humpback Whales are encountered regularly on spring, summer and fall trips from Narragansett, Rhode Island, mainly in July and August, and there are ad hoc encounters with some of the other species more familiar farther north.

Altogether, 18 cetacean species have been recorded off the coast of New England at one time or another and, while many of these are rarely seen, at least half a dozen are abundant or regular during the summer. Humpbacks are undoubtedly the stars of the show and are found on most trips. There are few other places in the world where whale watching is such a social occasion, as the on-board naturalists and researchers introduce individual Humpback Whales by name – animals they have known for years, or up to four decades, and can recognize by the distinctive markings on their tails – and tell stories and exchange information about their lives. The talk of the day is distinctly personal: about who is related to whom, who is travelling with whom and which mothers have new calves.

Stellwagen Bank National Marine Sanctuary

Stellwagen Bank, New England's whale-watching hotspot, is a massive kidney-shaped underwater plateau in the south-eastern corner of Massachusetts Bay. Named after the man who first mapped it properly, Henry S. Stellwagen, in 1854, it runs roughly north-south between Cape Ann in the north and the tip of Cape Cod in the south.

Some 30 miles east of Boston, it measures 19 miles long and a little under 6 miles wide at its widest point (at the southern end). It has an average depth of 112ft, though water depths over the bank can be as little as 66ft.

It is hard to believe but, in 1988, a developer proposed to place a 140-acre fixed platform on the bank, to house a major resort (including one of the largest casinos in the world). But this gave impetus to earlier efforts to make Stellwagen Bank a national marine sanctuary and, eventually, it was designated in 1992. With the full title Gerry E. Studds Stellwagen Bank National Marine Sanctuary, after a Member of Congress who was a staunch supporter of marine conservation, it covers a total area of 881 square miles.

This includes Stellwagen – which is the centerpiece of the sanctuary – as well as the southern portion of Jeffrey's Ledge. Jeffrey's is another major morphological feature in the Gulf of Maine with a good reputation for whales and dolphins. A long bank, averaging 3–6 miles wide (about 12 miles at its widest point) and stretching more than 60 miles from the northern end of Stellwagen to near Portland, Maine, it rises to within 160ft of the surface in places.

Most whale-watching trips head for the sanctuary. Those from Massachusetts usually go to Stellwagen and those from New Hampshire and Maine generally favor Jeffrey's Ledge.

It is open to vessels and both commercial and recreational fishing are allowed (though there are some restrictions, including catch limits or zero limits for certain species). The sanctuary is intensively used by a large number of boats and its proximity to urban areas (including Boston) adds pollution and other pressures. But certain activities are prohibited. These include sand and gravel mining, transferring petroleum products, and taking or harming marine mammals, birds and turtles. Over the years, there have been suggestions to expand the sanctuary (or create new ones) to include the rest of Jeffreys Ledge and the Great South Channel because, most summers, whales and dolphins divide their time between these three key areas.

Humpback Whales

It was in New England that the Humpback Whale acquired its scientific name, *Megaptera novaeangliae*, which translates as 'Big-winged New Englander'. New England was the origin of the first specimen described, in 1781, and its long flippers do look remarkably like wings.

Humpbacks start arriving in the Gulf of Maine in late winter or early spring (usually by the beginning of March). Females with calves are the last to arrive, usually by mid-May. About 700–800 of them spend the summer feeding primarily on huge aggregations of pencil-sized, pencil-shaped fish called Sand Lance (or Sand Eels – so-named because of their habit of burrowing into the seafloor to hide from the long list of animals that like to eat them). Wherever there are lots of Sand Lance, chances are there will be lots of Humpbacks. They also feed on Herring and krill. In between bouts of feeding, both adults and calves sometimes interact with whale-watching boats, investigating them closely and even spyhopping alongside.

Most of the Humpbacks feeding over Stellwagen Bank and Jeffrey's Ledge are known by name. Researchers and on-board naturalists can tell one individual from another by the black-and-white markings on the undersides of their tails. These range in color from pure white (so-called Type-1) to pure black (Type-5), with all sorts of variations in between (Type-2, -3 and -4). These pigmentation patterns (combined with scars) are much like our fingerprints – no two tails are exactly alike.

For scientific purposes, each whale is assigned a catalogue number. But they are also given names – Apex, Fracture, Midnight, Sockeye, Cygnus and so on – which are much easier to remember. The idea is to choose a name that jogs the memory, so Churchill has a V-shaped nick in his tail that resembles Winston Churchill's famous 'V for Victory' hand signal, while Orion has a pattern that looks like the constellation of the same name. Some of the whales are so familiar, and have been seen so many times, that they are like old friends to the researchers and naturalists who have been greeting them for so long on their return to Stellwagen every spring.

Each whale tail is photographed and the picture goes into two photo-identification catalogs: the Gulf of Maine Humpback Whale Catalog (Center for Coastal Studies) and the North Atlantic Humpback Whale Catalog (Allied Whale). These are an easy source of reference to all the Humpbacks that have been seen in the region. It works: one whale went 'missing' for 35 years between sightings, for example, but when it was seen again researchers were still able to confirm its identity. Most of the photographs in the catalogs were taken by researchers on whale-watch boats, or by amateur whale watchers, and they help to understand everything from family relationships and sexual maturity to day-to-day movements and migration patterns.

Information collected in this way on Humpback Whales in the sanctuary constitutes the longest and most detailed data set for any baleen whale anywhere in the world. The North Atlantic catalog now contains more than 9,000 different whales (including dead animals, of course) and the Gulf of Maine catalog contains 2,500.

The most famous whale in the catalogs – indeed, one of the most famous whales in the world – is the 'Grand Dame' of Stellwagen Bank, Salt. She was originally seen in 1976, in Massachusetts Bay, when whale biologist Stormy Mayo and Center for Coastal Studies researchers first began to keep records, and has been spotted around Stellwagen Bank every year since (bar one). For quite a while, no one knew whether Salt was male or female. It was not until 1980, when she turned up with a calf by her side (later named Crystal – because she was a little bit of Salt) that she disclosed her well-kept secret. She has had at least 13 calves since – Halos, Thalassa, Brine, Bittern, Salsa, Tabasco, Mostaza, Wasabi, Soya, Sanchal, Zelle, Epsom and, in 2016, Sriracha. When Thalassa had a calf of her own, in 1992, Grand Dame became a grandmother for the first time; she currently has no fewer than 15 grandchildren and two great-grandchildren.

Salt is easy to recognize, with a large white marking on the front side of her dorsal fin – as if someone has sprinkled salt on her back – and is unusual because she was

named for that rather than the distinctive patterns on her tail. She will go down in history as the whale that confirmed a link between the Humpback Whale feeding grounds in Stellwagen Bank National Marine Sanctuary and their breeding grounds 1,600 miles away in the Caribbean. Biologists had long suspected that they migrated between the two places twice every year, but there was no firm evidence until Salt was positively identified, in 1978, off the coast of the Dominican Republic.

More recent evidence has shown that the warm waters of the Caribbean, over shallow banks in the West Indies, are the most important winter breeding grounds for Humpbacks from all over the North Atlantic. The only other known wintering ground in the North Atlantic (outside the Caribbean) is a much smaller one, 3,300 miles away in the Cape Verde Islands.

North Atlantic Right Whale

One of the most endangered visitors to Stellwagen Bank and Cape Cod Bay – indeed one of the rarest of all whales – is the North Atlantic Right Whale. There are estimated to be no more than 525 individuals in the population altogether, with the vast majority in the western North Atlantic.

Males and non-calving females spend most of their year in cold, productive waters in the northeastern US and the Canadian Maritimes: in particular, the Great South Channel, Cape Cod Bay and Massachusetts Bay, Roseway Basin, the Gulf of St Lawrence and the lower Bay of Fundy. Meanwhile, mothers and calves, as well as many juveniles, spend winter in the warm waters off South Carolina, Georgia and Florida, where they stay from December to March; then they return to the northeast feeding grounds in early spring.

Each year the central Gulf of Maine (and, in particular, Jeffrey's Ledge and Stellwagen Bank National Marine Sanctuary) serves as a wintering ground for up to one-third of the world population of this endangered whale. Numbers increase from October onwards, reaching a peak in early April, and then decrease again into May. They are seen sporadically throughout the summer, though very rarely in July and August (when many are in the Bay of Fundy). The Great South Channel, Nantucket Sound and Cashes Ledge, about 80 miles off the coast of Cape Ann, are also important areas. They are certainly feeding in the Gulf at this time of year, but recent evidence suggests that they may also be mating. Sometimes they swim so close to Cape Cod, in particular, that they can be observed surface-feeding from the old clapboard beach houses and traditional homes of Provincetown lining the shore.

There has been a phenomenal effort over the years to care for the whales. North Atlantic Right Whales are particularly vulnerable to vessel strikes, because they are large and slow, difficult to see (with no dorsal fin) and tend to feed near the surface; worse, they have an unfortunate habit of aggregating in major shipping lanes. The busy international shipping lanes in and out of Boston Harbor – routing roughly 3,500 large cargo ships, tankers and passenger vessels right across Stellwagen Bank National Marine Sanctuary every year – were among the many areas along the east coast of North America where vessel strikes have occurred. Together, they have accounted for a large number of mortalities and this, at least partly, explains why the population has not bounced back after centuries of whaling, despite protection (entanglement in fishing gear has been another major problem).

But a variety of mitigation measures have successfully been introduced. In particular, those shipping lanes were moved to avoid areas of the sanctuary that are known to be used by Right Whales (and other species, of course). The lane changes, together with speed restrictions, are estimated to have reduced the risk of collisions between ships and North Atlantic Right Whales by an impressive 80–90 per cent. Other mitigation

Up to one-third of all North Atlantic Right Whales winter in the Gulf of Maine.

measures include using human observers and acoustic detection buoys to direct vessels away from the whales in real time.

Other species

Fin Whales, Minke Whales and Atlantic White-sided Dolphins are all abundant in the Gulf of Maine, while a number of other species are seen from time to time.

Minke Whales are particularly common, and seen on about three-quarters of whale-watching trips, though they tend to be overshadowed by Humpbacks and their other larger and often more flamboyant relatives. Fin Whales are most common in the sanctuary from April–November, and they are seen on more than half of all whale-watching trips. Some Fin Whales, at least, are believed to winter off Cape Cod.

There were virtually no sightings of Sei Whales before 1986 but, since then, they have been irregular visitors (which is typical of this species in most parts of its range). It is possible to go several years without seeing a single one, then dozens move into the area almost overnight. For a brief period they are seen on many whale-watching trips, particularly during the spring, then they disappear again.

They are most common between October and May around Jeffrey's Ledge, Stellwagen Bank and the Great South Channel, feeding on similar prey to Right Whales.

Atlantic White-sided Dolphins are present year-round, though they are most common in the winter and early spring. Therefore they are best seen at either end of the whale-watching season: in the spring (April–May) or fall (September–October). They are typically in pods of 15–50, but schools of 300 or more are not uncommon and some trips have logged as many as 2,000. They have not always been so common in the area: before the 1970s, they were quite rare and the most frequently seen species was the White-beaked Dolphin, but now it is the other way round. One likely explanation is a shift in prey abundance – there are more Herring, which Atlantic White-sided Dolphins prefer to eat, and fewer of the fish species and squid which White-beaked Dolphins prefer.

There are occasional sightings of Risso's, Striped and Bottlenose Dolphins, while Short-beaked Common Dolphins are being seen more often in recent years (they sometimes venture quite close to the shore

Fin Whales are seen on many whale watching trips in the Gulf of Maine.

during the summer). No one knows why this is happening, or if the trend will continue. Harbor Porpoises are present year-round, with most sightings in late summer and fall.

Long-finned Pilot Whales are present in relatively small numbers year-round, though they are most common from September–April. They are not seen frequently on whale-watching trips because they prefer deeper waters, such as around the edge of Georges Bank and in the Great South Channel.

Rarer visitors include Blue Whales (it may be wishful thinking, but sightings seem to have increased in recent years), Sperm Whales, Killer Whales (mainly from mid-July to the end of September) and even Bowhead Whales and Belugas.

Whaling

New England was once home to a thriving commercial whaling industry. It began soon after 1620, when the Pilgrim fathers William Bradford and Edward Winslow wrote: 'Cape Cod was like to be a place of good fishing, for we saw daily great whales, of the best kind for oil and bone.'

By the 1670s, colonists from Long Island and Cape Cod Bay were actively hunting North Atlantic Right Whales close to the shore, with the help of their Native American neighbors. They worked from small sailing vessels, using harpoons with wooden floats attached to long ropes; when the animals were exhausted from dragging the floats, they would be killed with long lances and towed to shore for processing. But so many Right Whales were killed that, by 1730, there were few left in these coastal waters. Whalers began to use single-masted sailing vessels, called sloops, to pursue the whales in deeper water farther offshore.

It was around this time that everyone's attention turned to another species of whale, the Sperm Whale. The story goes that, in 1712, a Nantucket captain cruising for Right Whales near the shore was blown out into the Atlantic in his small boat, and made the most of his predicament by killing a Sperm Whale. The whale yielded a superior quality oil and this marked the beginning of the systematic hunting of a much more valuable species.

Sperm Whales became the target of American whalers for the next century and a half and, by 1774, there were no fewer than 360 vessels hailing from 15 ports along this

Atlantic White-sided Dolphins are best seen at the beginning or end of the season.

stretch of coast. The whalers continued to use the age-old technique, using a harpoon with a rope attached, and the harpooned whales would drag their open boats for a considerable distance before tiring enough to be killed: a ride that became known as the 'Nantucket sleigh ride'.

In many ways, this period was comparable to the gold rushes that later swept across western North America. Like prospectors searching for big strikes, whalers moved relentlessly from one hunting ground to another, killing all the animals in one place, then moving on to the next. First it was in deep waters off the coast of New England, then it was farther out into the North Atlantic, and eventually it was as far afield as the coasts of Guinea in Africa and Brazil in South America.

By the early 1800s, as Sperm Whale numbers across the length and breadth of the Atlantic declined, most voyages from New England were heading all the way to the Pacific. Sometimes they went by way of the dreaded Cape Horn, at the tip of South America, and sometimes by the much longer route around the Cape of Good Hope, at the tip of South Africa. Inevitably, whaling voyages became longer and longer – up to five years in some cases.

It was on one of these whaling voyages, aboard the *Acushnet*, that Herman Melville was inspired to write his book, *Moby Dick*. The ship sailed from New Bedford, rounded Cape Horn and travelled to the South Pacific for a voyage of several years, though Melville and a crewmate jumped ship in the Marquesas Islands after only 18 months. After being captured by local cannibals, boarding another whaling ship, the *Lucy*

Ann, and being thrown into jail for joining the crew in a mutiny, he eventually arrived home more than three years after he had left.

But despite the distances involved there was still big money to be made from commercial whaling. Nantucket and New Bedford, in particular, became exceedingly rich as the primary whaling ports of the time. The New Bedford fleet reached its peak in 1857, when it alone harbored 329 vessels employing more than 10,000 men. The community became known as 'the city that lit the world', due to the phenomenal amount of candle oil that was produced within the city limits from the waxy oil found inside Sperm Whales' heads.

Around the mid-1800s, American whaling for Sperm Whales started to decline. There were several reasons: serious over-hunting had decimated whale populations everywhere; the California gold rush of 1849 and the American Civil War (1861–65) diverted attention away from whaling; the value of whale oil dwindled with the discovery of petroleum in 1859; and the rise of modern whaling technology developed in Norway ultimately led to an enormous increase in the number of large whales of every species being taken (more efficiently) worldwide. Quite simply, there were more lucrative opportunities for the American whalers, in everything from railroads to mining.

There are a number of excellent museums in New England, with exhibits and information on the region's whaling history, as well as on the whales themselves: in particular, New Bedford Whaling Museum and Nantucket Historical Association Whaling Museum.

Eastern Seaboard: New York to Georgia

Whale and dolphin watching along the Eastern Seaboard is not as popular as in many other regions of North America, but there are some outstanding opportunities. The stretch of coast between New York and Georgia is home to everything from urban Humpback Whales and migrating North Atlantic Right Whales to strand-feeding Bottlenose Dolphins, occasional Clymene Dolphins and even Gervais' Beaked Whales.

New York State and New Jersey

The New York–New Jersey metropolitan area is the most populated region of the United States, with 20 million people living within 10 miles of the coast. Yet no fewer than 25 species of cetaceans have been recorded in the waters here – and whales are regularly seen within sight of the Manhattan skyline.

The main whale-watching area is the New York Bight, a shallow 'urban sea' between Long Island and New Jersey. Stretching from Montauk Point in the north to Cape May in the south, it includes Long Island Sound, New York Harbor and the Jersey Shore. The sandy seabed of the Bight is relatively shallow, but it is bisected by the Hudson Canyon, which begins as a 15–130ft depression at the mouth of the Hudson River and drops to a depth of more than half a mile at the shelf edge.

Fin Whales are the most abundant large whales in the eastern New York Bight and nearshore waters off New Jersey. Although

Overview

Main species: Humpback Whale, Fin Whale, Minke Whale, Short-beaked Common Dolphin, Common Bottlenose Dolphin.

Occasional species: North Atlantic Right Whale, Blue Whale, Sei Whale, Sperm Whale, Short-finned Pilot Whale, Cuvier's Beaked Whale, Gervais' Beaked Whale, Clymene Dolphin, Atlantic Spotted Dolphin, Risso's Dolphin, Harbor Porpoise.

Other wildlife highlights: Gray Seal, Harbor Seal, River Otter, Bald Eagle, Osprey, Northern Gannet, Laughing Gull, Ring-billed Gull, Royal Tern, Roseate Tern, Forster's Tern, Black Skimmer, Audubon Shearwater, Great Shearwater, Cory's Shearwater, Sooty Shearwater, Wilson's Storm Petrel, Leach's Storm Petrel, American Alligator, Leatherback Turtle, Green Turtle, Kemp's Ridley Turtle, Loggerhead Turtle, Hawksbill Turtle, Blue Shark, Basking Shark, Ocean Sunfish.

Main locations: Montauk, New York City (New York); Cape May, Atlantic City, Avalon, Wildwood (New Jersey); Lewes (Delaware); Virginia Beach (Virginia); Nags Head, Manteo, Wanchese, Cape Hatteras (North Carolina); North Myrtle Beach, Kiawah Island, Bowens Island, Beaufort, Hilton Head Island (South Carolina); Savannah, Tybee Island, Wilmington Island, St Simons Island (Georgia).

Types of tours: one-hour to full-day trips; multi-day research expeditions; kayaking tours.

When to go: year-round (see specific locations for different seasons).

Regulations and guidelines: NOAA Whale Watching Guidelines Northeast Region; Whale SENSE program; US Federal Regulations; Marine Mammal Protection Act (1972); strictly enforced 500-yard rule for North Atlantic Right Whales.

Wildlife species are listed systematically (not in order of abundance) and frequency of sightings varies with location and season.

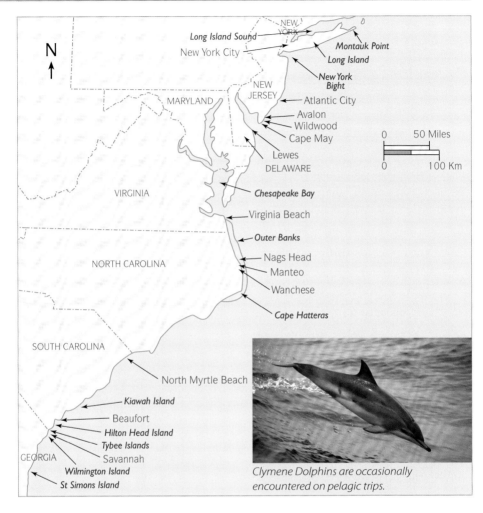

Clymene Dolphins are occasionally encountered on pelagic trips.

their distribution varies with the seasons, they are present in good numbers year-round. There are believed to be 200–400 in this population. They tend to be closest to shore (within a mile of the eastern coast of Long Island) from January–March, farther away (up to 30 miles) from April–August, and farthest away (60 miles or more along the shelf edge) from September to early December. They are seen on many whale-watching trips, sometimes in feeding aggregations of 20 or more individuals in the summer (usually three to four during the winter).

Humpback Whales also occur regularly in the Bight, and they are becoming increasingly common. In a good year, during the peak months of May to November, they are frequently quite close to the shore in places like Block Island Sound, Gardiners

Bay, the south shore of Long Island and occasionally even within New York Harbor.

Minke Whales are common and frequently seen on whale-watching trips (although they tend to ignore or avoid boats in this part of the world). Sei Whales appear from time to time, depending on the year, and Blue Whales are known to be some distance offshore (but they enter the Bight only once in a while). North Atlantic Right Whales were regularly caught off Long Island by shore whalers in the late 1600s and early 1700s. Nowadays, they use the New York Bight as a migratory corridor and can sometimes be seen travelling between their wintering grounds in the south and their summering grounds in the north. There are usually a few individuals in the area year-round (acoustic surveys have, on average, detected them about one day in every five) and these sometimes include females with calves that appear to be feeding.

Sperm Whales have always been considered rare in the Bight, but experts now believe that they are more common than previously thought. The best way to see them is by joining one of the pelagic trips, which venture much farther offshore. Sperm Whales are known to occur consistently in deep waters near the continental shelf, but have occasionally been recorded in shallower waters off Montauk Point. They are usually around in the fall, winter and late spring (rarely during the summer). Long-finned Pilot Whales also live in these deeper waters and are seen from time to time year-round.

There are two distinct populations of Bottlenose Dolphins in the Bight: one living offshore, from Long Island north; and the other living in coastal waters, from Long Island south. They are regularly seen on dedicated dolphin-watching trips. Short-beaked Common Dolphins and Harbor Porpoises are also fairly common. Risso's Dolphins, Atlantic White-sided Dolphins, White-beaked Dolphins, Pantropical Spotted Dolphins, Striped Dolphins, Killer Whales, Pygmy Sperm Whales, Belugas and Cuvier's Beaked Whales have all been recorded to varying degrees.

There are opportunities to join occasional research trips from Montauk, at the eastern end of Long Island. There are basically two options: shorter, six-hour trips that stay within the Bight, and over Hudson Canyon, where the main targets are Fin Whales and dolphins; and multi-day trips that travel as far afield as the Great South Channel and Stellwagen Bank, looking for more uncommon species.

There are also trips from Queens, in New York City, which focus on a population of Humpback Whales that usually spend the summer feeding just beyond Coney Island. Numbers have been increasing in recent years and, while they are not exactly frolicking around the Statue of Liberty, they are regularly seen with the Manhattan skyline as an unlikely backdrop. There are currently 48 individuals in Gotham Whale's New York City Humpback Whale Catalog. Bottlenose Dolphins are often seen on these trips too, and they are fairly common just outside the Harbor.

Farther south, in New Jersey, there are trips from Cape May, Atlantic City, Avalon and Wildwood to see Fin Whales, Humpback Whales, Minke Whales, Bottlenose Dolphins and other species. Many of the sightings are within 10 miles of shore, and even inside Delaware Bay. There are two options: short inshore trips to see the local Bottlenose Dolphins (there are more than 70 individuals in the Cape May photo-identification catalog alone) or longer trips to look for whales farther afield.

Full-day pelagic birding trips to places like Wilmington Canyon, 60 miles offshore, can be good for deep-water species such as Sperm Whales and even beaked whales, while anything from North Atlantic Right Whales to Striped Dolphins is possible.

Delaware to Virginia

There are whale-watching and dolphin-watching trips from Virginia Beach in Virginia. Whale-watching trips predominantly target Humpback Whales, from late December to mid-March (with guaranteed sightings until mid-February). They are often very close to shore, sometimes inside Chesapeake Bay and even within sight and sound of the city, though some trips have to venture as far as about 10 miles offshore to find them. Many of these whales are merely passing through, on their way between their breeding grounds in the Caribbean and major feeding grounds in the Gulf of Maine and beyond, but others (particularly juveniles) are known to stay for longer.

Bottlenose Dolphins are seen frequently too, particularly in the southern and central parts of Chesapeake Bay (reports of them in the Bay date back to the 1800s and they are now considered fairly abundant). Cape Charles, James River and Elizabeth River are particular hotspots, though they have been known to travel all the way up the Potomac River as far as Washington DC. Most pods within the Bay contain fewer than 10 individuals, though many more seem to travel together farther offshore. Fin Whales are encountered on quite a few trips, while Minke Whales, Short-beaked Common Dolphins, Harbor Porpoises and even North Atlantic Right Whales are seen from time to time. There are also shorter dolphin-watching trips, close to the shore, from mid-March to mid-October.

There are occasional pelagic birding trips from Virginia Beach – involving very long days at sea – that encounter a variety of cetaceans. They often head for Norfolk Canyon, 75 miles away on the shelf edge. Atlantic Spotted Dolphins and Bottlenose Dolphins tend to be quite common, while Sperm Whales, Short-finned Pilot Whales, Risso's Dolphins and a variety of other species are possible.

There are dolphin-watching trips from Lewes, in Delaware, to see the local Bottlenose Dolphins. It is also possible to join a two-hour kayaking tour here that focuses on the dolphins, which are often close to the shore, and can be quite curious and playful. Shore-based dolphin watching is popular in mid-summer: the long golden beaches around Dewey Beach can be good and, from mid-June to mid-August, there are dolphin-watching walks, guided by rangers, in Cape Henlopen State Park. There are also limited opportunities to see Bottlenose Dolphins as part of scenic cruises from Ocean City in Maryland.

North Carolina, South Carolina and Georgia

There is relatively little whale watching in this corner of the country, but there are some good opportunities for watching both resident and transient Bottlenose Dolphins and there is great potential for whale watching farther offshore along the shelf edge.

Most trips are in North Carolina and the place to head for is the Outer Banks, a 175-mile-long string of barrier islands off the coast (which also includes a small portion of Virginia). The islands are largely composed of sand, generally low-lying (apart from some 100ft dunes) and rarely more than a mile wide. They cover at least half of the North Carolina coastline,

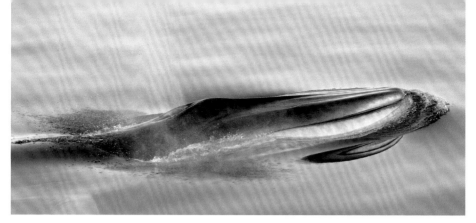

Fin Whales are frequently seen along the Eastern Seaboard.

separating Currituck Sound, Albemarle Sound and Pamlico Sound from the North Atlantic.

Most dolphin watching takes place in the sheltered waters of Roanoke Sound, on the inside of the Outer Banks, where Bottlenose Dolphins are the stars of the show. There are trips from mid-May to early October, though there are dolphins here year-round. A six-year study in Roanoke identified 1,092 individual dolphins in the area; most of these are transient, coming and going for a day or two at a time from late spring to early fall, but there is also a relatively small resident population of about 60 animals.

Land-based dolphin watching is popular here and sightings are common from certain hotspots. Cape Hatteras National Seashore, Cape Lookout, Cape Lookout National Seashore and the beaches around Corolla are all good. Cape Fear (south of the Outer Banks) is another popular spot for land-based watching. Bottlenose Dolphins are the most commonly seen, but other cetaceans turn up from time to time.

Cape Hatteras, near the southern end of the Outer Banks, is rapidly gaining a reputation as a cetacean hotspot, with 20 species recorded so far. In particular, there is great potential for whale watching along the edge of the continental shelf which,

at its nearest point, is only about 25 miles from here. Long-day pelagic birding trips from Hatteras have encountered a variety of cetaceans over the years – including some unusually good views of Gervais' Beaked Whales. Indeed, aerial surveys have revealed a significant year-round population of beaked whales along this stretch of the shelf edge, with most sightings between May and August; Cuvier's Beaked Whales appear to be the most abundant, but rarely seen True's Beaked Whales are also in the area. As well as beaked whales, Bottlenose Dolphins are seen on most of these pelagic birding trips and Atlantic Spotted Dolphins on many, while North Atlantic Right Whales, Humpback Whales, Sperm Whales, Short-finned Pilot Whales, Clymene Dolphins and Risso's Dolphins are all possibilities. They run on and off year-round.

In South Carolina, there are dolphin-watching trips in the sheltered estuarine waterways around Hilton Head Island, Bull Island and Pinckney Island National Wildlife Refuge, as well as farther north around Kiawah Island and Folly Beach. Some are dedicated dolphin trips, targeting resident populations of Bottlenose Dolphins as well as occasional transients, while many combine dolphins with other wildlife or sightseeing. Trips are mostly in small boats,

South Carolina is the best place to watch Bottlenose Dolphins strand-feeding.

year-round, and it is also possible to kayak with the dolphins.

The creeks and marshes along this stretch of the South Carolina coast is where Bottlenose Dolphins use a remarkable feeding technique called 'strand-feeding'. In an extraordinary cooperative behavior, small groups of them herd schools of Mullet and other fish together into a tightly packed 'bait ball' before forming a line and rushing forwards to create a pressure wave that drives the fish onto the saltmarsh mudbanks. Then the dolphins launch themselves out onto the shore to catch their prey, before wriggling back into the water. No one knows why, but they always strand-feed on their right-hand sides. Females teach their calves how to strand-feed on banks steeper than those preferred by experienced adults, allowing easier and safer re-entry into the water. This behavior is unique to South Carolina and Georgia (although Bottlenose Dolphins in the Gulf of Guayaquil, Ecuador, have recently been discovered using a similar technique). It can be seen year-round, usually within three hours of low tide, and Bull Creek is a particular hotspot. This behavior is not commonly seen on regular dolphin-watching trips – chartering a small boat specifically for the purpose would increase the odds.

In Georgia, there are short tours to see Bottlenose Dolphins from Savannah and nearby Tybee and Wilmington islands, as well as St Simons Island. Most of these operate from March–November, and they usually combine dolphin watching with sightseeing. Cumberland Island National Seashore, in the south, is a popular spot for land-based whale and dolphin watching.

The official state marine mammal of Georgia is the North Atlantic Right Whale, because this is the heart of its only known calving ground. In late fall, near-term pregnant females, and a few others, migrate south from their feeding grounds in the Gulf of Maine and the Bay of Fundy, to the relatively calm, warm, predator-free waters of Georgia and northern Florida (and, to a lesser extent, South Carolina). They spend several months here, appearing off the Carolinas in November, with peak numbers off Georgia and northern Florida in January and February. Most births are before the beginning of January (calf numbers vary greatly between years, from 1 to 39). Sadly, Georgia's North Atlantic Right Whales are rarely seen from land, because they are typically 5–25 miles offshore (they are more often seen close to shore in Florida).

Florida & the Gulf States

There is very little whale watching in Florida and the Gulf States, but more than 100 operators offer countless short trips to see Bottlenose Dolphins. In fact, there are few communities in Florida, at least, without dolphin-watching trips of one kind or another.

Bottlenose Dolphins are present throughout much of the region year-round and are easily accessible close to shore. They frequently enter inlets and bays – even around popular tourist resorts – as well as mangrove forests and bayous (slow-moving, swampy sections of rivers, lakes and inlets). There are numerous sizeable resident populations (numbering hundreds of dolphins or more) and many distinctive individuals are recognized by researchers, boat operators and locals who have been observing them for years.

Many operators guarantee sightings – with a free second trip if you are unlucky – while others promote dolphins on a more opportunistic basis. Some of the trips are as short as 45 minutes, though most are one to two hours and a few are as long as four hours, and at least two operators use glass-bottomed boats to view the animals underwater.

There are trips on and off all day every day throughout the year – even popular early evening trips, which combine dolphin watching with dinner and time to admire the sunset. Most operators are in Florida (particularly from the Keys to the Panhandle), Alabama and Texas, and there are also many do-it-yourself opportunities

Overview

Main species: Common Bottlenose Dolphin.

Occasional species: North Atlantic Right Whale, Humpback Whale, Short-finned Pilot Whale, Atlantic Spotted Dolphin.

Other wildlife highlights: West Indian Manatee, Bald Eagle, Osprey, White Ibis, Roseate Spoonbill, American White Pelican, Anhinga, Black Skimmer, Great Blue Heron, Great Egret, Tricolored Heron, American Avocet, American Alligator, Loggerhead Turtle, Green Turtle, Hawksbill Turtle, Kemp's Ridley Turtle, Leatherback Turtle, Tarpon.

Main locations: St Augustine, Daytona Beach, Flagler Beach, Ponce Inlet, New Smyrna Beach, Cape Canaveral, Cocoa Beach, Merritt Island, Indialantic, Melbourne, Vero Beach, Fort Pierce, Stuart, Jupiter, Fort Lauderdale, Miami Beach, Key West, Everglades City, Marco Island, Isles of Capri, Naples, Sanibel Island, Captiva Island, Manasota Key, Englewood, Cape Coral, Fort Myers, Venice, Sarasota, Anna Maria Island, St Petersburg/Clearwater, Tampa, St Pete Beach, Tarpon Springs, Homosassa, Crystal River, Panama City, Destin, Pensacola, and others (Florida); Orange Beach (Alabama); Galveston, Port Aransas, Port Isabel, South Padre Island (Texas); pelagic birding trips (with ad hoc cetacean sightings) from Venice and Port Fourchon (Louisiana), Padre Island and Port Aransas (Texas).

Types of tours: 45-minute to half-day trips; half-day research trips; kayaking tours; full-day pelagic (primarily birding) trips.

When to go: year-round; occasional North Atlantic Right Whale sightings December–March (peak in February).

Regulations and guidelines: Dolphin SMART voluntary program; NOAA Guidelines for Viewing Marine Mammals; US Federal Regulations; Marine Mammal Protection Act (1972); strictly enforced 500-yard rule for North Atlantic Right Whales.

Wildlife species are listed systematically (not in order of abundance) and frequency of sightings varies with location and season.

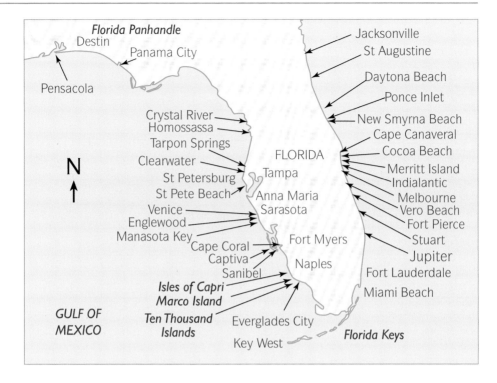

with boat-hiring facilities (keeping in mind the federal guidelines for remaining at least 50 yards away from the dolphins).

Dolphin SMART program

Unfortunately, while many operators are responsible and have the dolphins' best interests at heart, that is certainly not the case with all of them. An entire entertainment industry has grown up around the animals: several offer dolphin watching from jet skis, for example, some boast about the size of the wake their boats create (arguing that the dolphins like to play in it) and one even has clothing-optional dolphin tours.

There is also a major controversy over a few unscrupulous operators who have been feeding the dolphins, in order to guarantee close encounters for tourists, even though this practice is illegal in the US. It changes the dolphins' behavior and leads to potentially dangerous interactions with boats, fishing gear and people, and can distract them from remaining vigilant for predatory sharks. It can also be bad for the animals' health. There have been many reports of people feeding them hotdogs, beer and other inappropriate foods. One well-known dolphin near Sarasota, Florida, called Beggar, developed a taste for human food being given to him, illegally, by private boaters. As a result, he eventually died in 2012, dehydrated, with fishing tackle in his stomach and with a number of propeller injuries. There has been an official crackdown on dolphin feeding – particularly in places like Panama City, Florida, which has been the number-one hotspot for this practice for over 20 years –

but some operators persist in feeding and, when they are caught, receive hefty fines.

Swim-with-dolphin trips are another area for concern. There are a great many half-day trips, particularly in the Florida Keys, that take tourists in small boats to swim with wild Bottlenose Dolphins. Many operators boast of their long-developed relationships with certain local dolphins and imply that the dolphins benefit as much as the people, but the truth is usually different: it is highly stressful for the dolphins and disrupts their natural resting, feeding and social behavior. There are already proposals to ban swimming with dolphins in Hawai'i, and many would like to see the same happen in Florida.

The best operators abide by voluntary regulations developed by the Dolphin SMART program, which aims to promote responsible viewing of wild dolphins by commercial operators. A partnership between the National Oceanic and Atmospheric Administration (NOAA), the National Marine Fisheries Service, Whale and Dolphin Conservation and the Dolphin Ecology Project, the program began in 2007 and is now being adopted by more than a dozen operators in the Florida Keys, southwest Florida and Alabama. The guidelines include staying 50 yards away from the dolphins, keeping the engine in neutral when dolphins are near and refraining from feeding, touching or swimming with them.

The bottom line is simple: do not join swim-with-dolphin tours, and look for operators with Dolphin SMART flags and signs (make sure they display the current year). Hopefully, as more people push for operators to take responsibility, the overall standard of dolphin watching in this part of the world will improve.

Florida

Florida's west coast, in particular, has a long history of dolphin watching and, indeed, dolphin research. The resident population of about 160 identifiable Bottlenose Dolphins in Sarasota Bay – spanning at least five concurrent generations – has been studied since 1970, making it the longest-running study of a dolphin population anywhere in the world.

Farther south, in the Ten Thousand Islands, a chain of islands and mangrove inlets off the coast of southwest Florida, there is a long-established photo-identification study of a resident population of Bottlenose Dolphins. More than 200 individuals have been identified to date and paying passengers can help to spot, count and identify them. You'll need binoculars for a positive identification – if the operator remains the requisite 50 yards away from the dolphins – but if you discover a 'new' dolphin during the trip, you get to choose a name for him or her.

Unfortunately, Florida is also where the training of captive dolphins was pioneered. The first large oceanarium was developed as part of the film industry, when Marine Studios opened in 1938, just south of St Augustine, to film movies underwater (it later became Marineland of Florida). Scenes from the 1950s classic *Creature from the Black Lagoon* were filmed there. Visitors went to Marine Studios to see dolphin feedings and that ultimately evolved into training the animals to perform shows. It was also in Florida – at Miami Seaquarium – that the dolphins used in the famous TV series *Flipper* were trained, during the 1960s. Dolphin shows are still popular in Florida and, indeed, there are more captive facilities in the state than almost anywhere else in the country.

There are countless short trips to see Bottlenose Dolphins in Florida.

North Atlantic Right Whales are sometimes seen from shore in northeastern Florida.

The irony is that, in Florida, it is almost as easy (and often cheaper) to see Bottlenose Dolphins in the wild. They can be observed relatively easily from land on both sides of the state. Even in busy and touristy places like Naples, with all its intensive shopping, dining and golfing, there are good vantage points for dolphin watching (such as Naples Municipal Fishing Pier) and numerous boat operators offering trips to see them.

Indeed, there are so many places to see dolphins in Florida, particularly in the southwest, that it would almost be easier to list where you *cannot* find them. They can be seen from waterfront hotels, apartments, bars and restaurants (one restaurant, on Marco Island, boasts 'Come by boat, come by car. Watch the dolphins from the Chickee Bar!'). They can be seen in many sheltered bays, such as Choctawhatchee, Apalachicola, Sarasota and Biscayne, and they are readily spotted from bridges and causeways linking islands or crossing inland waterways. It is even possible to see them from many beaches, such as Fort Myers Beach, and those along the southern tip of Barrier Island, on Sanibel Island and along Lemon Bay. Some ferries offer dolphin-watching opportunities, too – for example, the 20-minute Caladesi Island ferry, between Honeymoon Island and Caladesi Island, north of Clearwater, is known for its dolphin sightings.

Though there are no dedicated whale-watching trips in Florida, Humpback Whales and several other species are sometimes seen from shore, mainly along the Atlantic coast. In particular, in the northeast, there are limited opportunities to see North Atlantic Right Whales. The Atlantic coast between Jacksonville and Cape Canaveral marks the southern end of their only known calving ground. In late fall, near-term pregnant females, a few males and assorted juveniles – on average around 100–150 whales throughout the season – migrate south from their feeding grounds in the Gulf of Maine and the Bay of Fundy, to the relatively calm, warm waters of northern Florida (others do not reach as far as Florida – they spend the winter off Georgia and, to a lesser extent, South Carolina). They spend several months here, from December to late March, and this is where the females have their calves (most births are before the beginning of January).

There are typically about 75 sightings of North Atlantic Right Whales off the Florida coast each winter, but this varies greatly from year to year. The best time tends to be February, though they can be seen any time between November and April (with a peak from December to March). The greatest chances tend to be along the stretch of coast between St Augustine and Daytona Beach and there are four fishing piers that potentially make good spots to watch from: St Augustine Beach Pier, Flagler Beach Pier, Sunglow Fishing Pier in Daytona Beach and Daytona Beach Main Street Pier. It is also possible to attend an introductory talk by Marineland and become a volunteer Right Whale observer for the day.

Gulf of Mexico

There are numerous different cetaceans in the Gulf of Mexico, but not many opportunities to see them. No fewer than 31 species have been recorded in the region altogether, but it has a particularly wide and shallow continental shelf so most species are rarely seen except by venturing into deeper waters far from shore.

The Gulf of Mexico is a huge semi-enclosed sea, bordered by the US, Mexico and Cuba. Covering about 580,000 square miles, it is open to the North Atlantic via the narrow Straits of Florida in the east and to the Caribbean Sea through the Yucatán Channel in the southeast.

The Gulf is basically a large pit with a broad, shallow rim. It is bordered by a wide

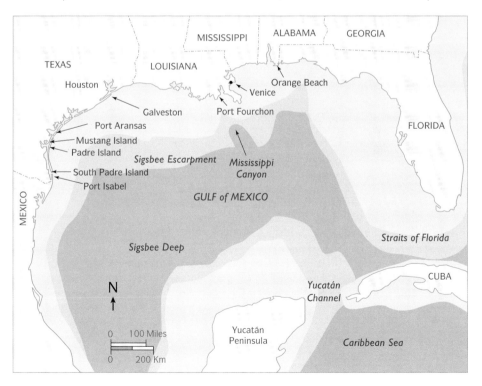

Resident Bottlenose Dolphins are a familiar sight in the Gulf of Mexico.

intertidal area less than 70ft deep, then the continental shelf (no more than 600ft deep) stretches to an average of 30 miles offshore (though it is up to 150 miles wide off parts of Florida, Louisiana and Texas). The deeper waters beyond the shelf are particularly interesting for their whale-watching potential, as where the shelf drops away is a landscape full of deep holes, ridges, canyons and cliffs. The significant deeper areas are the 75-mile-long Mississippi Canyon, south of Louisiana, which drops to a depth of more than 4,000ft (this is where the *Deepwater Horizon* drilling rig exploded on 20 April 2010); the Straits of Florida (where depths drop to about 2,800ft); the Yucatán Channel (to about 6,600ft); and the appropriately named Sigsbee Deep, the abyssal plain, which drops to a maximum depth of 12,300 –14,400ft (the actual figure is disputed) in the southwest.

Baleen whales are rare here, but many of the toothed whales are abundant. Fairly common species in the deeper waters

include Sperm Whale, Short-finned Pilot Whale, Melon-headed Whale, Rough-toothed Dolphin, Risso's Dolphin, Bottlenose Dolphin, Pantropical Spotted Dolphin, Atlantic Spotted Dolphin, Spinner Dolphin, Clymene Dolphin, Striped Dolphin and Fraser's Dolphin. Several other species are not as common but are encountered frequently during research surveys, including Bryde's Whale, Pygmy Sperm Whale, Dwarf Sperm Whale, Killer Whale, False Killer Whale, Pygmy Killer Whale and Gervais' Beaked Whale.

There are some long-day pelagic birding trips from various locations around the Gulf that head for the Mississippi Canyon or the shelf edge, some 40–50 miles away (depending on the departure point). These focus on birds, of course, but they often see Atlantic Spotted Dolphins and Bottlenose Dolphins, and sometimes encounter Sperm Whales, Short-finned Pilot Whales, Melon-headed Whales, Striped Dolphins, Pantropical Spotted Dolphins, Spinner Dolphins, Clymene Dolphins, Rough-toothed Dolphins, Risso's Dolphins and other species, including beaked whales.

There are also numerous short trips to see Bottlenose Dolphins close to the shore, many with guaranteed sightings. Apart from Florida, most operators are in Alabama and Texas (with limited opportunities in Mississippi and Louisiana). There are more than 20 operators in Orange Beach, Alabama, offering excursions to see mainly resident populations in the surrounding bays and bayous. In Texas, trips run from South Padre Island, close to the Mexican border, as well as nearby Port Isabel. They also leave from Port Aransas on Mustang Island and from Galveston farther round the coast near Houston.

CANADA

Canada was probably the first country in the world to attempt commercial whale watching. In the early 1900s, Humpback Whales in Howe Sound (stretching from Squamish to the Strait of Georgia, opposite southern Vancouver Island) became an attraction for trail-blazing tourists from nearby Vancouver, where they could go on boat excursions, organized by local entrepreneurs, specifically to see the whales. Unfortunately, whaling from the station at Page's Lagoon (now Piper's Lagoon) in Nanaimo, from 1907–10, wiped out the local whale population and put an end to the enterprise.

Canada's next attempt at whale watching was not until 1970, when the Montreal Zoological Society began offering trips into the Gulf of St Lawrence, Quebec, to see Fin Whales, Minke Whales, Belugas and other cetaceans (incidentally, these were the first commercial whale-watching trips anywhere on the east coast of North America). They were a huge success and became a regular event – and prompted such an interest in whale watching in Canada that the industry grew exponentially.

Nowadays, Canada attracts more whale watchers than almost any other country in the world (after the US and Australia). There are major hotspots on both the Atlantic and Pacific coasts, as well as in the country's Arctic and sub-Arctic regions and, depending on where you go, it is possible to see everything from Blue Whales, Humpback Whales and Bowhead Whales to Killer Whales, Narwhal and Belugas.

A breaching Killer Whale off the west coast of Canada.

CANADA: WEST COAST

British Columbia

Whale watching in British Columbia officially began in 1980, when tourists were taken from historic Telegraph Cove, BC's last boardwalk community, on the northeast corner of Vancouver Island, to see the local Killer Whales. Vancouver Island is now virtually synonymous with Killer Whales and is widely considered to be one of the best places in the world to see them.

Whale watchers concentrate on two main areas: Johnstone Strait, in the north, which is a critical habitat for the so-called Northern Resident Killer Whale community; and Georgia Strait, Haro Strait, Boundary Pass, Swanson Channel, Puget Sound and Juan De Fuca Strait, in the south, in waters shared between Canada and the US, which is a critical habitat for the much smaller Southern Resident Killer Whale community. A transient (Bigg's) Killer Whale population

(named in honor of the late Dr Michael Bigg, a pioneering whale researcher) roams the Pacific coast of the US and Canada and their pods turn up frequently, too; there are currently several hundred individuals in this particular population.

Whale watching on the west coast of Vancouver Island focuses on the northward migration of as many as 18–21,000 Gray Whales, travelling between their winter breeding grounds in Baja and their summer feeding grounds in the Bering, Chukchi and Beaufort seas. There are also opportunities to watch Gray Whales outside the migratory season, because a small number of them prefer to spend their summers along the west coast of Vancouver Island, rather than migrating all the way to the Arctic.

But there is much more to Vancouver Island than Killer Whales and Gray Whales (as if they aren't enough). Humpback Whales are being seen increasingly frequently, with more group lunge-feeding than ever before; they have also become much friendlier in recent years, sometimes almost mugging the whale-watch boats for a scratch (making it tough for the operators to keep to strict local regulations). Minke Whales are also a feature of the summer season. There are abundant populations of Dall's and Harbor Porpoises, Pacific White-sided Dolphins are encountered year-round and many other species turn up from time to time.

Farther north, there are opportunities for whale watching around Haida Gwaii (formerly the Queen Charlotte Islands). The species list for this spectacular archipelago

Canada's Killer Whales have been studied intensively for more than 40 years.

Performing for whale watchers in Johnstone Strait, northeastern Vancouver Island.

of 150 islands is similar to Vancouver Island, and it has among the highest density of Humpback Whales in British Columbia waters. Fin Whales are seen quite frequently here, too. There are a variety of other species, particularly off the Pacific coast, including Blue Whales, Sperm Whales and beaked whales, though the chances of seeing them are small. In 2013, researchers even encountered a critically endangered North Pacific Right Whale just off the coast. This is also a good place – in relative terms – to see offshore Killer Whales, which are far less well known than any of the other Killer Whales in the Northeast Pacific. The best way to see Haida Gwaii's cetaceans is by joining one of several multi-day live-aboard expeditions that include whale watching as part of more varied itineraries. They leave from Sandspit or various pick-up points on the mainland.

The Great Bear Rainforest can also be good for Fin Whales, Humpback Whales, Killer Whales and Dall's Porpoises, in particular; Pacific White-sided Dolphins were commonly seen until a few years ago, but these days are encountered less frequently within the waterways of the forest itself (they are still being seen offshore). Again, there is no dedicated whale watching, but there are lodges and a variety of multi-day live-aboard expeditions that focus on bears and other wildlife, and include whale watching on an ad hoc basis.

Finally, there is some outstandingly good land-based whale watching in British Columbia and some great viewing opportunities from the many BC Ferries that regularly ply these whale-and-dolphin-rich waters (some ferry captains actually announce sightings).

Vancouver Island (Johnstone Strait)

The maze of islands and protected waterways in Queen Charlotte Strait, Blackfish Sound and Johnstone Strait (the now-famous 68-mile channel that separates northern Vancouver Island from the rest of Canada) is the core summer and fall range of many family groups belonging to a world-famous community of Killer Whales called the Northern Residents. This is one of three main populations of resident Killer Whales

in the Northeast Pacific, the others being the Southern Residents and the Southern Alaska Residents. At this time of year, salmon funnel into the narrow waterways here on their way to spawning rivers, and the Killer Whales congregate to intercept them.

The Northern Residents do turn up periodically around northeastern Vancouver Island in the winter, though only in small numbers. During the colder months they are normally spread out, and consequently more difficult to find: over the course of a year, their range includes many thousands of miles of inlets, channels, passes and straits in coastal waters from roughly the midpoint of eastern Vancouver

Overview

Main species: Humpback Whale, Minke Whale, Killer Whale, Pacific White-sided Dolphin, Dall's Porpoise, Harbor Porpoise.

Occasional species: Gray Whale, Fin Whale.

Other wildlife highlights: Black Bear, Brown Bear, Wolf, Sea Otter, River Otter, American Mink, Steller Sea Lion, California Sea Lion, Harbor Seal, Northern Elephant Seal, Bald Eagle, Harlequin Duck, Cassin's Auklet, Rhinoceros Auklet, Common Murre, Marbled Murrelet, Ancient Murrelet, Red-necked Phalarope, Rufous Hummingbird; migrating birds on Pacific Flyway.

Main locations: Telegraph Cove, Port McNeill, Alert Bay, Port Hardy, Sointula; there are also tours from Campbell River and Heriot Bay (Quadra Island), farther south (which used to involve a longer journey, by bus or boat, through Discovery Passage to the whale watching grounds in Johnstone Strait, but now focus on improved sightings of Humpback Whales and transient Killer Whales in the northern Salish Sea).

Types of tours: three-hour to full-day tours; multi-day live-aboard expeditions; multi-day kayaking tours; land-based whale watching.

When to go: May–October; Northern Resident Killer Whales concentrated during the salmon run, July–October; May to mid-June tours tend to focus on Humpback Whales (with the added possibility of transient (Bigg's) Killer Whales).

Regulations and guidelines: Be Whale Wise Marine Wildlife Guidelines endorsed by Fisheries and Oceans Canada and BC Parks; See a Blow? Go Slow! Guidelines endorsed by Marine Education & Research Society; Marine Mammal Regulations (under the Fisheries Act) prohibit any form of harassment of cetaceans (including repeated attempts to pursue, disperse or herd whales); Fisheries and Oceans Canada is currently preparing countrywide enforceable regulations for whale watching.

Wildlife species are listed systematically (not in order of abundance) and frequency of sightings varies with location and season.

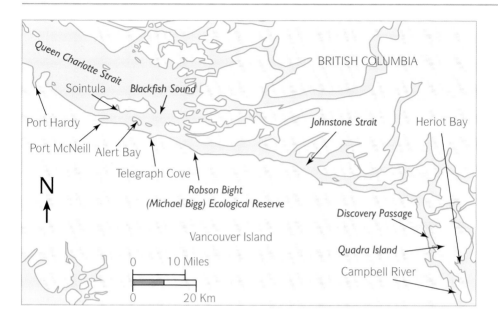

Island north to Southeast Alaska (though they do sometimes occur as far south and west as the Juan De Fuca Strait). Indeed, Northern Residents and Southern Residents (which are the focus of whale watching at the southern end of Vancouver Island) have somewhat overlapping ranges. But they have different 'languages' and culture, and do not associate with one another.

Consisting of 16 pods from three clans (Clan A: pods A1, A4, A5, B1, C1, D1, H1, I1, I2, and I18; Clan G: pods G1, G12, I11 and I31; and Clan R: pods R1 and W1) and currently totalling about 290 individuals, the Northern Residents are some of the best-known whales in the world. Field studies in this corner of northern Vancouver Island began in 1972 and have continued every year since. Most members of the community are known personally by researchers (and, of course, by the best whale-watch operators) and many of their lives have been studied from the day they were born.

They are given names and numbers: for example, Ripple (A43) is an adult female born in 1981, while Blackney (A38) is an adult male born in 1970. The most famous has to be A1 – more affectionately known as Stubbs – which was the very first whale in the Northern Resident community to be named. She had a severely damaged dorsal fin, which looked as if it had been cut in half (probably by a boat propeller) and resembled a stub. It was Stubbs who gave whale researchers the idea of photographing the dorsal fin and saddle-patch of each Killer Whale they encountered – to tell one individual from another – a technique that has been used with great success ever since. She died in 1974, aged about 45 years.

Corky

Another famous Northern Resident is Corky, or A16, who was captured in Pender Harbor, British Columbia, in 1969 and – along with five of her close relatives – taken into captivity. In fact, all 12 members of the pod (A5) were temporarily penned and Corky was one of six unlucky individuals selected for sale to oceanariums. It was the second time it had happened in two years, because six other members of the same pod had been captured and sold the previous year. Corky is the only survivor and still lives, and performs, at SeaWorld in San Diego. She has spent 48 of her 53 years in captivity. Meanwhile, there are now 12 members of A5 pod swimming free in the wild, and they continue to travel the waters of Johnstone Strait every summer.

Dr Michael Bigg Ecological Reserve at Robson Bight

The famous Dr Michael Bigg Ecological Reserve at Robson Bight, 10 miles southeast of Telegraph Cove, in Johnstone Strait, is a special sanctuary set aside for the Northern Resident Killer Whales. Established in 1982, and comprising 6.6 miles of shore-line, it is a unique area where some of the whales often rub themselves on smooth rocks, pebbles and gravel in the shallow water near the beach. They probably visit Robson Bight more than any other single locality in the region (often several times a day when they are in western Johnstone Strait) and spend a considerable amount of time here resting and socializing. It is possible that other groups not known to use Robson Bight have an equivalent – as yet unknown – rubbing beach somewhere else on the coast. Boats (including kayaks) are not allowed to enter the reserve, although it is possible to watch the whales from a safe distance (1 nautical mile) outside; there is no legal access from shore, either, except for wardens and researchers with permits.

Transient (Bigg's) Killer Whales

As well as resident Killer Whales, transient (Bigg's) Killer Whales are often encountered in the region. They belong to a community known as the West Coast Transients. Research from 1975–2012 identified 521 individual whales in this stock: 217 in a poorly known 'outer coast' sub-population and 304 in the well-known 'inner coast' sub-population. These Killer Whales roam along the entire length of the Pacific coast of Canada and the US, from California to Alaska, though many groups have strong site fidelity to smaller regions of the coast. While they are less easy to predict than residents, they can be encountered sporadically year-round. There is a peak in sightings around Vancouver Island during August and September, which is when Harbor Seal pups are being weaned (and most numerous) and are therefore particularly vulnerable to predation.

Many whale-watching boats have on-board hydrophones, to listen to the Killer Whales vocalizing underwater. Transient (Bigg's) Killer Whales are generally silent while they are foraging (because their mammalian prey can hear them), although they do vocalize after a successful hunt. The residents, on the other hand, can be highly vocal and make a variety of whistles, squeaks, screams, squawks and other sounds. Each pod has its own unique dialect and the best operators can tell one from another just by listening to them.

Other cetaceans in Johnstone Strait

As well as Killer Whales, there are many other cetaceans in Johnstone Strait and its environs during the summer. Sightings of Humpback Whales are becoming increasingly common. As the population recovers from depletion by whaling, it is reoccupying many areas where it was formerly abundant, and the inland waterways of northeastern Vancouver Island is one of those areas. As recently as the early 1980s, sightings of Humpback Whales in British Columbia were quite rare (most were off Haida Gwaii, with a small number off the north mainland coast and the northern end of Vancouver Island). But sightings have steadily increased since then and nowadays it is very common to see them back on their old feeding grounds in and around Johnstone Strait (the peak period is May to November). Research suggests that most of the Humpbacks here migrate to Hawai'i to breed (a small number migrate to Mexican and Central American breeding grounds instead).

Minke Whales are seen fairly frequently in the region, though it appears to be the same few whales that are being spotted repeatedly by whale-watching boats. Sightings are reported year-round, but most are in July and August. Many of them, if not all, probably migrate south for at least part of the winter (there are relatively few around from December to February).

A significant number of Gray Whales are present in British Columbia waters during the summer (probably around 100 or fewer in any given year). There are several key hotspots – one of which is near Cape Caution, on the mainland coast, at the northern end of Queen Charlotte Strait. They are not seen frequently on whale-watching trips in the Johnstone Strait area, but they are not too far away.

The Pacific White-sided Dolphin is one of the most abundant cetaceans in the region and is frequently seen year-round. Traditionally, there were seasonal peaks in spring and fall (the dolphins seemed to move offshore in large numbers during summer)

Bow-riding Dall's Porpoises.

but this seems to be changing. Herds of 300–400 are commonplace and there are occasional sightings of as many as 1,000 together. Until quite recently they were rarely seen in the inside coastal passages. But they began to appear with increasing regularity from the early 1980s onwards, first in the waters of Fitz Hugh Sound, then farther south into Queen Charlotte Strait, and then, in the late 1990s, they began to be seen in the Strait of Georgia. The frequency of sightings has increased steadily since then. No one knows why this has happened, but it is likely to do with changing distribution and abundance of their prey.

Dall's Porpoises and Harbor Porpoises are also frequently seen in the area and, in the inshore channels, passes and straits, are particularly common in areas of strong tidal mixing.

Vancouver Island (Salish Sea)

The Salish Sea is a large, biologically rich semi-enclosed sea shared between the southwestern portion of the Canadian province of British Columbia and the northwestern portion of the US state of Washington. Also known as the Emerald Sea, due to its color and nutrient content, it is a major hotspot for Killer Whales.

An intricate network of coastal waterways, it includes the Strait of Juan de Fuca, Haro Strait, the Strait of Georgia, Puget Sound and all their connecting channels and adjoining waters. It also contains no fewer than 419 islands, including Canada's Gulf Islands and the US's San Juan Islands. The Canada–US border runs right through the middle of the whale-watching area, but whale-watch boats can move freely back and forth across the border (though they are not allowed to land passengers outside their own country).

Best of all, from a whale-watching point of view, the Salish Sea is readily accessible from many towns and cities, including Vancouver, Seattle and Victoria. Throughout the summer and fall, there are a great many tours leaving on and off all day every day from many ports in the region. The Pacific Whale Watch Association – which is committed to research, education and responsible wildlife viewing in the region – has no fewer than 35 member companies operating about 100 vessels in the Salish Sea, departing from 20 different ports in British Columbia and Washington State. Between them, they carry more than 400,000 passengers every year. It is estimated that a further 100,000 or

Overview

Main species: Humpback Whale, Minke Whale, Killer Whale, Pacific White-sided Dolphin, Dall's Porpoise, Harbor Porpoise.

Occasional species: Gray Whale.

Other wildlife highlights: Black Bear, Steller Sea Lion, Northern Fur Seal, California Sea Lion, Northern Elephant Seal, Harbor Seal, River Otter, Sea Otter, Bald Eagle, Rhinoceros Auklet, Tufted Puffin, Pigeon Guillemot, Marbled Murrelet, Pacific Loon, Surf Scoter, Bonaparte's Gull, Glaucous-winged Gull.

Main locations: Vancouver Island: Victoria, Salt Spring Island, Sidney, Cowichan Bay, Sooke; mainland: Vancouver, Steveston, White Rock.

Types of tours: three- to five-hour tours; multi-day packages and kayaking tours; land-based whale watching.

When to go: April–October (some tours also operate in March and November); peak for Killer Whales June to late September, Humpback Whales May–November.

Regulations and guidelines: Be Whale Wise Marine Wildlife Guidelines endorsed by Fisheries and Oceans Canada and BC Parks; See a Blow? Go Slow! Guidelines endorsed by Marine Education & Research Society; Best Practice Guidelines developed by Pacific Whale Watch Association; specific regulations in different operating areas and Federal Regulations apply when whale watching on US side of border (with additional state laws regulating behavior near Southern Resident Killer Whales); Soundwatch Boater Education Program; Marine Mammal Regulations (under the Fisheries Act) prohibit any form of harassment of cetaceans (including repeated attempts to pursue, disperse or herd whales); Straitwatch; Fisheries and Oceans Canada is currently preparing countrywide enforceable regulations for whale watching.

Wildlife species are listed systematically (not in order of abundance) and frequency of sightings varies with location and season.

more watch the whales from private vessels.

There was one occasion in Haro Strait when no fewer than 107 commercial and recreational boats were observed following the same small pod of Killer Whales. That was exceptional, and at the height of the expansion of the whale-watching industry, but there is no doubt that it can get crowded and the number of vessels is the only downside to whale watching in the Salish Sea. The commercial whale-watch operators are mostly very careful in the way they maneuver around the whales, and they follow local guidelines to the letter, but private boaters are often either oblivious or not so responsible.

Fortunately, there are strenuous efforts to prevent vessel disturbance to Killer Whales and other marine wildlife in the region, such as through the Straitwatch program, operated by Cetus Research & Conservation Society. This puts staff and volunteers on the water every day during summer to educate recreational boaters on the least intrusive ways to watch whales in the wild and to monitor

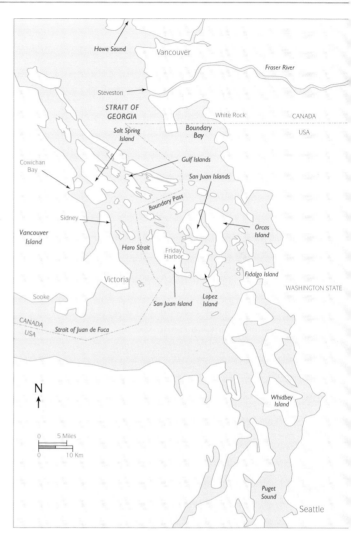

A Southern Resident Killer Whale in the Salish Sea.

all vessel activity near the whales. The Washington Department of Fish & Wildlife and the National Oceanic Atmospheric Administration also have patrol vessels monitoring the conduct of all boats around the Southern Residents during peak season. One of the aims is to spread the fleet out to different groups of whales, to minimize disturbance.

Southern Resident Killer Whales

The Salish Sea is the core summer and fall range of a famous community of Killer Whales called the Southern Residents. This is the smallest of the three resident Killer Whale communities in the Northeast Pacific, currently with 78 individuals in three pods: J-pod (24 members), K-pod (19 members) and L-pod (35 members). Northern Resident Killer Whales very occasionally appear this far south (they normally spend their summers off northeastern Vancouver Island), but they are seen no more than once every few years, on average.

Southern Residents congregate in the Salish Sea to intercept salmon – particularly Chinook, which is their favorite – as the fish funnel into the narrow waterways on their way to spawning rivers. Their favorite area tends to be off the western side of San Juan Island, but they forage as far as Swiftsure Bank (roughly between the northern end of the Strait of Juan de Fuca and Tofino) on the west coast, and as far as the Fraser River on the mainland in the east (the Fraser River being where most of the salmon go to spawn).

Increasingly, J-pod tends to remain in the same inshore waters for much of the winter, too, but the other two pods spend more time offshore, and travel as far south as Monterey in California and as far north as Haida Gwaii (formerly the Queen Charlotte Islands).

The Southern Resident Killer Whales have been studied intensively since 1976 and every individual is known to researchers (and, of course, to the best whale-watch operators). There are many well-known individuals among them. The first to be named was Ruffles, or J1, who was the icon of the Southern Residents for three decades, thanks to his exceptionally tall and wavy dorsal fin. There are claims that Ruffles was the most photographed Killer Whale in the world (sadly, he died in November 2010, aged about 60 – his death was reported in newspapers and on TV news bulletins worldwide). Ruffles was once actually captured to be sold and put on display in captivity but, in a twist of fate, was set free because he was too big.

Other members of the Southern Residents were not so lucky: Lolita, or Tokitae as she used to be known, was captured near Seattle in Penn Cove, Puget Sound, in 1970, when about four years old. She still lives in Miami Seaquarium and is the last survivor of 45 members of the Southern Resident community that were captured and sold for display in marine parks between 1965 and 1977. Lolita's 89-year-old mother, Ocean Sun, or L25, still swims freely in the Salish Sea with the rest of the family.

There are many other characters among the Southern Residents: Deadhead, named in honor of the rock band The Grateful Dead's lead singer, Jerry Garcia; Slick, who recently gave birth to her sixth young calf (who would have died without the help of Aunt Alki); Princess Angeline, who was one of three females in J-pod, all of whom were pregnant at the same time (they were affectionately known as 'The Pregnancy Club'); and many more.

Granny

But the real superstar has to be Granny, or J2, who was probably Ruffles's mother and was the oldest known Killer Whale in the world. It is estimated that she celebrated her 105th birthday in 2016. Still the matriarch leader of J-pod, she led her family group of no fewer than five generations (she outlived her children, but spent every day with her remaining grandchildren, great-grandchildren and great-great-grand-children) and was a fount of knowledge on all the best feeding, resting and socializing spots in the Salish Sea. She travelled up to 100 miles every day, and even breached. Sadly, she went missing in October 2016 and is now considered deceased.

Transient (Bigg's) Killer Whales

As their name suggests, transient (Bigg's) Killer Whales are indeed 'transient': they may be seen one day then move on to an entirely different area the next, or they may be seen several times before disappearing for weeks or even months. Similarly, some family groups are rare visitors to the area, while others come and go many times throughout the year.

However, it is becoming more and more common to see them in the central Salish Sea and Puget Sound. Local experts are even joking that some of the transients are almost becoming 'resident transients' – it's been dubbed the 'transient invasion'. The reason is probably a boom in the local seal and sea lion populations – which means plenty of food – although they also hunt porpoises in the area and, in April 2016, were observed attacking two adult Gray Whales in Puget Sound.

Many whale-watching boats have on-board hydrophones, to listen to the Killer Whales vocalizing underwater. Transient (Bigg's) Killer Whales are generally silent while they are foraging (because their mammalian prey can hear them), although they do vocalize after a successful hunt. The residents, on the other hand, can be highly vocal and make a variety of whistles, squeaks, screams, squawks and other sounds. Each pod has its own unique dialect and the best operators can tell one from another just by listening to them (you can listen to the hydrophone feeds – live – on OrcaSound.net).

Other cetaceans in the Salish Sea

Humpback Whales were once common in the Salish Sea but, between 1905 and 1925, more than 5,500 were killed by commercial whalers in the region. By 1925, they were so scarce that whaling stations shut down operations and catcher boats moved on to Alaska and California.

But after being absent for nearly a century, Humpback Whales began to return to the Salish Sea in the 1990s. Researchers have recorded a steady increase in numbers since then: each year has record sightings and then it is topped the following year. It has been dubbed the 'Humpback comeback'. Nowadays, they are seen in every month of the year and nearly every day during the peak period from May–November. There are no official estimates, but it is possible that as many as 15–25 different Humpbacks are present on some days. The Strait of Juan de Fuca is a particular hotspot.

One of the first recognizable individuals to return was a female called 'Big Mama' (or, more officially, BCY0324). She was first photo-identified in 1997 and has returned every year since 2003. In fact, since 2003, she has come back with no fewer than six different calves (she returned with her sixth in 2016). Big Mama used to feed mainly southwest of Victoria, but seems to have

Minke Whales are often seen in the Salish Sea from late spring to fall.

expanded her range in recent years into the Strait of Georgia.

Minke Whales are most often seen from late spring to fall, with peak sightings in July and August. They are most frequent around the Gulf Islands, particularly in Boundary Pass and Haro Strait, but can also be seen in the Strait of Juan de Fuca and elsewhere; they like to forage off Hein Bank and Salmon Bank, at the bottom of Haro Strait/East Entrance to Juan de Fuca. In winter, they probably move to warmer waters farther south to breed and, while sightings have been recorded in the Salish Sea in all months of the year, there are relatively few for December–February. There are records of the same individuals returning year after year – one particular Minke Whale has been sighted in the Salish Sea over a period of more than 20 years. Interestingly, they have been seen playing with resident Killer Whales in Haro Strait on several occasions – suggesting that they can distinguish between the harmless fish-eating residents and the potentially dangerous mammal-eating transients (which occasionally hunt Minke Whales).

Gray Whales are much more sporadic. On their way north, while migrating between their breeding grounds in Baja California, Mexico, and their Arctic feeding grounds in the Bering, Chuckchi and Beaufort seas, a few individuals wander into the Salish Sea region. Some are seen, most years, in Boundary Bay, south of Vancouver, for example, especially early in the season. There is also a core group of about 10–15 Gray Whales that take a little detour into Puget Sound and around Whidbey and Camano Islands to forage there for a few months, typically from February until May or June. Sightings in other parts of the Salish Sea are sparse.

For much of the past century, Pacific White-sided Dolphins were rarely encountered in British Columbia's inside coastal passages, but that seems to be changing. Since the early 1980s they have been appearing with increasing regularity. Nowadays, they are seen increasingly often in the Salish Sea, typically in pods of 50–150 (sometimes more than 300), with particular hotspots including the southern Strait of Georgia and Howe Sound, near Vancouver. The increase in sightings in the past 10 years, in particular, has been nothing short of remarkable.

The only other species seen regularly in the Salish Sea are Dall's Porpoises and Harbor Porpoises. However, others do turn up from time to time: Fin Whales, for example, have been recorded but are extremely rare, with only 10 confirmed sightings since 1930 (intriguingly, four of which have been recent – in 2013, 2015 and 2016, when there were two). And a pod of Short-beaked Common Dolphins appeared in Juan de Fuca in June 2016.

Vancouver Island (West Coast)

Whale watching on the west coast of Vancouver Island focuses on two main species: Gray Whales and Humpback Whales.

The season officially begins in March with the Pacific Rim Whale Festival, which celebrated its 30th birthday in 2016. Hosted jointly by Tofino, Ucluelet and the Pacific Rim National Park Reserve, with nine days and nights of events it celebrates coastal traditions, the unique local environment and the spring return of the Gray Whale.

As well as boat trips from the villages of Tofino (mainly in and around Clayoquot Sound), Ucluelet and Bamfield (mainly in and around Barkley Sound), there is also some excellent land-based whale watching here. People from all over the world flock to the area, from late February to May, to watch the Grey Whales migrating north. Hotspots include the Amphitrite Point Lighthouse, in Ucluelet, and Kwistis Visitor Center and Radar Hill, in Pacific Rim National Park Reserve.

Migrating Gray Whales

Almost the entire world population of 18–21,000 Gray Whales migrates along the western shore of Vancouver Island, between the breeding grounds in Baja California, Mexico, and the primary feeding grounds in the Bering, Chukchi and Beaufort seas. For the majority of these whales, British Columbia waters serve solely as a migration corridor.

On their way south, they pass Vancouver Island between November and January (with a peak during the latter half of December). But they are difficult to observe at this time of year, because the weather is often quite poor, they swim relatively fast and they usually pass some distance from shore.

They are more readily seen on their way north. Northbound whales swim closer to shore (usually within 3 miles) and at a more

Overview

Main species: Gray Whale, Humpback Whale, Harbor Porpoise.

Occasional species: Minke Whale, Killer Whale, Pacific White-sided Dolphin, Dall's Porpoise.

Other wildlife highlights: Black Bear, Black-tailed Deer, Raccoon, Sea Otter, River Otter, Steller Sea Lion, California Sea Lion, Harbor Seal, Rhinoceros Auklet, Pigeon Guillemot, Marbled Murrelet, Harlequin Duck, Surf Scoter, White-winged Scoter, Common Loon, Pacific Loon, Wilson's Phalarope, Red-necked Phalarope.

Main locations: Tofino, Ucluelet, Bamfield.

Types of tours: 2.5- to 5.5-hour tours; land-based whale watching.

When to go: mainly March to mid-October (to early November in Tofino); some tours offered year-round.

Regulations and guidelines: Be Whale Wise Marine Wildlife Guidelines endorsed by Fisheries and Oceans Canada and BC Parks; See a Blow? Go Slow! Guidelines endorsed by Marine Education & Research Society; Marine Mammal Regulations (under the Fisheries Act) prohibit any form of harassment of cetaceans (including repeated attempts to pursue, disperse or herd whales); Straitwatch; Fisheries and Oceans Canada is currently preparing countrywide enforceable regulations for whale watching.

Wildlife species are listed systematically (not in order of abundance) and frequency of sightings varies with location and season.

moderate pace. They begin to appear off Vancouver Island in late February, increase to a peak in the last two weeks of March, then decline in numbers during April and May. The best time to see them is during March and April, when there are maximum numbers passing through and the weather is generally better.

Summer Resident Gray Whales

But a significant number of Gray Whales are also present during the summer (mainly May–October). These 'Summer Residents' were first noted by researchers in British Columbia waters in the early 1970s and, since then, some 200 have been identified between northern California and Southeast Alaska. They are known as the 'Pacific Coast Feeding Group'. Fewer than half this number are believed to occupy British Columbia waters in any given year. However, there are several key hotspots and one of these is along the southwestern shore of Vancouver Island, including in and around Clayoquot and Barkley Sounds.

Remarkably, the 'friendly' Gray Whales from the breeding lagoons in Baja are becoming increasingly common and are beginning to seek out interactions with boaters in other areas, including the west coast of Vancouver Island. While thrilling for the whale watchers there is concern that, away from the safety of the lagoons, it carries risks to the whales, which may be inadvertently injured by boat propellers or entangled in fishing gear.

Humpback Whales

The other highlight of whale watching here is the Humpback Whale, which is found throughout the inshore, outer coastal, continental shelf and offshore waters of British Columbia. At one time, it was the most abundant large whale along the British Columbia coast. But after years of commercial whaling – nearly 2,000 Humpbacks were killed by coastal whaling operations here between 1903 and 1966 – the species virtually disappeared from the region. The population is recovering, though, and Humpbacks are beginning to reappear in some of their former feeding grounds. They are seen off the west coast of Vancouver Island year-round, though mainly from April–November (with a peak in June–September).

A small number of Gray Whales spend every summer in British Columbia.

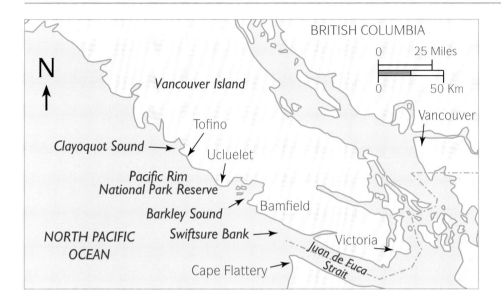

There have been fewer Humpbacks in Clayoquot and Barkley Sounds in the past few years. It appears that their favorite prey, Sardines, moved away – and the whales either followed them or shifted to different prey species in different locations. But they are still being found farther offshore and there is every chance that they will return to their old haunts in years to come.

The two sounds lie more or less on the border between regions where Humpback Whales migrate either to Hawai'i or Mexico and Central America. Most go to Hawai'i – the largest breeding ground in the North Pacific – but some do head south.

Killer Whales

Killer Whale sightings on the west coast are far less frequent than elsewhere around Vancouver Island. However, they are encountered year-round – with sightings on whale-watch trips averaging roughly every one to three weeks. Southern Residents frequently forage during summer on Swiftsure Bank, which is roughly between Tofino and the northern end of the Juan De Fuca Strait. Transient (Bigg's) Killer Whales are less easy to predict, and do not show the regular patterns of seasonal distribution seen with residents. But there seem to be more of them around during August and September, which is when Harbor Seal pups are most numerous and vulnerable to predation.

Other cetaceans on the west coast

Harbor Porpoises are seen on many trips, while there are less frequent encounters with Dall's Porpoises, Pacific White-sided Dolphins and Minke Whales (most encounters with Minkes are in July and August). There are also Blue Whales, Fin Whales, Baird's Beaked Whales, Cuvier's Beaked Whales, Risso's Dolphins and several other species off the west coast of Vancouver Island, but they are normally in deeper waters farther offshore and rarely seen during whale-watching trips.

CANADA: EAST COAST

Bay of Fundy

Sandwiched between Nova Scotia and New Brunswick, at the northern end of the Gulf of Maine, the Bay of Fundy is a huge semi-enclosed sea covering an area of some 6,200 square miles. Roughly 170 miles long and 30–50 miles, it is famed for having the highest tidal range in the world – the difference between high and low tide can be as much as 55 feet (the range is highest where the Bay narrows at the head).

These powerful tides help to produce vigorous upwellings that bring cold nutrient-rich water to the surface. This is the cause of the infamous Fundy Fog (warm air drawn into the Bay from the southwest passes over the cold water and condenses) but it's also what makes the Bay of Fundy so rich in wildlife.

The hotspot for whale watching is the mouth of the Bay, where it meets the Gulf of Maine and the Atlantic Ocean. This is an important summer feeding area and nursery ground for a variety of whales, dolphins and porpoises, as well as seals and seabirds, and

Overview

Main species: North Atlantic Right Whale, Humpback Whale, Fin Whale, Minke Whale, Harbor Porpoise.

Occasional species: Atlantic White-sided Dolphin.

Other wildlife highlights: Harbor Seal, Gray Seal, River Otter, Bald Eagle, Osprey, Peregrine, Atlantic Puffin, Razorbill, Black Guillemot, Common Loon, Sooty Shearwater, Great Shearwater, Manx Shearwater, Wilson's Storm Petrel, Leach's Storm Petrel, Northern Gannet, Northern Fulmar, Bonaparte's Gull, Red-necked Phalarope, Red Phalarope, Semi-palmated Sandpiper, Leatherback Turtle, Basking Shark, Thresher Shark, Porbeagle Shark, Atlantic Bluefin Tuna, Ocean Sunfish.

Main locations: New Brunswick: St Andrews By-the-Sea, Campobello Island (Welshpool, Wilsons Beach), Grand Manan Island (Seal Cove, North Head); Nova Scotia: Brier Island (Westport), Long Island (Freeport, Tiverton), East Ferry, Digby; United States: Eastport, Lubec (both opposite Campobello Island).

Types of tours: two- to five-hour tours; good whale-watching opportunities on several ferry routes; land-based whale watching.

When to go: mid-June to mid-October; North Atlantic Right Whales traditionally mid-August to late October (occasionally June until late November) with a peak in August–September; other baleen whales mainly summer and fall, but smaller numbers present year-round; Atlantic White-sided Dolphins mainly August–October; Harbor Porpoises year-round.

Regulations and guidelines: voluntary Code of Ethics for Bay of Fundy Marine Tour Operators; Marine Mammal Regulations (under the Fisheries Act) prohibit any form of harassment of cetaceans (including repeated attempts to pursue, disperse or herd whales); Fisheries and Oceans Canada is currently preparing countrywide enforceable regulations for whale watching.

Wildlife species are listed systematically (not in order of abundance) and frequency of sightings varies with location and season.

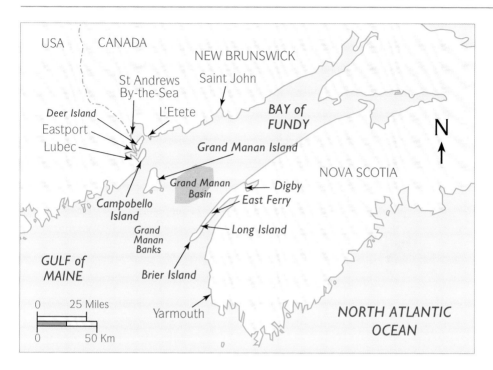

it is where most whale watching takes place. There are operators on both sides of the Bay, and on some islands, based in Canada and the United States; several operators assist with research by providing sightings data to scientists, for example, and contributing photographs to the North Atlantic Humpback Whale and North Atlantic Right Whale photo-identification catalogs.

North Atlantic Right Whales

The jewel in the Bay of Fundy crown is undoubtedly the endangered North Atlantic Right Whale, one of the rarest whales in the world. Females calve during the winter in the coastal waters of Florida and Georgia, then spend the summer and fall in cold, productive waters farther north: the Great South Channel, Cape Cod Bay, Roseway Basin, the Gulf of St Lawrence and, of

course, the Bay of Fundy. They enter the Bay to feed on copepods, and to socialize, but some two-thirds of the females also bring their several-month-old calves and use it as a nursery area (the location of a second nursery for the other one-third remains unknown); many of these adult females had first been brought to the Bay by their own mothers, when they were calves.

Right Whales are traditionally found mainly in the upper Grand Manan Basin, in waters 300–800ft deep, where the densest concentrations of copepods have been found. This is a seasonally important area for the species and monitoring surveys using photo-identification to distinguish individuals have been conducted annually since 1980 by New England Aquarium researchers, based in Boston, Massachusetts. In record years, up to two-thirds of the entire

The Bay of Fundy is the best place in the world to see North Atlantic Right Whales.

surviving population of about 525 North Atlantic Right Whales have been sighted in the Bay, mostly in this region; in normal years, some 100–150 are present. They traditionally arrive in mid-August (though there was an eight-year period when they arrived as early as June) and typically stay for a couple of months; however, how long each individual whale remains in the Bay is not well understood.

There has been tremendous variation in the number of Right Whales seen in the Bay over the past three and a half decades of research. In particular, far fewer individuals were observed between 2012 and 2015. Only five were seen during surveys in 2013 – the lowest count in 34 years. There were about 60 in 2014 (mostly during a three-week period) and only eight in 2015. Admittedly, other Right Whales were observed by whale watchers and researchers outside of these survey periods (and are not included in the figures) but numbers were undoubtedly very low.

Researchers believe that rising sea temperatures affecting phytoplankton blooms may be responsible, leading to a decline in copepods in the Bay and forcing the whales to change their migration patterns. It is unlikely that Right Whale numbers are declining – they just seemed to be spending their summers elsewhere. A greater number of sightings have been reported in the Gulf of St Lawrence (especially east of the Gaspé Peninsula), for example, but it is unclear where the majority are spending the summer.

However, at least 70 (and possibly as many as 100) turned up in late July, August and September 2016, and stayed for the rest of the season. Perhaps, should conditions improve as they seem to have done in 2016, they will reappear in large numbers in the Bay of Fundy in years to come.

There has been a phenomenal effort over the years to care for the whales. North Atlantic Right Whales are particularly vulnerable to vessel strikes, because they are large and slow, difficult to see (with no dorsal fin) and tend to feed near the surface; worse, they aggregate in major shipping lanes. The Bay of Fundy is one of many areas along the east coast of North America where vessel strikes have occurred: large tankers, cargo ships, bulk carriers and container ships use shipping lanes in and out of the Bay where fog, foul weather and large tides are common navigational hazards. Over the years, vessel strikes throughout the range of the Right Whale have accounted for a large number of mortalities and this at least partly explains why the population has not bounced back after centuries of whaling, despite protection.

But a variety of mitigation measures have successfully been introduced. In particular, in summer 2003, whales were officially given right of way by the Canadian Government and the mandatory shipping lanes into the port of Saint John were moved 4 miles to the east. This was a huge and unprecedented undertaking – not least because it required changes to seven nautical charts by the Canadian Hydrographic Service (at a cost of CA$30,000 per chart) and forced ships to take a slightly longer passage through the Bay. To their eternal credit, local fishermen agreed to the lane shift in order to protect the whales.

In US waters, there are several other mitigation measures. These include using human observers and acoustic detection buoys to direct vessels away from the whales, and seasonally regulating the speed of vessels approaching nine ports between Florida and Massachusetts.

Another hazard for Right Whales (and, of course, for other whales) throughout their range is entanglement in fixed or anchored fishing gear; a shocking 83 per cent of the North Atlantic Right Whale population carries scars from entanglement. The whales are powerful and can usually break free from fixed fishing gear, but they often take rope with them (wrapped around their bodies or tangled up in their baleen). In the lower Bay of Fundy, the volunteer Campobello Whale Rescue Team responds to entanglements and does its best to free the whales, but it is a difficult and dangerous task. There are all sorts of efforts to reduce the risk of entanglement, including educational programs and campaigns to reduce the amount of rope in fishing operations. But in recent years, with increasingly stronger ropes and more intensive fishing efforts throughout the whales' range, death from entanglement has become a bigger problem than vessel strikes. There are now fears that it could cause a population decline.

To acknowledge the importance of the Bay of Fundy to Right Whales, the Canadian Government has declared an area located roughly between Digby and Grand Manan as a North Atlantic Right Whale Critical Habitat, under the Canadian Species at Risk Act. This area traditionally supports the highest concentrations of copepods in the Bay, together with associated large numbers of whales. There is a similar area 30 miles south of Nova Scotia, in the Roseway Basin; since 2008, vessels have been asked to avoid this area altogether from June–December.

Other species

With or without Right Whales, whale watching in the Bay of Fundy is still outstanding. Several other species feed here on schooling fish in significant numbers: Humpback Whales, Fin Whales, Minke Whales and Harbor Porpoises, in particular. They tend to be most active, and feed more, on an incoming tide when their prey is most concentrated, but can be seen at any time of day and often very close to shore.

Humpback Whales are a common sight and, during a typical summer, there can be as many as 50 of them at any one time in the entrance to the Bay, including several mother–calf pairs; some 150–200 different individuals are identified annually. They frequently associate closely with the whale-watching boats and small numbers are sometimes present year-round.

Fin Whales are most often seen during the summer and fall (though they are also seen year-round), with mother–calf pairs occasionally present early in the season. In some areas, where food sources are good, pods of 10 or more Fin Whales can be seen feeding cooperatively; this is also when rare surface social activity can be observed, such as rolling on one side and exposing the tail flukes.

Minke Whales are present year-round, with larger numbers throughout the summer and fall. It is not unusual to have several Minkes feeding in the same area. This can be a good place to see them breaching: repeated breaches (sometimes up to 70 times in a row) are reported by whale-watch operators most weeks. There are occasional reports, too, of curious individuals approaching boats closely.

Atlantic White-sided Dolphins are around throughout the summer and fall, mainly (though not exclusively) over Grand Manan Banks, in the Grand Manan Basin and off Brier Island; on rare occasions, they have been sighted in the upper reaches of the Bay, and they sometimes strand. They tend to move farther offshore during winter. With a little luck, it is sometimes possible to see them riding the bow waves of some of the ferries.

Sei Whales were relatively common in the 1990s, but nowadays are seen only from time to time. Before 1970, White-beaked Dolphins were the dominant dolphin species in the Bay and, after a lull in sightings for many years, they now seem to be making a bit of a comeback. Pods of Killer Whales are occasionally seen, and a lone male Killer Whale, called Old Thom, has been visiting the Bay every year since 2008. Blue Whales, Sperm Whales (during the past decade), Long-finned Pilot Whales (some of which have been matched to individuals frequenting the waters off Cape Breton) and solitary Belugas have been recorded; there was even a lone Bowhead Whale, in 2012. Everything from Northern Bottlenose Whales and Pygmy Sperm Whales to Striped Dolphins and Bottlenose Dolphins have stranded (but they are considered wanderers outside their normal range).

Harbor Porpoises are common and are frequently seen in coastal waters - and far from the shore if fish schools are present. They are here year-round and sometimes venture well up into the Bay, chasing Gaspereau and other small schooling fish. Unfortunately, they have a habit of following Herring into fishing weirs and become trapped. They can swim, feed and breathe inside, but often do not swim out on their own, so experts from the renowned Harbor Porpoise Release Program (developed by the Grand Manan Whale & Seabird Research Station) have been helping local fishermen to remove the animals safely without affecting their Herring catch. The success rate is about 94 per cent and, since the program began in 1991, more than 750 Harbor Porpoises have been released from Herring weirs around Grand Manan Island. The fishermen have received formal training from the Release Program staff and, nowadays, are able to release the Harbor Porpoises themselves. The problem is not as serious as it once was; since there are fewer Herring close to shore, the number of weirs has dropped by about 80 per cent. Minke Whales also sometimes swim into the weirs and, on rare occasions, Humpbacks, North Atlantic Right Whales and even two Fin Whales have been trapped. They can usually be released unharmed, if they do not find or force their own way out.

Ferries

A number of different ferries operate in the Bay of Fundy and these offer some excellent opportunities for whale watching. The crossing from Blacks Harbor to Grand Manan is particularly good – it takes about 1.5 hours and passes through a key feeding area for marine mammals and seabirds;

Atlantic White-sided Dolphins sometimes ride the bow waves of Fundy's ferries.

there are usually more sightings later in the season. The best views are from the top deck and it's possible to see Humpback, Fin and Minke Whales as well as Atlantic White-sided Dolphins, Harbor Porpoises and, very occasionally, North Atlantic Right Whales. Other good crossings include: between Saint John and Digby; to Deer Island from L'Etete; and the seasonal (mid-June to mid-September) Campobello–Deer Island–Eastport and Grand Manan–White Head ferries; even the short ferry trip between Long Island and Brier Island can encounter whales en route. The fast ferry from Yarmouth to Portland, Maine, which runs from June–September, also travels through good whale-watching territory.

Land-based Whale Watching

There is some good land-based whale watching here, too. On Grand Manan Island, the best locations include: Long Eddy Point (or the Whistle), Southwest Head, White Head Island (Gull Cove) and Swallow Tail (perched on the cliff near the ferry terminal at North Head). Some of these places have steep cliffs and, if you

are lucky, it is sometimes possible to look straight down on a whale and see it in its entirety. The best viewing times tend to be early in the morning or late in the evening, or on specific tide phases when the prey is being concentrated. However, it can also be worth going to the top of the hill at Swallow Tail, after sunset, to see if you can hear the Herring boiling – an extraordinary sound that wakes people up in the nearby campground – and you may hear the Harbor Porpoises and Minke Whales chasing them.

East Quoddy Head Lighthouse, in the far north of Campobello Island, can also be very good; it is possible to walk across to the lighthouse at low tide, or try sitting on the bench on top of the cliff opposite. Blacks Harbor's Pea Point Lighthouse, where the ferry departs for Grand Manan, can be a good spot to watch from before getting on the ferry. Digby Neck, southwestern Nova Scotia, is a frequent summer and fall feeding ground for Humpback, Fin and Minke whales. Other possible lookouts include Northern Light, at the northern tip of Brier Island (about a mile north of Westport).

The Gully

Roughly 125 miles southeast of the Atlantic coast of Nova Scotia, lies The Gully: the largest submarine canyon in eastern North America. Sitting right on the edge of the Scotian Shelf, this steep-sided chasm is astoundingly rich in nutrients and hosts a spectacular diversity of marine life. Indeed, as an area of such great ecological

Overview

Main species: Northern Bottlenose Whale, Long-finned Pilot Whale, Short-beaked Common Dolphin, Atlantic White-sided Dolphin.

Occasional species: Blue Whale, Fin Whale, Humpback Whale, Sperm Whale, Sowerby's Beaked Whale, Striped Dolphin.

Other wildlife highlights: Gray Seal, Harbor Seal, Northern Fulmar, Atlantic Puffin, Roseate Tern, Great Shearwater, Sooty Shearwater, Wilson's Storm Petrel, Leach's Storm Petrel; Ipswich Sparrow on Sable Island.

Main locations: Sable Island best starting point.

Types of tours: no dedicated whale-watching tours, but sometimes included in multi-day expedition cruises.

When to go: mid-June–August (best for weather and greater variety of species).

Regulations and guidelines: Marine Mammal Regulations (under the Fisheries Act) prohibit any form of harassment of cetaceans (including repeated attempts to pursue, disperse or herd whales); Fisheries and Oceans Canada is currently preparing countrywide enforceable regulations for whale watching.

Wildlife species are listed systematically (not in order of abundance) and frequency of sightings varies with location and season.

importance, in May 2004 it became Atlantic Canada's first marine protected area (protecting it from oil and gas development and restricting commercial fishing to its least vulnerable zones).

Plunging down to more than 1.6 miles at the mouth, its deepest point, and measuring some 40 miles long and 9 miles wide, The Gully contains large concentrations of plankton, fish and squid. Best of all, it is considered one of the most important habitats for cetaceans on the east coast of Canada. Since studies began in 1986, 20 different species have been documented within the canyon and it is clearly a critically important site for several of these. One is Sowerby's Beaked Whale – known from only a handful of sightings and strandings elsewhere in its range across the northern North Atlantic – which is being observed more and more frequently in The Gully and nearby canyons. Other species, such as North Atlantic Right Whale, Sei Whale, Minke Whale, Killer Whale, Cuvier's Beaked Whale, Risso's Dolphin, White-beaked Dolphin and Bottlenose Dolphin are known to occur at least from time to time. And a further two species, Blainville's Beaked Whale and Fraser's Dolphin, have been tentatively identified.

But the prize residents of The Gully are Northern Bottlenose Whales. This is probably the best place on the planet to observe this rarely seen species and, indeed, it is one of the few places where beaked whales of any kind can be observed routinely. A sub-population – including mothers and calves, adult males and juveniles – is resident year-round and can be seen relatively easily. Researchers have found their natural behavior a little difficult to study simply because they are so curious about boats: they are readily attracted to

The best place in the world to see Northern Bottlenose Whales is The Gully.

small, stationary vessels, and sometimes even approach larger vessels.

There are approximately 140 individuals in and around The Gully altogether (precise estimates from the most recent count, in 2010–11, range from 129–156). The sub-population is likely still recovering from whaling in the 1960s, when about 60 animals were killed.

At any one time, more than half these Northern Bottlenose Whales are typically in a 5 miles by 12 miles core area at the entrance to The Gully, where they are believed to feed principally on squid. There are smaller numbers elsewhere in the canyon, and in nearby Shortland and Haldimand canyons (the three large canyons are arranged along the shelf edge at intervals of approximately 30 miles). They are rarely seen outside these three hotspots, or in water less than 1,640ft deep; in The Gully itself, they routinely dive to the sea floor over 4,600ft below the surface.

Sowerby's Beaked Whales are being seen more often in The Gully and nearby canyons.

Unfortunately, The Gully is a difficult place to visit. The nearest land of any kind is Sable Island, about 25 miles to the west. This wild and windswept island, just 26 miles long and 0.8 miles across at its widest point, is one of Canada's most distant offshore islands. It is accessible by air from Halifax (though this involves chartering a small seven-seater plane and landing on a beach) or by sea (for which you'll probably need your own boat). However, while there are currently no organized whale-watching tours, some expedition cruises do include a visit to The Gully in itineraries primarily exploring Sable.

Newfoundland

The craggy isle of Newfoundland, in the province of Newfoundland and Labrador, is the easternmost region in Canada. Nearly the size of England, but with less than one-hundredth of the human population, it is renowned for its dramatic and convoluted coastline, thick boreal forests, ancient rock formations and unspoilt wilderness.

The southeastern tip of Newfoundland is where the cold Labrador Current from the Canadian High Arctic and Greenland meets the warm Gulf Stream from the south. The Labrador Current is rich in nutrients and carries a huge biomass of plankton, while mixing of these two titanic forces kick-starts a great profusion of marine life.

It is, indeed, the site of the legendary Grand Banks. These relatively shallow underwater plateaus – ranging in depth from 80–330ft – underlie one of the most productive ecosystems on the planet. The once-great quantities of Cod in this natural fish-producing factory were the draw for most early European excursions to North America. Famously, of course, decades of overfishing caused a catastrophic population collapse that reduced the Cod stock to a minuscule fraction of its former self.

Overview

Main species: Humpback Whale, Fin Whale, Minke Whale, White-beaked Dolphin, Atlantic White-sided Dolphin, Harbor Porpoise.

Occasional species: Blue Whale, Sei Whale, Sperm Whale, Killer Whale, Long-finned Pilot Whale, Beluga, Short-beaked Common Dolphin.

Other wildlife highlights: Polar Bear (sporadic spring sightings northeast coast), Black Bear, Caribou, Moose, Harp Seal, Hooded Seal, Gray Seal, Harbor Seal, Bald Eagle, Atlantic Puffin, Common Murre, Thick-billed Murre, Razorbill, Northern Gannet, Black-legged Kittiwake, Ivory Gull, Arctic Tern, Great Shearwater, Sooty Shearwater, Manx Shearwater, Leach's Storm Petrel, Leatherback Turtle, Basking Shark, Ocean Sunfish, Atlantic Bluefin Tuna.

Main locations: boat trips: St John's, Holyrood, New Bonaventure, Trinity, Twillingate, Lewisporte, Roddickton, Williamsport, St Anthony, Rocky Harbor, Norris Point, Woody Point, Cox's Cove, Cape Broyle, Mobile, Witless Bay, Bay Bulls, Petty Harbor; land-based whale watching: Cape Spear, Signal Hill and the North Head Trail, East Coast Trail, Holyrood Arm, Bay de Verde, Trinity, Cape Bonavista, Salvage, Twillingate's Long Point Lighthouse, White Bay, St Anthony, Cape Norman to Lobster Cove Head Lighthouse, Cape St George, Cape St Mary's, St Vincent's Beach, Cape Race, Witless Bay and others.

Types of tours: one-hour to full-day tours; multi-day expedition cruises; kayaking; wilderness lodges; excellent opportunities for land-based whale watching.

When to go: mid-May to end of September (peak season mid-June–August).

Regulations and guidelines: local code of conduct, but no official regulations; Marine Mammal Regulations (under the Fisheries Act) prohibit any form of harassment of cetaceans (including repeated attempts to pursue, disperse or herd whales); Fisheries and Oceans Canada is currently preparing countrywide enforceable regulations for whale watching.

Wildlife species are listed systematically (not in order of abundance) and frequency of sightings varies with location and season.

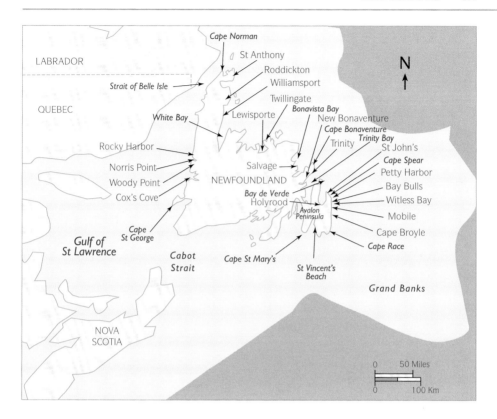

But this is still a phenomenally productive ecosystem and 'The Rock', as Newfoundland is affectionately known, is a veritable magnet for whales, dolphins and porpoises. Some 22 species have been spotted over the years and, while some of these are extremely rare, others occur in significant numbers.

Many of them come to Newfoundland not for Cod, but for a small silvery fish called Capelin (traditionally spelt 'Caplin' in Newfoundland). This is the vital link in the Northwest Atlantic food chain between plankton and larger predators – it was what attracted Cod to the region in the first place – and is a major source of food for everything from larger fish and seabirds to seals and whales.

Capelin spend much of their lives offshore, moving inshore only to breed. Spawning in Newfoundland takes place mainly during June and July, and the fish literally throw themselves onto the seashore – a behavior known locally as the 'Capelin Scull' – to deposit their spawn in beach gravel. Evenings will find local families down on the beaches collecting Capelin literally by the bucket-load. The scull attracts a host of other wildlife, too, and a quite extraordinary whale-watching experience takes place at one of these spawning grounds: near St Vincent's Beach in St Mary's Bay, on the southern shore of the Avalon Peninsula. Here, the cobblestone beach drops abruptly into deep water and, during the peak period (usually mid-June to mid-July) Humpback Whales sometimes feed within a few yards of the shore. You can sit and watch them rushing headlong toward the beach, then veering away at the last second – it is quite a spectacle.

Whale watching is a long-established industry in Newfoundland. There are about 20 operators altogether, and some have been taking people out to see whales for several decades. The majority are clustered around the Avalon Peninsula, a vaguely H-shaped landmass in the southeastern corner (it is even possible to join trips from downtown St John's, the province's capital) and along the north coast, but others are dotted around the island. They offer a wide variety of tours on everything from Zodiacs to large catamarans.

Humpback Whales

Newfoundland is a primary feeding ground for Humpback Whales and they are the focus of most whale-watching trips. They migrate here from their Caribbean breeding grounds to gorge themselves on Capelin and, to a lesser degree, other small schooling fish. They are typically present from April–October (with a peak from May–September) but a small number remain on the feeding grounds year-round and do not make the annual migration south. They first began appearing close to shore in the late 1970s, when the Capelin were seriously depleted on the Grand Banks farther offshore, and their distribution around the island is still strongly correlated with the distribution of this key prey species.

Entanglement of Humpbacks and other large whales in commercial fisheries has been a consistent problem around Newfoundland for decades. The Whale Release and Strandings Program, launched in 1979, was designed to release captured animals and reduce costs to fishermen; it is currently being run by the independent Whale Release and Strandings Group. Since then, nearly 1,300 large whale entanglements have been recorded in Newfoundland and Labrador: the vast majority were Humpback Whales, but there were also a significant number of Minke Whales, and smaller numbers of other species. The entanglement problem has declined significantly in recent years, with changes in the fishing industry, though it has also shifted to more offshore waters – which are more difficult to monitor and tackle.

Fin Whales and Minke Whales

Fin Whales are fairly common around Newfoundland during summer and, while there is debate about what they are eating, incidental observations suggest that they are feeding on Capelin, too. They do not come close to shore every year, but in good years are most commonly seen in the southeast, with particular hotspots including Witless Bay, Trinity Bay and Bonavista Bay. Minke Whales are present year-round, though they are most common from spring to early fall, when they are seen on many whale-watching trips.

Killer Whales

Killer Whales are seen mainly during the spring and summer (with a peak from June–September). However, some are known to remain year-round and it is possible that certain pods venturing into the Canadian High Arctic, during summer, spend their winters off the Atlantic coast of Newfoundland. Most sightings are close to the shore, though they have been observed far offshore in depths of over 10,000ft. Researchers believe that about 500 Killer Whales, including lots of calves, spend the

Humpback Whales are the focus of most whale watching trips in Newfoundland.

summer in Newfoundland and Labrador (particularly around Newfoundland), and numbers are rising. There are more than 200 recognizable individuals in the Newfoundland photo-identification catalog. They are not seen regularly on whale-watching trips, though there are hotspots (such as the Strait of Belle Isle, separating Labrador from Newfoundland) and there have been more sightings in recent years. Also, they seem to be particularly curious in Newfoundland, often approaching whale-watching boats and even offering to share prey.

It is unclear which ecotypes occur here. Predation on fish and seabirds as well as marine mammals has been recorded – even by the same animals. One particular pod was observed fishing for Cod and Salmon, moved on to eat some auks, and then harassed a few Humpback Whales (Newfoundland's Humpbacks appear to be some of the most Killer Whale-scarred on Earth, with over 20 per cent along the east coast showing obvious scarring from Killer Whale attacks). Dolphins are a favorite prey item, with Minke Whales a close second. Yet there is also a lone male, dubbed Old Thom, who frequently hangs out with dolphins. And, for the first time in living memory, Killer Whales are hunting Harp Seals along the edge of the pack ice. There may be specialist pods here – the population dynamics of at least some seem to be similar to those of transients in the North Pacific – but there are generalists, too.

Long-finned Pilot Whales

Anywhere around Newfoundland can be good for Long-finned Pilot Whales, though the southeast is where most sightings occur. They can be seen inshore, as early as May and as late as October, wherever squid, their primary food, is plentiful. In winter, they are believed to range from the Grand Banks as far south as North Carolina. They used to be hunted here, using the same 'drive' technique (that involves forcing groups ashore to be killed in the shallows) that is still being used in the Faroe Islands. During 1947–71, this drive fishery is estimated to have taken 54,000 animals and to have reduced the local population substantially. But Canada's 1972 ban on commercial whaling put an end to the barbaric practice.

Sperm Whales

Some 424 Sperm Whales were hunted in Newfoundland and Labrador between

1904–72. They are seen inshore occasionally during summer and fall, particularly in deep-water bays such as Trinity and Placentia, and certain individuals are known to stick around in these areas for months at a time; they occasionally overwinter here, too. However, their main concentration is farther offshore, over the Grand Banks. Only males – indeed, mostly young males – are found in Newfoundland; the females remain in lower latitudes year-round.

Dolphins and porpoises

White-beaked Dolphins, Atlantic White-sided Dolphins and Harbor Porpoises are encountered regularly, too, and all are believed to be present year-round. Harbor Porpoise numbers seem to be increasing, thanks to the closure of the inshore Cod fishery and the removal of thousands of fishing nets, and they are seen on at least half of the whale-watching trips. Locals have their own names for some of these more common species: Harbor Porpoises are called 'Puffing Pigs', for the grunting sound they make when they blow; White-Beaked Dolphins are referred to as 'Squidhounds'; and Atlantic White-sided Dolphins are known as 'Jumpers'. Short-beaked Common Dolphins are also being seen – more frequently now than a few years ago – and pods of several hundred are encountered from time to time.

Other species

A number of other species turn up occasionally. Some 1,500 Blue Whales were taken in Newfoundland and Labrador between 1898 and 1915. These days, they are mainly seen during the spring, summer and fall in the Strait of Belle, and during the winter off the south and southwest coasts, though they have been recorded at all times of the year. There also appears to

be a concentration of Blue Whales in the offshore Orphan Basin area, which is about 250 miles north-east of St John's. Sei Whales are sporadic visitors and tend to be more pelagic, but they are seen on whale-watching trips occasionally. There have also been about a dozen sightings of endangered North Atlantic Right Whales since 1990. Other rare sightings have included Bowhead Whale, Sowerby's Beaked Whale and Narwhal.

On 25 April 2009, the citizens of St Anthony, on the north coast, woke up to a never-before-seen spectacle: more than 1,000 Belugas had suddenly appeared right on their doorstep. Occasionally, young Belugas become separated from their pods and end up in Newfoundland, where they are often very social and will associate closely with people and boats (which can be a problem – they are sometimes injured by propellers). There are nearly always one or two youngsters hanging around various coastal communities, including sometimes even in St John's.

Land-based whale watching

Land-based whale watching is particularly popular and productive in Newfoundland. The island rises above the continental shelf like a giant viewing station and its sheer cliffs offer some fantastic sweeping views ideal for spotting cetaceans. Any time during the summer, you can plonk yourself down on a rock with a view and have a good chance of seeing whales pretty much anywhere around the island. The main hotspots are in the northwest and southeast, but there are good observation points on the other coasts, too. Try asking local fishermen where the Capelin and squid are – these are likely to be the best places to look.

There are many good sites, but here are a few of the best. On the Avalon Peninsula:

Whale watching from the shore near Trinity, in Newfoundland.

try walking from downtown St John's to the North Head Trail, which follows the rocky northern edge of the harbor and offers dramatic sweeping views of the rugged coastline and a good chance of cetacean sightings; Cape St Mary's is a good place to see Humpback Whales, Minke Whales and sometimes Long-finned Pilot Whales and Atlantic White-sided Dolphins; Holyrood Arm, the southernmost inlet of Conception Bay, also sometimes attracts Long-finned Pilot Whales. And do not forget St Vincent's Beach (mentioned above). On the northern coast Humpbacks sometimes feed close to the shore near St Anthony, where it is possible to watch them from the clifftop as they hunt for spawning fish among the seaweeds.

Many of these cetaceans can also be seen from the Marine Atlantic Ferries, operating between Nova Scotia and Newfoundland. There is a year-round, daily service between North Sidney, Nova Scotia, and Port aux Basques, in southwestern Newfoundland, and a June–September service between North Sidney and Argentia, on the Avalon Peninsula. The short ferry journey between St Barbe on Newfoundland's northwest coast and Blanc Sablon on the Quebec–Labrador border crosses the Strait of Belle

Isle, which can also be good for whale watching. And there are also some good local ferries, particularly those travelling between remote communities along the southern coast.

Newfoundland's coastline is teeming with seabird colonies. All the major ones are on islands (though the most iconic is a particularly spectacular one on Cape St Mary's, on the southwestern tip of the Avalon Peninsula) and they contain literally millions of birds of about a dozen different species. The most numerous resident breeder is the Leach's Storm Petrel, with more than 3 million pairs (Baccalieu is the largest Leach's Storm Petrel colony in the world), while undoubtedly the most popular is the Atlantic Puffin – hundreds of thousands of pairs nest here every year. There are often lots of icebergs, too, adding a dramatic additional feature to the seascape, mainly from mid-May to early June. They take a couple of years to float down so-called 'Iceberg Alley' from the Canadian Arctic and Greenland, to make their last stand in the waters around Newfoundland before melting away. It was, of course, one of these icebergs that sank the *Titanic* about 370 miles southeast of Newfoundland, on 14 April 1912.

St Lawrence River & Gulf of St Lawrence

Québec has the largest whale-watching industry in Canada, and one of the largest whale-watching industries in the world. The main focus is on the St Lawrence River Estuary and the Gulf of St Lawrence – two vast waterways in the northeastern corner of the country – where a number of cetacean species occur in considerable numbers, and often quite close to the shore.

The St Lawrence River is Canada's Amazon, a behemoth of a river. Some 744 miles long, it flows from Lake Ontario, past Montréal and Québec City, all the way to the Gulf of St Lawrence. It is the outflow

Overview

Main species: Blue Whale, Fin Whale, Minke Whale, Humpback Whale, Beluga, Long-finned Pilot Whale, Atlantic White-sided Dolphin, White-beaked Dolphin, Harbor Porpoise.

Occasional species: North Atlantic Right Whale, Sei Whale, Sperm Whale.

Other wildlife highlights: Black Bear, Wolf, Coyote, Moose, White-tailed Deer, Gray Seal, Harbor Seal, Bald Eagle, Osprey, Common Tern, Arctic Tern, Black-legged Kittiwake, Atlantic Puffin, Common Murre, Thick-billed Murre, Razorbill, Black Guillemot, Northern Gannet, Manx Shearwater, Great Shearwater, Double-crested Cormorant, Greater Snow Goose, Common Eider, American Black Duck, Common Loon, Red-throated Loon, Basking Shark.

Main locations: St Lawrence River Estuary (boat trips): Saint-Siméon, Baie-Sainte-Catherine, Tadoussac, Grandes-Bergeronnes, Les Escoumins, Portneuf-sur-Mer, Baie-Comeau, Pointe-des-Monts, Berthier-sur-Mer, Trois-Pistoles, Rivière-Du-Loupe, Trois-Rivières; bus-boat packages from Québec City; St Lawrence River Estuary (land-based): Whale Route (from Tadoussac to Natashquan), Point-Noire, Godbout, Cap de Bon-Désir, Sault-au-Mouton, Pointe-des-Monts, Parc National du Bic, Baie Sainte-Marguerite; Gulf of St Lawrence (boat trips): Gaspé, Percé, Sept-Îles, Longue-Pointe-de-Mingan, Havre-Saint-Pierre, Cape Breton Island (Chéticamp, Pleasant Bay, Bay St Lawrence, Neil's Harbor); Gulf of St Lawrence (land-based): Mingan Archipelago, Forillon National Park, Cap Gaspé, Percé, Île Bonaventure, Cape Breton Island (Cabot Trail).

Types of tours: two-hour to full-day boat trips; opportunities to participate in research projects; multi-day expedition cruises; kayaking; excellent land-based whale watching.

When to go: May–October (peak season late June to late September); Blue Whales mainly August–December; Belugas year-round.

Regulations and guidelines: St Lawrence River Belugas must not be sought for whale watching from a boat; Marine Activities in the Saguenay-St Lawrence Marine Park Regulations; Eco-Whale Alliance's Guide for Eco-Responsible Practices for Captains/Naturalists; Guidelines for Best Practices for Watching Marine Mammals in Québec; Marine Mammal Regulations (under the Fisheries Act) prohibit any form of harassment of cetaceans (including repeated attempts to pursue, disperse or herd whales); Fisheries and Oceans Canada is currently preparing countrywide enforceable regulations for whale watching.

Wildlife species are listed systematically (not in order of abundance) and frequency of sightings varies with location and season.

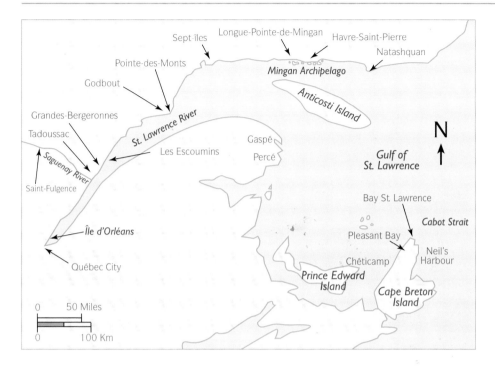

for the entire Great Lakes system. The river first encounters saltwater near Île d'Orléans, beyond Québec City, and is predominantly oceanic by the time it passes Tadoussac. It seems an unlikely place for whales – so far from the open sea – yet here they congregate throughout the spring, summer and fall. There are Fin Whales, Minke Whales and Belugas at least 180 miles upstream from the mouth of the river, and Blue Whales, Humpback Whales and other species farther downstream and in the gulf.

Pointe-des-Monts, about 6 miles from the village of Baie-Trinité, marks the end of the St Lawrence River Estuary and the start of the Gulf of St Lawrence; from here the south shore, roughly 21 miles away, appears merely as a distant blue line. The gulf itself is a semi-enclosed sea, covering an area of about 60,000 square miles and

fringing the shores of half the provinces in Canada: Québec, New Brunswick, Nova Scotia, Newfoundland and Labrador, and Prince Edward Island. It is connected to the Atlantic Ocean by Cabot Strait, in the southeast, and the Strait of Belle-Isle, in the north.

Most whale watching here takes place along the wilder and more rugged north shore of the estuary. But there are some operators and lookouts along the relatively built-up south shore and in the gulf. Indeed, the gulf is the best place to see Atlantic White-sided Dolphins and White-beaked Dolphins, as well as Long-finned Pilot Whales and occasional visitors such as North Atlantic Right Whales. Many operators carry hydrophones to listen to the whales, adding another dimension to the experience.

Whale watching in the estuary is unlike anywhere else in the world. When the ice thaws in the St Lawrence River every spring, more than half a dozen species frequent the region until fall. They are here largely because of the river bottom or, more precisely, the Laurentian Channel. This is a submarine trench, running 870 miles from the edge of the continental shelf south of Newfoundland, through Cabot Strait, right across the middle of the Gulf of St Lawrence, and all the way upstream in the St Lawrence River as far as Tadoussac and the Saguenay River. Some 1,800ft deep where it begins on the Scotia Shelf, it shallows to about 1,000ft at the estuary's mouth, and then rises abruptly to a depth of only 80–100ft roughly between Grandes-Bergeronnes and Tadoussac (it also narrows from 34 miles wide to about 6 miles). A complicated interaction of topography, tides, currents and temperature gradients drives nutrient-rich waters to the surface at the head of the Laurentian Channel, near Tadoussac, and effectively traps vast numbers of krill, copepods and fish as the enriched waters flow downstream. The result is a smorgasbord of whale food.

Tadoussac, and around the mouth of the Saguenay River, is where much of the commercial whale watching takes place: the core area is the 480-square-mile Saguenay-St Lawrence Marine Park, created in 1998 and administered jointly by Parks Canada and Parks Québec. Tadoussac was once a sleepy summer tourist town, but whale watching began here in the 1970s, and now it is eastern Canada's bustling main whale-watch center.

Another well-known hotspot is the Mingan Island Archipelago National Park Reserve, which encompasses about 40 islands and 800 islets along the north shore of the gulf. The village of Longue-Pointe-de-Mingan is home to the Mingan Island Cetacean Study Field Station, which has been studying Blue Whales and other large whales since 1979. This group pioneered photo-identification of Blue Whales and visitors are able to watch, and sometimes assist with, the research. It may involve bouncing around in rubber inflatables while dressed in Mustang survival suits (provided by the research team), but it affords a rare chance to see how world-renowned cetacean research is carried out.

Beluga Whales

The most famous inhabitants of the St Lawrence are the Beluga Whales. They are the only cetaceans living in the estuary year-round (although it is not impossible to see occasional large spouts of Blue Whales in ice-free areas, or get a fleeting glimpse of a Harbour Porpoise, even in the coldest months).

The annual range of the Belugas extends all the way from the gulf to the estuary, and into the Saguenay River, but the main concentrations vary seasonally. In spring, they can be found from the Gaspé Peninsula far upstream to Île aux Coudres. Their summer range extends from Île du Bic upstream to Île aux Coudres and the Battures aux Loups Marins (as recently as the 1940s, it was as far upstream as Québec City); and, in the Saguenay River, it extends about 60 miles upstream as far as Saint-Fulgence. At this time of year, the whales prefer coastal waters with strong currents, especially around river mouths, although cow–calf pairs tend to prefer protected bays. In winter, the population moves into the outer reaches of the estuary (between Forestville, or sometimes Les Escoumins, and Pointe des Monts) and into the northwestern sector of the gulf, where ice cover is less extensive.

Beluga Whales are the most famous inhabitants of the St Lawrence River Estuary.

Large herds, containing as many as 100 individuals, are often seen in spring and fall, and such gatherings may be related to these migratory movements.

This is the southernmost population of Belugas in the world. It is geographically isolated from other populations in the eastern Arctic – the nearest major summering ground is in Hudson Strait – though, of course, it is possible that individuals occasionally travel that far.

It is also one of the most threatened populations. In the mid-1880s, there were believed to be between 7,800 and 10,100 Belugas in the St Lawrence River Estuary. But the population declined because of hunting and, by the time it was stopped in 1979, there were only about 1,000 survivors. The current population is 1,150, but since the 1970s they have faced many new threats, including reduction in prey availability, human disturbance, habitat degradation and pollution.

In particular, they live downstream of a densely populated and highly industrialized corner of North America, and along a major marine highway. So, not surprisingly, the St Lawrence contains a wide range of pollutants. In the 1970s,

scientists revealed that the river's Belugas were carrying extremely high levels of toxic chemicals in their bodies – including PCBs, DDT, Mirex, mercury and lead. For some reason, probably to do with diet, these were affecting Belugas more than other cetaceans. They were so badly contaminated that, when some individuals died and washed ashore, their carcasses had to be classified as 'toxic waste'. The result of this contamination is scary: there is strong evidence that the Belugas' immune systems have been undermined, and alarmingly high rates of infections and cancers have been observed.

In the years since, huge efforts have been made to clean up the river, though contaminant concentrations in Beluga tissues are not decreasing quickly. The good news is that the Recovery Strategy for the Beluga Whale St Lawrence River Estuary Population believes there is hope, and still aims to increase the population to 7,070 individuals by the 2050s.

One thing whale watchers can do to help is to limit disturbance, especially since there are thousands of boats in the estuary between June–September, during the Beluga calving season. Local whale-watch operators have to abide by very strict regulations and are not allowed to target Belugas for observation, or even drift toward them. Indeed, if Belugas approach a whale-watching vessel, the captain must slowly move away until the animals are at a distance of at least 1,300ft.

So be prepared to see them only at some distance on boat trips. In fact, the best way to see the Belugas is from the shore, and there are many good lookouts on both coasts of the estuary. They sometimes congregate at remote Baie Sainte-Marguerite, about 25 miles up the Saguenay River from Tadoussac, for example, where there is a visitor center and a 2-mile nature trail that winds along the bay.

Blue Whales

Blue Whales can be seen in the St Lawrence Estuary, and in the northwestern sector of the Gulf of St Lawrence, from April–January (and sporadically in mid-winter). Abundance tends to increase throughout the summer, peaking in late August and early September. The area is a critically important feeding ground for this endangered species, which can often be seen very close to the shore.

The seasonal distribution of the whales varies from month to month, and from year to year. But the largest concentrations are usually in the waters off Sept-Îles and along the north shore of the lower estuary from Pointe-des-Monts to Grandes-Bergeronnes (where researchers have sighted up to 12 per square mile). Another hotspot is the eastern tip of the Gaspé Peninsula (between Cloridorme and Percé): they seem to pass by here on their way to the estuary, with sightings starting as early as April and peaking in June and July. The area between the Mingan Archipelago and Anticosti Island (especially along the northern shore of the Jacques-Cartier Passage) was another favorite feeding ground, but was abandoned in 1992–93, and has rarely been used since.

The St Lawrence Blue Whales are well studied and the local researchers' photo-identification catalog now contains over 495 individuals. No more than a third of these are sighted in any given year: some return to their feeding grounds annually, others more sporadically. On average, each individual Blue Whale is in the area for just 22 days, suggesting that they are highly mobile.

Other cetaceans

Minke Whales are usually the first baleen whales to arrive in the area once the ice has cleared: they appear in early spring, often by mid-March, and stay until December (with a peak from early July to early September). Where they go in mid-winter is still a mystery.

They occur in both the estuary and the gulf and can often be seen very close to the shore. They are seen daily in the estuary – on one day in 2006 researchers counted no fewer than 74 different individuals. A particular hotspot is along the north shore between Tadoussac and Grandes-Bergeronnes, and some venture as high as 12 miles up the Saguenay River. A photo-identification project operating since 1978 has so far catalogued over 300 individuals and shows that the same whales are appearing year after year. The vast majority appear to be females – there are about six females to every male – but very few mother–calf pairs have been observed, suggesting that the calves have been weaned before the females arrive in this area.

Fin Whales are also seen regularly on whale-watching trips. Researchers estimate a population of about 50 in the estuary, plus more in the gulf, though there seems to be a downward trend. The head of the Laurentian Channel, between Tadoussac and Grandes-Bergeronnes, is a hotspot. Their winter distribution is poorly known, but they are believed to over-winter off Nova Scotia, just outside the pack ice.

Humpback Whales come here from their breeding grounds in the West Indies. They are a familiar sight and their numbers have noticeably increased since the late 1990s. They also seem to be feeding in the estuary more often and for longer than they used to. More than 870 individuals have been observed in the estuary and the gulf and many of them are well known to researchers, returning year after year, often with their calves.

North Atlantic Right Whales are regular, albeit sporadic, visitors to the gulf (they are rarer in the estuary). They have been seen more often since the mid-1990s – with about 1–10 individuals spotted in a typical year – and seem to have adopted the region since 2012 (when they largely abandoned their traditional feeding grounds in the Bay of Fundy). Indeed, in 2016, there was an explosion in numbers, with more than 50 individuals recorded. Most sightings are from July–September, in shallow coastal waters along the Gaspé Peninsula. Percé can be a good vantage point. Other hotspots include Chaleur Bay, to the south of Percé, the Magdalen Islands and the gulf's lower north shore.

Long-finned Pilot Whales are summer residents in the gulf, especially off the Gaspé Peninsula and Cape Breton Island (and along the southeast coast of Newfoundland). Large pods are commonly seen on trips around Cape Breton – indeed, that is what these trips tend to focus on – and they often associate very closely with the boats.

Some 1,500 different individuals have been identified off the coast of Cape Breton since 1998. They rarely enter the estuary (though there was a mass stranding in 1920).

Two species of dolphin are encountered regularly in the gulf. Throughout summer, the coast of the lower north shore is a particularly good place to look; in spring and fall, they are regularly observed along the Gaspé Peninsula. Sightings in the estuary are rare and short-lived. The commonest, with an estimated population of 12,000, is the Atlantic White-sided Dolphin, which sometimes occurs in pods of more than 500 animals; Cape Breton Island is particularly good for this species. White-beaked Dolphins are less common, with an estimated population of a couple of thousand.

Harbor Porpoises are the most commonly seen toothed whales in the area. From the end of June to the end of September, they are often seen close to shore both in the estuary and the gulf – especially in fjords, bays, estuaries and ports. Their winter habitat is poorly understood and, while some individuals may stay in the estuary, most are believed to move offshore to avoid the ice.

Several other species occur from time to time. Young male Sperm Whales are seen occasionally, mainly from May–October; they are believed to be seeking new feeding grounds, while at the same time avoiding competition with older males. According to records from the 1940s, Killer Whales were once abundant in the area, but they are rarely seen these days, with about two dozen sightings since the early 1980s. However, there was an exceptional period during the 1990s, when a pod of four or five Killer Whales regularly visited the gulf (particularly the Jacques Cartier Strait) but they have not been seen for years. Northern Bottlenose Whale

Whales and people live alongside each other in the St Lawrence River.

sightings are extremely rare, normally as stranded animals, and Short-beaked Common Dolphins and Striped Dolphins occasionally travel through.

Land-based whale watching

The St Lawrence waterways are particularly good for land-based whale watching, with many proper lookouts – some with telescopes, experienced naturalists on hand and covers. In particular, there is an official Whale Route that runs 550 miles along the north shore, from Tadoussac to Natashquan, and includes some of the best spots where sightings of whales, dolphins and porpoises are frequent; simply follow the blue signs with the white whale.

Other land-based hotspots in the estuary include Pointe-Noire Interpretation & Observation Center, overlooking the juncture of the St Lawrence and Saguenay rivers, and Cap de Bon-Désir Interpretation & Observation Center, farther east. There is also an excellent Marine Mammal Interpretation Center in Tadoussac. In the gulf, good spots include Île Bonaventure, Cap Gaspé and Percé, and Forillon National Park. And the Mingan Island Cetacean Study Interpretation Center at Longue-Pointe-de-Mingan is definitely worth a visit.

Capelin is a favorite prey of several cetacean species here, including Fin Whales, Minke Whales and Humpbacks, so take note when the locals say 'the Capelin are rolling'. This means they have come to spawn on the beaches and there are likely to be thousands of them in very shallow water – a particularly good time to observe whales close to shore.

Whale watching from ferries

It is possible to see whales from some of the ferries plying the St Lawrence waterways. Short shuttles across the estuary – such as Godbout and Baie-Comeau to Matane, Forestville to Rimouski, Les Escoumins to Trois-Pistoles, Tadoussac to Baie-Sainte-Catherine, and Saint Siméon to Rivière-du-Loup – can all be good. They sometimes have sightings of Fin Whales, Minke Whales, Belugas and others. The much longer ferry journey between Rimouski and Sainte Barbe, in the Strait of Belle Isle, includes the entire northern sector of the gulf, with multiple stops along the way, and often have sightings of Blue Whales and others. The weekly coastal supply vessel and ferry between Rimouski and Blanc Sablon can also be very good.

CANADA: ARCTIC AND SUB-ARCTIC

Nunavut

Nunavut is Canada's newest territory. Although it has been continuously inhabited for several thousand years, it was officially carved out of the Northwest Territories as recently as 1999.

Covering an area of 800,000 square miles, it is roughly the size of Western Europe. Yet it has a human population of fewer than 34,000 (Western Europe's population is nearly 400 million) which means there is just one person for every 24 square miles. One of the least inhabited regions on the planet, it is renowned for its vast expanses of pristine wilderness.

Much of Nunavut is high above the Arctic Circle. Indeed, the territory is home to the northernmost permanently inhabited settlement on the planet – Alert, at 82°28'N, on Ellesmere Island – which has a registered population of just five people living only 508 miles from the North Pole. Summer days are long and, in the most northerly communities, the sun never completely sets below the horizon for up to five months

---

Overview

Main species: Bowhead Whale, Narwhal, Beluga.

Occasional species: Killer Whale; species off southeastern Baffin Island in summer: Blue Whale, Fin Whale, Sei Whale, Minke Whale, Humpback Whale, Northern Bottlenose Whale, Long-finned Pilot Whale, Harbor Porpoise.

Other wildlife highlights: Polar Bear, Brown Bear, Wolf, Wolverine, Arctic Fox, Arctic Hare, Muskox, Caribou, Arctic Ground Squirrel, Walrus, Bearded Seal, Harp Seal, Hooded Seal, Ringed Seal, Snow Goose, Gyrfalcon, Snowy Owl, Ivory Gull, Thayer's Gull, Glaucous Gull, Sabine's Gull, King Eider, Ptarmigan, Rock Ptarmigan, Snow Bunting, Horned Lark, Greenland Shark.

Main locations: Ellesmere Island (Grise Fjord); northern coast of Somerset Island; Baffin Island (Pangnirtung, Qikiqtarjuaq, Isabella Bay, Clyde River, Pond Inlet, Arctic Bay); Cornwallis Island (Resolute); Foxe Basin (Igloolik, Hall Beach, Kugaaruk); Hudson Bay (Repulse Bay, Coral Harbor, Chesterfield Inlet, Whale Cove, Arviat, Sanikiluaq).

Types of tours: full-day trips by boat or snowmobile from local communities; several wilderness lodges and permanent or temporary camps; multi-day expedition cruises; some opportunities for land-based whale watching from community shores.

When to go: May to early September (see entries for specific dates, depending on species and location).

Regulations and guidelines: Marine Mammal Regulations (under the Fisheries Act) prohibit any form of harassment of cetaceans (including repeated attempts to pursue, disperse or herd whales); 100-meter distance under Nunavut regulations; Fisheries and Oceans Canada is currently preparing countrywide enforceable regulations for whale watching.

Wildlife species are listed systematically (not in order of abundance) and frequency of sightings varies with location and season.

(and, of course, it never rises for nearly five months every winter, when the Moon provides the only natural light).

Nunavut is not the easiest place to explore. You can only get there by air or sea and there are no roads connecting the widely separated communities. The locals (some 84 per cent of Nunavut's inhabitants are Inuit) get around by boat, *qamutiq* (a traditional Inuit sledge pulled by a snowmobile or dog team) or ATV (all-terrain vehicle). For visiting whale watchers, there are basically four choices: join an expedition cruise on a ship with an ice-strengthened hull; join an organized tour that arranges all the necessary travel over ice, snow or water, and sets up a temporary camp; fly in to a remote lodge or permanent camp; or use a local community as a base and explore from there with the help of Inuit guides (if they are available – booking ahead is strongly recommended).

Professional photographers, film crews and anyone wanting tailored arrangements can also organize for specially prepared private camps to remote fly-in-only areas. These are obviously more expensive, but by going remote have the added advantage of avoiding areas where there is hunting.

Independent travel is not to be recommended – due to the potential risks of Polar Bear attack, for example, and constantly changing ice conditions – except for experienced Arctic adventurers. Bear in mind that much of what happens in Nunavut is strictly governed by ice.

Nunavut's whales

Nunavut is the best place in the world to see all three truly Arctic whale species – Bowhead Whale, Beluga and Narwhal – and these are the only cetaceans living in the heart of the territory year-round.

Bowheads can be seen in many places, but there are two main hotspots: along the east coast of Baffin Island (the 7,300-strong Baffin Island-Davis Strait sub-population – good places include Pangnirtung, Qikiqtarjuaq, Isabella Bay, Clyde River and Pond Inlet); and in the northern Hudson Bay/Foxe Basin region (where there is a population of about 3,600 – good places include Cape Dorset, Igloolik, Hall Beach, Repulse Bay, Kugaaruk and Coral Harbor).

Narwhal are more difficult to find though they, too, can be seen in many places. Indeed, more than three-quarters of the world population of Narwhal spends the summer in Nunavut's ice-free bays, fjords and island passages. A particularly good time to see them is when they are on their spring migration, travelling along predicable routes between their wintering and summering grounds: in May, June and July (the precise timing depends on location), as they are moving north and west, they crowd at the edges of the fast ice (sea ice attached to the coast). But they can be seen throughout the summer, almost anywhere along the east and north coasts of Baffin Island, in Eclipse Sound and Lancaster Sound and into the Northwest Passage, as well as in Foxe Basin and northern Hudson Bay. The best places are Arctic Bay and Pond Inlet, but Resolute, Grise Fiord and Repulse Bay are all very good.

Belugas are common near many Nunavut communities. Tens of thousands of them spend the summer in shallow coastal waters, especially around river estuaries, where they often occur in dense concentrations. Hotspots include: Hudson Bay (Coral Harbor, Chesterfield Inlet, Whale Cove, Arviat and Sanikiluaq); Cape Dorset in Foxe Basin; Resolute on Cornwallis Island (they can often be seen close to town); the

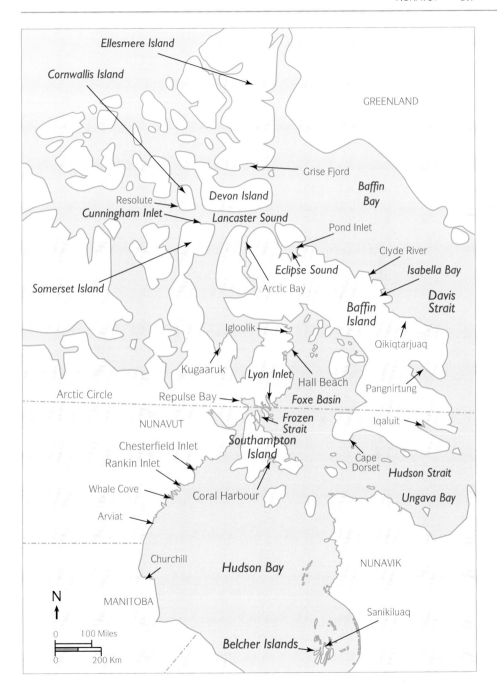

Ellesmere Island

Cornwallis Island

GREENLAND

Grise Fjord

Baffin Bay

Resolute

Devon Island

Cunningham Inlet

Lancaster Sound

Pond Inlet

Clyde River

Eclipse Sound

Isabella Bay

Arctic Bay

Davis Strait

Somerset Island

Baffin Island

Igloolik

Qikiqtarjuaq

Kugaaruk

Lyon Inlet

Hall Beach

Pangnirtung

Arctic Circle

Repulse Bay

Foxe Basin

NUNAVUT

Frozen Strait

Iqaluit

Chesterfield Inlet

Southampton Island

Cape Dorset

Hudson Strait

Rankin Inlet

Whale Cove

Coral Harbour

Ungava Bay

Arviat

Churchill

Hudson Bay

NUNAVIK

N

MANITOBA

Sanikiluaq

0   100 Miles

0   200 Km

Belcher Islands

northern coast of Somerset Island; Jones Sound, between Devon Island and Ellesmere Island; and the eastern coast of Baffin Island (particularly from Qikiqtarjuaq and Clyde River as far north as Pond Inlet).

Other cetaceans can sometimes be seen in Nunavut during the summer, mainly off southeastern Baffin Island. Blue Whale, Fin Whale, Sei Whale, Minke Whale, Humpback Whale, Northern Bottlenose Whale, Long-finned Pilot Whale and Harbor Porpoise are all encountered from time to time.

Killer Whales have been present in parts of the Canadian Arctic since at least the 1800s, though the number of reported sightings has dramatically increased in the past 50 years. Nowadays, they are regular if not particularly common visitors wherever the sea is relatively ice-free (intriguingly, they frequently enter pack ice in the Antarctic – there is even an ecotype called the Pack Ice Killer Whale – but they rarely do so in the Arctic). They are known to feed here mainly on Bowhead Whales, Belugas and Narwhal (one estimate suggests that they could be killing 200–300 Narwhals on their summer feeding grounds every year), but will also take several seal species. Sightings gradually increase from June to a peak in August, and then decrease again in September and October; they are very rarely seen in the region during winter. But with melting sea ice (due to global warming) and increasing numbers of Bowhead Whales, Killer Whales are pushing farther north, venturing into areas they have rarely been seen before, and staying for longer.

It is worth taking a hydrophone on any whale-watching trip to Nunavut. The potentially long wait for Narwhal to pass the floe edge, for example, can be enlivened by the most remarkable underwater cacophony: singing Bowhead Whales, and the riotous symphonies of Narwhal and Belugas, as well as everything from Bearded Seals to Walruses.

Hunting

Whale watching in Nunavut sounds almost too good to be true and, indeed, there is a catch. Hunting is a traditional way of life here and the local Inuit hunt everything from Polar Bears and Walruses to Narwhal and Belugas. There are quotas and harvest limits for many species, but for Narwhal, in particular, these may not be sustainable. Also, the number shot but never retrieved or counted is a concern – many Narwhal in Nunavut bear deep bullet wounds on their heads and backs. Each year, three Nunavut communities are given licenses to harvest one Bowhead Whale each.

The Inuit diet is high in protein and fat and, because it is impossible to cultivate plants in the Arctic, much of their vitamin C comes from whale skin with the adhering blubber (known locally as *muktuk*). Consequently, there are signs of hunting in every community, and whale watchers may inadvertently witness the hunts.

Baffin Island

Pangnirtung Fondly known as 'Pang', this medium-sized community of 1,650 people lies 30 miles south of Arctic Circle, in Pangnirtung Fjord on the northern side of Cumberland Sound. Renowned for its famous 'Pang hat' (a crocheted winter hat very popular all across Nunavut) and as the gateway to Auyuittuq National Park, it is a good area for all three Arctic whale species – Bowhead Whale, Narwhal and Beluga. The floe edge off Kekerten Island is a particular hotspot in May and June. Bowheads are frequently seen in

Isabella Bay is a critical feeding, resting and socializing site for Bowhead Whales.

Cumberland Sound and Inuit elders have noticed increasing numbers at the floe edge south and southwest of Pang (sometimes as early as March and April, when the floe edge is farther offshore). They disperse in summer, after the ice breaks up, and the overall rate of sightings decreases. Commercial whaling by Scottish and American whalers began in Cumberland Sound in 1820 – there was a whaling station on nearby Kekerten Island – but the whales were 'fished out' by the mid-1860s; it is only quite recently that numbers have noticeably increased. The community caught its third Bowhead Whale in living memory in September 2016. Killer Whales are seen every year, and a small number may remain during the summer; reported sightings appear to be increasing, but they are still relatively rare (when they are around there tend to be fewer Bowhead Whales). There is 24-hour daylight in Pangnirtung from 8 June–4 July.

Qikiqtarjuaq This small community of about 550 people was formerly known as Broughton Island, the same name as the island on which it is located. It lies 60 miles north of the Arctic Circle, off the eastern coast of Baffin Island, and faces the Davis Strait. Often called 'Qik' for short, it is known as the iceberg capital of Nunavut, since it captures many of the bergs that travel down Davis Strait from Greenland. It is great for whale watching. Qik is best known for Bowhead Whales and, indeed, much of eastern Baffin Island (particularly from Qik to Clyde River) is good for them. Elders report an increase in numbers in recent decades. The clear, shallow waters south of Qik are exceptional – one Bowhead scientist describes it as the best place in the world to see and photograph these whales. Large numbers now gather in nearby Merchants Bay, as well. August and September are the peak months. Qik can also be a good place to see Belugas and, sometimes, Killer Whales.

Narwhal frequently enter nearby Muktuk Fiord, in Auyuittuq, but it is closed to visitors when they arrive, to allow hunting. Rare sightings over the years have included North Atlantic Right Whales, Blue Whales (which sometimes travel up Davis Strait to feed) and Sperm Whales. There is 24-hour daylight from 29 May–15 July.

Isabella Bay (Igaliqtuuq) Isabella is a critical Bowhead Whale feeding, resting and socializing site. It is estimated that at least 200 whales use the Bay on and off during summer and fall (with as many as 100 recorded at one time – making this the single largest concentration of Bowheads anywhere in Canada). The peak period is August–September, but varying numbers of whales are present from mid-July to early October (the bay is covered in ice for up to nine months of the year). Most of the whales are adults and sub-adults; mothers and calves are rarely seen (they move farther north and west through Lancaster Sound). The Bay has a shallow shelf at the entrance, where much of the social activity takes place, and there are two deep troughs offshore that are rich in copepods and form a critical feeding ground. The area is known locally as 'the place where fog sits' but, on a clear day, it is often possible to see Bowhead Whales from the shore; a well-known spot is Cape Raper, a coastal headland on the northeastern corner of the bay, which is now officially known as 'Baleana Lookout'. Narwhal are also sometimes seen in the area. Isabella Bay (including its shoreline and islands, as well as the adjacent ocean out to 12 nautical miles from shore) was designated a Bowhead Whale Sanctuary, known as the Niginganiq National Wildlife Area, in 2010. It was the first ever Inuit-initiated whale sanctuary. Access is from Clyde River, 75 miles to the north, though it is very weather-dependent.

Clyde River (Kangiqtugaapik) The Inuktitut name for this scenic community of about 1,000 people means 'nice little inlet' and, indeed, it is located in a beautiful sheltered cove called Patricia Bay. It is possible to see all three Arctic whale species here. Bowheads can be seen almost anywhere along this coast (particularly from Qikiqtarjuaq to Clyde River). In particular, around Clyde River they are sometimes near the community from August until freeze-up some time in September. Elders report an increase in numbers in recent decades. Narwhal are hunted in Patricia Bay and, for the first time in over a century, a Bowhead Whale was killed by Inuit whalers about 12 miles from the community, in August 2014. Clyde River is considered the artistic center of Inuit whalebone carving in Nunavut. There is 24-hour daylight from 13 May–1 August.

Pond Inlet (Mittimatalik). This large community of about 1,700 people is located on the northeastern tip of Baffin Island, near the eastern entrance to the Northwest Passage. Some 435 miles north of the Arctic Circle, it overlooks Eclipse Sound and, 16 miles away, the migratory bird sanctuary of Bylot Island (reputedly home to a million nesting seabirds). It is world renowned as one of the best places in the Arctic to see Narwhal, which migrate past the floe edge here on their way north, particularly from the end of May to mid-June. It is also possible to see Bowhead Whales, which often approach the floe edge very closely, and occasionally Belugas. There are guided trips using snowmobiles and qamutiqs to travel from the community of Pond Inlet across the sea ice to the floe edge (typically some five to seven hours away, depending on conditions). Participants camp on the ice, in temporary but comfortable safari-style heated tents, and stand (or sit) on the floe edge looking for whales. This is a great place to use a hydrophone – the underwater world here hosts a veritable orchestra of singing marine mammals. Inuit elders report an increase in Bowhead numbers in recent decades, and now they can be seen in the area throughout the summer. Narwhal can be seen around Pond Inlet later in the summer, too, and will often swim right past the community; they can be found almost anywhere in the Eclipse Sound/Milne Inlet area. There is 24-hour daylight in Pond Inlet from 5 May–7 August.

Arctic Bay (Ikpiarjuk) Located on the northwest corner of Baffin Island, this vibrant community of nearly 900 people lies in Adams Sound, which feeds into Admiralty Inlet and ultimately into Lancaster Sound and the Northwest Passage. Large populations of Narwhal gather in the region, and this is undoubtedly one of the best places in the Arctic to see them. They frequently hang around for longer than the travelling Narwhal that pass by the floe edge at Pond Inlet, but the principle for whale watching is the same: guided trips use snowmobiles and qamutiqs to travel from nearby Victor Bay across the sea ice to the floe edge (typically some five to seven hours away, depending on conditions). Participants camp on the ice, in one of the most northerly camps on the planet, in temporary but comfortable safari-style heated tents, and stand (or sit) on the floe edge looking for whales. Belugas are often seen here, too, and Bowhead Whales turn up from time to time. This is a great place to use a hydrophone, with a good chance of hearing all three Arctic whales and other species such as Bearded Seals and Walruses. June is usually the best month. Narwhal can be seen anywhere in Admiralty Inlet

Whale watchers look for Narwhal from the ice edge at Pond Inlet.

and Lancaster Sound. Killer Whales are seen on and off throughout the summer, and there are significant numbers in Admiralty Inlet. There is 24-hour daylight from 6 May–6 August.

Somerset Island

Somerset Island is a wild and remote island of some 9,570 square miles, with lots of wildlife (including Muskox, Arctic Foxes and Polar Bears) and no permanent human residents. But it is best known for its Beluga Whales.

The traditional place to see them is Cunningham Inlet. Some 500 miles north of the Arctic Circle, and about 56 miles from Resolute, the inlet lies on the northern tip of Somerset Island, overlooking the Northwest Passage. When Beluga Whales were being studied here in the late 1990s there were believed to be as many as 2,000 of them during a typical summer, nursing their calves and molting their skin in the relatively warm, shallow water. But in the years since, Beluga numbers have been very up and down: some years, if the ice does not melt, there are no whales at all. The peak months are usually July–August (primarily mid-July to mid-August) but ice conditions – and whale numbers – are inexorably linked and impossible to predict. In good years, however, the whales can readily be observed from the shoreline (no boats are permitted in Cunningham Inlet) and they seem to be completely unperturbed by their human admirers. There is a permanent safari-style tented camp – one of the most northerly permanent camps in the world – on the southern shore of the inlet.

There are a number of alternative sites for Belugas around northern Somerset Island. Irvine Bay and Garnier Bay, to the east of Cunningham Inlet, can be good; Prince Leopold Island, off the northeast coast, has smaller numbers of Belugas which frequently cruise along the base of the island's colossal seabird colonies. Coningham Bay, on neighboring Prince of Wales Island, is another good place to see Belugas, especially immediately after the ice break-up.

Ellesmere Island

Grise Fiord, or Aujuittuq, lies on Jones Sound, at the southern end of Ellesmere Island, and is a good place to see large pods of Narwhals and Belugas. 'The place that never thaws out' is a tiny hamlet of about 160 people, at 76°24'N and 720 miles north of the Arctic Circle, with a reputation for being one of the coldest inhabited places on Earth. It lives up to its Inuktitut name: for 10 months of the year the sea around Grise Fiord is frozen. Summer temperatures can sometimes rise above freezing to as high as 5°C, but winter temperatures frequently drop to -40°C; the average yearly temperature is -16.5°C. The season is inevitably short, but Narwhals and Belugas migrate past the floe edge every spring (typically about 30 miles east of the community). Bear in mind, though, that this is open ocean floe edge and it is much more dangerous than inlet floe edges. Grise Fiord does have a short airstrip, despite its remoteness, but it is a very difficult and expensive place to get to. There is 24-hour daylight from 22 April–20 August.

Cornwallis Island

Located on the southern shore of Cornwallis Island, right in the middle of the Northwest Passage, Resolute or Qausuittuq ('the place with no dawn') is remote by any standard. Some 370 miles north of the Arctic Circle, it often serves as the starting point for expeditions to the North Pole, 1,250 miles

Beluga Whales gathering in shallow water on the north coast of Somerset Island.

away. With a population of just 250 people, it is one of the most northerly communities in both Nunavut and Canada. It is good for Belugas, which routinely swim past on their way to and from their prime summering grounds and can sometimes be seen from the beach right in front of town (especially in the fall). It is occasionally visited by Narwhals. There is a good airstrip with a scheduled jet service and several hotels, but there is also a good chance of being 'weathered in' here. There is 24-hour daylight from 29 April–13 August.

Foxe Basin

Igloolik The 'place of igloos' lies on a small island in Foxe Basin, just off the northeastern corner of Melville Peninsula (which is part of the mainland). With a population of about 2,000 people, it is best known for the award-winning movie *Atanarjuat – The Fast Runner*, which was produced and filmed here and stars many local residents. Icebergs and ice floes drift past the island, through the narrows of Fury and Hecla Strait, which also funnels migrating whales

to within easy viewing distance. There are large numbers of Bowhead Whales in this part of northern Foxe Basin, mainly during June–July (though they can be seen well into September). The area north of Igloolik seems to be a particular hotspot and local people observe that numbers have been steadily increasing since the mid-1980s. Belugas are seen fairly frequently, and Narwhals occasionally (they tend to be farther north, the other side of Fury and Hecla Strait). Small numbers of Killer Whales are observed most summers, particularly in August–September, depending on ice conditions; they appear to be following the Bowhead Whales and tend to keep to the center of Foxe Basin (though sometimes travel through Fury and Hecla Strait). The area is also renowned for Walruses and large numbers can be seen hauled out on the ice floes and, once the ice has disappeared in August, on rocky islands. It is possible to stay in a safari-style tented camp on Igloolik Point, about a one-hour qamutiq ride from town. There is 24-hour daylight from 18 May–26 July.

Hall Beach (Sanirajak) Hall Beach lies about 43 miles south of Igloolik on the northeastern side of Melville Peninsula (part of the Canadian mainland). It has a population of about 800. Looking out across Foxe Basin, it is a haven for marine mammals and is a good place to see Bowhead Whales. Small numbers of Killer Whales are observed most summers, depending on ice conditions; they appear to be following the Bowhead Whales and tend to keep to the center of Foxe Basin or move past the community fairly quickly. Hall Beach is also one of the best places in Nunavut to see Walruses, which haul out on the ice floes. It is possible to organize whale-watching trips locally, with Inuit guides. There is 24-hour daylight from 21 May–22 July.

Kugaaruk (Arvilligjuaq) Strictly speaking, Kugaaruk is a long way outside Foxe Basin, and access involves an entirely different route through Yellowknife, but it is home to the same populations of whales. Its alternative name, Arvilligjuaq, means 'place of many Bowhead Whales' and, indeed, it provides a good base for seeing this species. Home to about 950 people, it lies on the southeastern shore of Pelly Bay, off the Gulf of Boothia (the community was known as Pelly Bay, until the name was formally changed in 1999). This can also be a good place to see Narwhal. Kugaaruk has a history of making traditional kayaks and there is great potential to try and use them to watch whales here. There is constant 24-hour daylight from 21 May–22 July.

Hudson Bay

Repulse Bay (Naujaat) This medium-sized community of about 1,000 people lies on the Arctic Circle, in the extreme northern corner of Hudson Bay. Home to all three Arctic whale species – Bowhead Whale, Narwhal and Beluga – it is very much an adventurer's destination. Bowheads are seen in spring and early summer along the floe edge (with a peak in June and early July) while Repulse Bay and nearby Frozen Strait and Lyon Inlet harbor important summer concentrations of Narwhal (they can be seen from June–September). However, the community has a substantial annual Narwhal quota and takes almost all of them within a few days of their arrival in early summer; this is not a good time to visit – tourists are not welcome during the hunt – and there are bullets flying across the bay. Inuit observers have noted a growing number of Killer Whales in this area and they are observed most summers, depending on ice conditions; there seems to be a regular movement along this stretch of coast: when they are seen in Igloolik or Rankin Inlet, quite often about a week later they are seen in Repulse Bay. Killer Whales have even been observed chasing Narwhals and causing them to beach themselves right in front of the town (making easy prey for local hunters). There is 24-hour daylight from 4 June–9 July.

Coral Harbour (Salliq) Located on the southern shore of Southampton Island, overlooking Hudson Bay, Coral Harbour is renowned for its wildlife. It is a medium-sized community, with a population of about 900 people, and can be a place to see Belugas and, increasingly, Bowhead Whales. Both species are reasonably abundant at the floe edge off the southern coast of the island during May–June, including mothers and calves (but bear in mind that this is open ocean floe edge, which is much more dangerous than inlet floe edge). Later in the season, Belugas can be anywhere in this region and

Narwhal can be seen at a number of places in Nunavut.

Bowheads are in open water throughout the summer. Killer Whales are being seen more frequently in recent years.

Chesterfield Inlet (Igluligaarjuk) Lying on the northwestern shore of Hudson Bay, Chesterfield Inlet is the oldest permanent settlement in Nunavut. At one time there were as many as 700 people living here, when European and American whalers first arrived and began using the place as a safe winter harbor for their vessels, but nowadays the population is closer to 400. This is a particularly good place to see Belugas.

Whale Cove (Tikirarjuaq) A pretty little hamlet of about 460 people, Whale Cove sits on a long peninsula of the Canadian mainland that projects into northwestern Hudson Bay. About 50 miles south of Rankin Inlet, its English name comes from the great abundance of Belugas that congregate here every fall, often very close to shore. There is a big Beluga Whale's Tail Monument on the hill overlooking the settlement, which has become a familiar local symbol. Sightings of Bowhead Whales are rare, but numbers have slowly been increasing in recent years.

Arviat Previously known as Eskimo Point, the southernmost mainland community in Nunavut is a sizeable place, with a population of around 2,600 people. It lies on the western shore of Hudson Bay, about 160 miles north of Churchill and gets its name from the Inuktitut word '*arviq*' meaning 'Bowhead Whale' – literally translated, it is 'The Place of the Bowhead Whale'. Bowheads do sometimes occur along the west coast of Hudson Bay, from Arviat through Roes Welcome Sound and farther north, throughout the summer, but they are not particularly common. A notable landmark is the Whale's Tail Monument – two Bowhead tails with splendid views of Arviat and its surroundings. These days, the community is better known for its Belugas: pods often gather in the many small bays near the community, especially during late summer and fall. Killer Whales are also seen from time to time, when the ice is clear, and sightings have increased in recent years.

Churchill

Lying at the mouth of the Churchill River, on the western shore of Hudson Bay, Churchill was used as a seasonal hunting ground as long as 4,000 years ago. The area was later established as a remote fur-trading post by the Hudson's Bay Company, in the late 1600s, and the town itself became a major northern shipping harbor in the late 1920s and early 1930s. Its 800 permanent residents are surrounded by wilderness, where the boreal forest meets the Arctic tundra, and the closest sizeable settlement is 250 miles away to the south. It is an enchanting place, with the feel of a frontier town and yet plenty of modern facilities.

Churchill lies at 58°77'N – roughly the same as Juneau or Inverness – and is actually about 500 miles south of the Arctic Circle. But its winters, and wildlife, are more Arctic in character than its latitude might suggest. Better known as the 'Polar Bear Capital of the World', it is also one of the best places to see Belugas.

Beluga congregation

In July and August it is almost impossible to look out across the Churchill River estuary, which is right next to town, and not see Belugas. The water is often teeming with them – there can be so many that, at first glance, it looks as if the estuary is covered in whitecaps.

Hudson Bay is an immense semi-enclosed sea, covering an area of some 475,000 square miles. It is connected to the Atlantic Ocean via Hudson Strait and to the Arctic Ocean via Foxe Basin. There are two main summer gatherings of Belugas in the bay: approximately 57,000 in the west and

Overview

Main species: Beluga.

Occasional species: Killer Whale.

Other wildlife highlights: Polar Bear, Arctic Fox, Red Fox, Caribou, Arctic Hare, Collared Lemming, River Otter, Bearded Seal, Harbor Seal, Ringed Seal, Gyrfalcon, Snowy Owl, Northern Hawk Owl, Ivory Gull, Thayer's Gull, Sabine's Gull, Bonaparte's Gull, Smith's Longspur, Spruce Grouse, Snow Goose, Tundra Swan.

Main locations: Churchill, Seal River; for other whale-watching locations in Hudson Bay, see Nunavut (page 267).

Types of tours: two to three-hour jet-boat and Zodiac tours; three-hour snorkeling and kayaking tours; two-hour paddleboarding tours; good land-based whale watching.

When to go: late June, July and August.

Regulations and guidelines: no official guidelines or regulations; Marine Mammal Regulations (under the Fisheries Act) prohibit any form of harassment of cetaceans (including repeated attempts to pursue, disperse or herd whales); Fisheries and Oceans Canada is currently preparing countrywide enforceable regulations for whale watching.

Wildlife species are listed systematically (not in order of abundance) and frequency of sightings varies with location and season.

about 2,000 in the east. Altogether, it is the summer home of roughly one-third of all the Belugas in the world.

They tend to congregate in river estuaries to calve and moult – they rub against the smooth river rocks and feed on the plentiful Capelin – and, in the west, there are particular hotspots around the Nelson, Churchill and Seal estuaries. It is not unusual to have as many as 3,000 of the white whales in the Churchill River estuary alone, making it one of the most accessible large concentrations of these whales anywhere on the planet.

The exact timing of the Belugas' arrival in Churchill varies from year to year, according to the break-up and melting of the Hudson Bay ice. Also, the main season has changed slightly in recent years due to global warming: there are now four extra ice-free weeks in the summer than there were just 10 years ago. Traditionally, the whales were around only in July and August, but now the first pods are turning up more often in early June and some are staying into early September. They remain throughout the summer to calve, molt and feed on shoals of Capelin and other fish, before migrating north to their wintering grounds in polynyas (areas of open water surrounded by sea ice) in Hudson Strait, Ungava Bay, the Labrador Sea and southwest Davis Strait.

Whale-watching tours

It's much quieter in Churchill at this time of year (it can be busy during Polar Bear season in the fall and early winter) and the tundra is ablaze with wildflowers and full of birds. The only catch is the huge clouds of omnipresent blackflies and mosquitos, but it is a small price to pay for such good whale watching. It is not unusual to see hundreds of Belugas during a single trip, and they often approach very closely and turn on their sides for a better look at the whale watchers on board. Most of the boats have hydrophones on board, too, to listen to the extraordinary cacophony of groans, roars, whistles, squawks, moos, buzzes and trills that Belugas are so well known for (they have one of the most diverse vocal repertoires of any cetacean).

Depending on weather, tides and visibility, it is also possible to get into the water with the whales and snorkel with them. The guide simply locates a relaxed pod and the snorkelers slip over the side of the boat into the decidedly chilly water. An Arctic wetsuit, complete with gloves, boots and hood, provides surprisingly good insulation from the cold, and you can stay in the water quite comfortably for well over an hour. The snorkelers hold onto a rope and the boat either drifts or gently tows them along at a very slow speed – this encourages the whales to swim alongside.

It is sometimes difficult to tell who is supposed to be watching whom. Belugas can be very inquisitive and will come within a yard or two, even bringing their calves to have a closer look. The sea here tends to be green or tea-colored and the whales first appear as ghostly apparitions in the water, appearing and disappearing, approaching from in front, behind, underneath and either side. There can be layers and layers of these ethereal, white glows underneath, looking up curiously. They will often mimic whatever the snorkelers do and seem to respond to singing and humming.

It is possible to kayak with the whales, too, for a more intimate sea-level encounter (a safety Zodiac accompanies every tour). And there are paddleboarding tours – indeed, Churchill may be the only place in the world where there are organized tours to paddleboard with whales.

Other cetaceans around Churchill

No other cetaceans are seen regularly around Churchill. However, Killer Whale presence in Hudson Bay has increased exponentially over the past 50 years, thanks to global warming. Extensive writings from European explorers, dating from the early 1600s, contain no mention of them before 1900. But areas that were historically blocked by ice are now

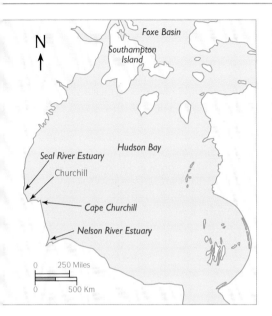

increasingly ice-free for longer periods and, as elsewhere in the Arctic, this is allowing the predators to penetrate further and stay longer. Killer Whales are still quite rare around Churchill but since the 1960s there has been a small, but steady, increase in sightings. In 2014, a pod of 11 individuals turned up about a mile from town and killed several Belugas (individuals that had wandered too far from the safety of the shallow river estuary); there have also been sightings in late summer 2015 and 2016. It is anticipated that they will become more frequent in years to come.

Minke Whales have been recorded and a small number of Bowhead Whales have been encountered in recent years (after an absence of about a century).

Polar Bear Capital of the World

Finally, it is impossible to talk about Churchill without mentioning its other star attraction – it does, after all, bill itself as the 'Polar Bear Capital of the World'. Polar Bears spend most of their time living on the ice that covers 90 per cent of Hudson Bay for about eight months of the year, where they feed on seals. But when the ice has completely melted (usually by the end of July or early August) they have to come ashore for three to four months until it freezes again some time in early November. During this enforced hunting break, they laze around to conserve energy and eat very little (surviving mainly on fat reserves). Gradually, they make their way to Cape Churchill, to the east of town, and wait for the big freeze (Cape Churchill and the Churchill Wildlife Management Area is usually where it happens first).

It is this impressive fall congregation that bear-watchers go to see. Peak viewing varies from year to year, ranging from early October to the end of November depending on ice formation, but mid-October to mid-November tends to be the peak period (with the historic freeze-up being 15 November). Of course, there are never any guarantees. The good news is that bears can be seen around Churchill throughout the Beluga season. The population is scattered along the coast all summer and, while there are far fewer of them near town, with the help of a local guide they can often be found on the treeless terrain.

Seal River

Seal River Heritage Lodge, near the Seal River estuary and approximately 37 miles north of Churchill, offers another chance to see, hear and snorkel with Belugas. The whales gather in the estuary every summer. Other wildlife in the area includes Polar Bear, Caribou, Moose, Red Fox, Arctic Fox, Wolf and many different birds. Access is by plane, via Churchill.

The 'Polar Bear Capital of the World' is also a good place to see Beluga Whales.

Inuvik

Sprawled across northern Canada, between the Yukon and Nunavut, the Northwest Territories is twice the size of France yet has a population of only 44,000 people. The northern coast of this breathtaking wilderness faces the eastern Beaufort Sea and Amundsen Gulf – renowned areas for Bowhead Whales and Belugas.

Inuvik

The center for whale watching is Inuvik ('Living Place' – not 'Place of Man' as it is often mistranslated), a small town of about 3,500 people, at the top of the famous 457-mile-long Dempster Highway. This is literally the end of the road – it is the farthest north you can drive on a public highway in North America – unless, of course, you wait for the winter freeze and follow the ice road carved across the Mackenzie River and into the Arctic Ocean. The road is currently being extended and, by 2018, it will be possible to drive another 87 miles to Tuktoyaktuk to the northeast (and then it is likely that most whale watching trips will leave from there instead of Inuvik). Whale watching here is not well established – and it is often combined with trips to traditional whaling camps – but there is some potential.

Beluga concentrations

Inuvik sits on the east channel of the Mackenzie River delta (about 60 miles south of the Beaufort Sea). This is the summer home of a large population of Belugas. There are estimated to be about 40,000 Belugas in the eastern Beaufort Sea altogether and the outer delta is one of their favorite gathering grounds (a survey in 2012, when the ice

Overview

Main species: Bowhead Whale, Beluga.

Rarely seen species: Gray Whale, Killer Whale.

Other wildlife highlights: Polar Bear, Brown Bear, Black Bear, Wolf, Arctic Fox, Muskox, Moose, Caribou, Beaver, Arctic Hare, American Marten, Bearded Seal, Ringed Seal, Bald Eagle, Golden Eagle, Gyrfalcon, Snowy Owl, Ivory Gull, King Eider, Tundra Swan, Sandhill Crane.

Main locations: Inuvik.

Types of tours: half-day tours; kayaking tours; multi-day boat trips; aerial scenic tours.

When to go: mid-June to early September.

Regulations and guidelines: no specific guidelines; Marine Mammal Regulations (under the Fisheries Act) prohibit any form of harassment of cetaceans (including repeated attempts to pursue, disperse or herd whales); Fisheries and Oceans Canada is currently preparing countrywide enforceable regulations for whale watching.

Wildlife species are listed systematically (not in order of abundance) and frequency of sightings varies with location and season.

break-up was unusually early, counted 755). They calve, feed and molt here, and the shallow waters are a good place to hide from predatory Killer Whales.

The whales normally arrive in June and are present until September, when they move farther offshore. July tends to be the peak month. There are half-day boat trips and multi-day boat excursions to Herschel Island and some of the other Arctic islands in the Beaufort Sea, that include whale watching as part of the itinerary. There are also full-day sightseeing tours by air that often see whales. And there are ad hoc opportunities to see them from any of the smaller settlements in

There is potential for seeing Bowhead Whales in the Northwest Territories.

the area, since the whales occur along the entire Northwest Territories coast.

Bowhead Whales

Bowhead Whales are sometimes seen on these trips, especially around Herschel Island. The freshwater pouring into the Beaufort Sea from the Mackenzie River provides rich feeding conditions for them – areas off King Point, Shingle Point, Mackenzie Bay and Herschel Island have all been identified as potentially important areas. Sightings by researchers vary from year to year: in some years the whales stick to shallow ice-free waters and in others they are found farther offshore. The Tuktoyaktuk Peninsula is a good location for Bowheads, and they sometimes feed close to shore here. The peak period is usually from mid-August to late September (and into October near Herschel). Then the whales slowly make their fall migration back into the Bering Sea.

Subsistence whaling

Whales are hunted for subsistence here, with several traditional whaling camps along the Mackenzie coastline used by the communities of Tuktoyaktuk, Inuvik and Aklavik; communities outside the delta (Paulatuk, Sachs Harbor and Ulukhaktok) also harvest whales at sea. On average, 100 Belugas and one Bowhead are landed in the region per year.

MEXICO

Mexico was the first country in Latin America to begin whale watching. It spread from southern California in the early 1970s, when American cruise ships took people into the Gray Whale breeding lagoons in Baja California, in the hope of meeting some of the newly discovered 'friendlies'. After Canada and California, it is the third oldest whale-watching area in the world (and the place where multi-day whale-watching tours began).

The hotspot for whale watching in Mexico is undoubtedly Baja, on the west coast. This is one of the world's best-known whale-watching venues and the indisputable highlight is its Gray Whales: safely sheltered from the pounding surf of the North Pacific, thousands of them gather to socialize, mate and calve in a string of magical lagoons beside the desert. Best of all, they have become so friendly that they frequently approach small whale-watching boats to be scratched, tickled and splashed.

Understandably, the rest of Baja tends to be overshadowed by San Ignacio and the other lagoons, and it has remained a surprisingly well-kept secret. But the Pacific coast, the southern tip and, on the other side, the Gulf of California or Sea of Cortez offers some of the best whale watching on the planet. On a good day, it is possible to see as many as 8–10 different species – everything from Blue Whales and Humpback Whales to lesser-known Dwarf Sperm Whales and rarities such as Peruvian Beaked Whales. The Gulf is also home to the most critically endangered cetacean in the world, the Vaquita or Gulf of California Porpoise.

There is some excellent whale watching farther south, too, in Banderas Bay and along the coast of Guerrero state, with further opportunities to see whales and dolphins in the Revillagigedo Archipelago. Despite considerable potential, there are fewer opportunities on the east coast of Mexico: currently just dolphin watching on the Yucatán peninsula.

Mexico has established a number of important marine and whale reserves – including, in 1972, the world's first whale refuge at Ojo de Liebre Lagoon. In May 2002, it created the Mexican Whale Refuge (Refugio Ballenero Mexicano) and became one of the few countries in the world to make its entire Exclusive Economic Zone (about 1.2 million square miles) a national whale sanctuary.

A friendly Gray Whale in San Ignacio Lagoon.

MEXICO: WEST COAST

Baja California

Look at a map of North America and, down in the bottom left-hand corner, you will see a long stretch of land that looks rather like a giant chilli. This is Baja California – one of the world's great whale-watching hotspots.

With a little luck, in a couple of weeks, you can tickle implausibly friendly Gray Whales under the chin, listen to Humpback Whales singing their haunting, unearthly songs, enjoy unforgettably close encounters with gargantuan Blue Whales, travel with thousands of boisterous Common Dolphins, and see a host of other species from Sei Whales and Sperm Whales to Dall's Porpoises and even Peruvian Beaked Whales. Along the way, you can snorkel with playful California Sea Lions and Whale Sharks.

One of the longest peninsulas in the world, stretching 800 miles south from the Californian border, Baja is unusual because it is both a breeding ground and a feeding ground for cetaceans. This means that you can see an unusually great variety of species.

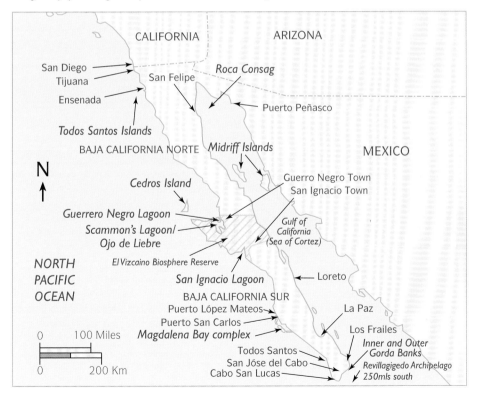

Gray Whale breeding lagoons

The Pacific side of this 'Mexican Galapagos' is best known as the winter home of practically the entire world population of Gray Whales.

Once on the verge of extinction, due to hunting, Gray Whales have bounced back thanks to intensive conservation efforts. Now as many as 18–21,000 of these inveterate travellers migrate back and forth along the entire length of the western North American coastline, between their feeding grounds in the Arctic and their breeding grounds in Baja. The round-trip distance can be as much as 12,400 miles, making their journey one of the longest migrations of any mammal.

They gather in four main lagoons: Guerrero Negro and Scammon's (Ojo de Liebre), about 470 miles south of the US border; San Ignacio, about 560 miles south of the border; and Magdalena Bay complex, about 750 miles south of the border. These lagoons are government-protected marine parks and whale watching is strictly controlled: it is only allowed in small boats (called *pangas*) operated by trained and licensed local guides.

Recognizing the importance of the Gray Whales' breeding lagoons, the Mexican government established Ojo de Liebre (Scammon's Lagoon) as the world's first whale refuge, in 1972. San Ignacio Lagoon was given official protection in 1979 and Guerrero Negro in 1980. Then, in 1988, El Vizcaíno Biosphere Reserve was created. Covering an area of 9,833 square miles, the reserve includes three of the four main Gray

Overview

Main species: Gray Whale, Common Bottlenose Dolphin; Long-beaked Common Dolphin (Ojo de Liebre and Magdalena Bay only).

Other wildlife highlights: Coyote, California Sea Lion, Osprey, Magnificent Frigatebird, Surf Scoter, Caspian Tern, Royal Tern, Elegant Tern, Heermann's Gull, White Ibis, Brant Goose, large numbers of waterbirds and shorebirds, Green Turtle, Loggerhead Turtle, Hawksbill Turtle, Pacific Ridley Turtle.

Main locations: San Ignacio Lagoon; Scammon's Lagoon or Ojo de Liebre; Magdalena Bay complex; packages (including long overland journeys) from San Diego, Cabo San Lucas, Todos Santos, La Paz and Loreto.

Types of tour: 1.5- to 3-hour tours in open skiffs (known locally as *pangas*), typically carrying 6–12 people; 12-day marine safaris on live-aboard boats from San Diego, California (which stop off for 2–3 days in San Ignacio Lagoon); multi-day kayaking trips in Magdalena Bay complex.

When to go: late December to late April (precise season varies with lagoon).

Regulations and guidelines: official regulation NOM-131-SEMARNAT-2010; whale-watch boats require official permits; further local regulations.

Wildlife species are listed systematically (not in order of abundance) and frequency of sightings varies with location and season.

Whale breeding lagoons (Ojo de Liebre, Guerrero Negro and San Ignacio) and a 3-mile-wide coastal strip on both sides of the peninsula (in the Pacific and the Gulf of California). It also includes Sierra de San Francisco in the east and the vast Vizcaíno desert at its center. San Ignacio and Ojo de Liebre became World Heritage Sites in 1993.

In reality, the winter Gray Whale population spreads itself out between

San Ignacio is the original home of the famous 'friendlies'.

southern California and the Gulf of California: the whales come and go day by day and week by week. Some females return to the same lagoon to give birth, while others switch lagoons from one birth to the next. Many whales – especially single males and females – visit different lagoons during the same season. They rarely stay for more than a few days or weeks at a time, presumably moving around the winter aggregation areas looking for opportunities to mate.

But although no more than a few thousand Gray Whales are present at any one time, the lagoons can appear impressively crowded. These are some of the greatest concentrations of large whales on Earth.

San Ignacio Lagoon

San Ignacio is the original home of the famous 'friendlies' – the Gray Whales that actively seek out human company to be tickled, scratched and splashed.

It's almost impossible to exaggerate how thrilling, uplifting and all-round life-changing a few days in San Ignacio can be. The Gray Whales here literally nudge the sides of the small whale-watching boats, or pangas, and lie alongside waiting to be petted. It's a breathless, and for some initially a rather nerve-wracking experience, but it's arguably one of the greatest wildlife encounters on Earth.

Yet it's hard to believe that these very same Gray Whales once had a reputation for being ferocious and dangerous. They were hunted ruthlessly in the second half of the nineteenth century, and again in the early twentieth century, until there were almost none left. Yankee whalers entered the Baja lagoons in small wooden rowing boats (roughly the same size as today's whale-watching pangas) and harpooned them. But the whales fought back – chasing the whaling boats, lifting them out of the

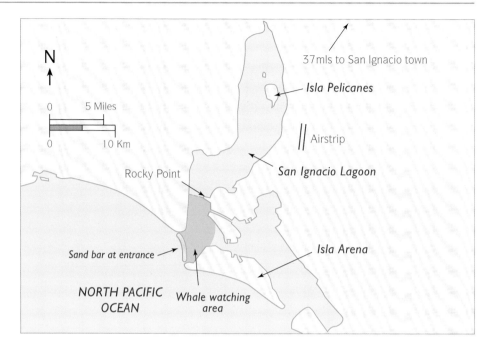

water like big rubber ducks, ramming them with their heads and dashing them to pieces with their tails. They would 'fight like devils', so the Yankee whalers dubbed them 'devilfish'.

Nowadays, the whales positively welcome tourists into their breeding lagoons. Somehow, they seem to understand that we come in peace and, far from smashing our small boats to smithereens, welcome us with open flippers. They are as trusting and playful as kittens, albeit kittens up to 49ft long. They seem to have forgiven us for all those years of greed, recklessness and cruelty. They trust us, when we don't really deserve to be trusted. It's a humbling experience. And all this in the world's last truly undeveloped Gray Whale breeding lagoon.

All encounters are from small 8- or 10-seater skiffs, operated by local fishermen, which are amazingly stable and perfect for close encounters and close-up photography. And, if you're wondering if it's a good policy to encourage people to touch wild animals, consider this: if you don't scratch and tickle them, the whales simply go and find a boatload of people who will. And if, for any reason, they are not interested, they simply go their separate ways: all encounters are entirely on their terms.

The first people to meet one of San Ignacio's friendly Gray Whales were two fishermen, Jose Francisco 'Pachico' Mayoral and Santa Luis Perez. Early one morning, in February 1972, they were fishing for Black Sea Bass in the lagoon, from their panga, when the head of a whale suddenly popped out of the water and began rubbing against the side of their boat. As children, the two men had been taught to stay away from Gray Whales, because of their reputation for smashing up small boats. But the whale stayed around for almost an hour and, eventually, Francisco plucked up the courage to reach out. Far from reacting aggressively, the whale allowed him to touch it.

Word spread among the local fishermen and others tried, sometimes successfully, to pet the whales. It took a while but, eventually, news of their extraordinary encounters reached the outside world. Whale watchers and scientists began to visit San Ignacio to see if they, too, could make friends with the whales.

To begin with, it was just a few individuals that displayed friendly behavior. In 1977, for example, there was a particular young female dubbed 'Amazing Grace' or 'Gracie' who acquired a multitude of fans by being particularly approachable. Gradually, others became more friendly. But it took some individuals a while to become fully aware of their own strength: in those early days, several nudged the small boats with such high-spirited enthusiasm that passengers were knocked overboard; and one particular whale, called 'Bopper', seemed to enjoy coming up underneath small boats and giving them a good whack.

Nowadays, while lone adults are often friendly, and enjoy being scratched and tickled, most of the friendly behavior is with playful calves. They tend to be most friendly when the water is calm, and least friendly when it is choppy.

San Ignacio is a large lagoon covering an area of about 62 square miles (though only some 35 square miles is sufficiently deep to be accessible to the whales). In a good year, there appear to be whales almost everywhere. They begin to arrive in early December, reach peak numbers around the middle of

Whale watching in Baja California is unlike whale watching anywhere else in the world.

February, and a few stragglers remain well into May. Around St Valentine's Day there are typically 300–450 adults and calves in the lagoon (plus others outside in the surf beyond the lagoon entrance). Most mating activity takes place in January and early February. After mid-February, the number of single whales (males and females without calves) in the lagoon steadily decreases until, by the end of March, virtually all that are left are mothers and calves.

Most calves have been born by mid-February, but counts of mothers and calves continue to increase week by week until well into April. No one knows why, but San Ignacio appears to be a staging post for mothers and calves from other lagoons, in preparation for their long migration north.

The only other cetacean in the lagoon is the Bottlenose Dolphin. There is a sizeable resident population of about 100 animals, but hundreds of others join them at intervals to feed on huge schools of Sardines. It's hard not to feel sorry for the dolphins here: in most parts of the world, they get heaps of love and attention but, in San Ignacio, they have to compete with the friendliest whales in the world.

There are two ways to 'do' San Ignacio: join a 12-day marine safari from San Diego, on a live-aboard boat (these spend two or three days in the lagoon as part of the trip). Or it is possible to stay in one of the more than half a dozen safari-style camps (tents or wooden huts) dotted along the shoreline. Some of the camps are so close to the whales that you can lie in bed listening to the evocative sound of their blows at night. Each camp has its own fleet of pangas and no more than 16 pangas are allowed in the whale observation area (near the mouth in the southern part of the lagoon) at any one time.

Access is via the oasis town of San Ignacio – about 560 miles south of San Diego – which is just over 30 miles away. The road used to be difficult and daunting, but recently the first 27 miles has been paved; the final stretch is a rough dirt road, though it is still manageable in a two-wheel-drive compact car. Alternatively, most of the camps offer packages that include a charter flight from Tijuana or Ensenada (the plane lands on a sandy airstrip nearby).

Scammon's Lagoon (Ojo de Liebre) – Guerrero Negro Lagoon complex

Scammon's Lagoon and Guerrero Negro Lagoon are two lagoons within the same complex (Guerrero Negro is also the name of the local town, which is the main center for whale watching in the area). A handful of Gray Whales sometimes enter Manuela Lagoon, immediately to the north, but it is not considered a breeding lagoon.

There is no organized whale watching in Laguna Guerrero Negro ('Black Warrior'), the smaller of the two. Named after an American whaling ship that was wrecked on the sand bars near the mouth of the lagoon in 1858, this is the northernmost of the four Gray Whale breeding lagoons. But the whales here have a chequered history, and very few use the lagoon these days.

There is a huge salt-making facility near Guerrero Negro town. Extracting salt from Scammon's Lagoon, it is one of the largest salt mines in the world (producing up to 9 million tonnes each year). During the early days of extraction, from 1957–67, its port facilities were at Puerto Venustiano Carranza, near the entrance to Guerrero Negro Lagoon; consequently, there was heavy shipping traffic across the lagoon and constant dredging operations to maintain a sufficiently deep shipping channel. During this period, Gray

Whales abandoned Guerrero Negro altogether. Since then, the cargo ships have been leaving from El Chaparrito, in Scammon's, and Guerrero Negro has been relatively disturbance-free. The whales returned in small numbers (the highest count was in 1981, when there were 43 single whales and 164 mothers with calves) but, since the 1980s, the population has plummeted again. There were fewer than 13 adult whales inside the lagoon in the late 1990s and early 2000s and, while there hasn't been an official count since, numbers have remained low. It is unclear why they have not bounced back, but local fishermen suggest it may be due to the natural closure of the lagoon entrance caused by accumulating sand (possibly the result of physical changes in the lagoon after the original dredging operations).

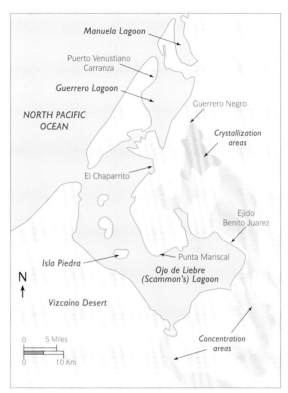

Guerrero Negro town sprang up to service the salt factory and is the headquarters of Exportadora de Sal (ESSA), one of the largest salt producers in the world: in the early 1990s, ESSA proposed a new project to expand its operations to San Ignacio Lagoon; thankfully the plan has been shelved, at least for the time-being, after a massive international outcry.

Meanwhile, the town is still a major hub for whale watching, offering a good base with hotels and restaurants suitable for day trips to see the whales. Boat trips operate in Scammon's Lagoon (named after the prolific nineteenth-century whaling captain, Charles Melville Scammon, who was the first to hunt Gray Whales along the Baja coast). It is otherwise known as Ojo de Liebre which, literally translated, means 'Eye of the Jackrabbit' – a reference to the large number of jackrabbits along this stretch of coast. Scammon's is several times larger than Guerrero Negro and unlike either of the lagoons farther south.

In many ways, it is an unlikely place for whale watching. Much of it is unmistakably industrial, vast areas of the shoreline and surrounding desert are covered in salt evaporation and crystallization ponds, and every day barges transporting cargos of salt ply in and out of the lagoon to holding facilities on Cedros Island (about 60 miles to the north).

Nevertheless, vast areas of Scammon's remain untouched and it usually harbors

A Gray Whale shows off its baleen plates.

more whales than any of the other breeding lagoons. There are frequently as many as 1,600 Gray Whales in the lagoon at one time (typically 600 mother–calf pairs plus 400 adults without calves) and, since 2013, numbers have hit a record-breaking 2,000 individuals. Arguably, this is the greatest concentration of large whales in the world. In any given year, more than half of all Gray Whale calves are born in this lagoon. There is a lot of friendly behavior, too.

Whale watchers can stay at a motel in town, or in a safari-style camp on the shore of the lagoon. There are three main whale-watching areas and embarkation points, depending on the operator. El Chaparrito is the nearest, just half an hour's drive from town and close to the salt loading facility; whale watching here focuses on the whales that congregate near the lagoon entrance; this area can be affected by strong winds and large waves rolling in from the Pacific, but has a reputation for lots of breaching. Punta Mariscal is considerably farther south, so it's a longer drive; but whale watching here concentrates on the whales around Isla

Piedra and tends to be less crowded. Finally, there is Ejido Benito Juarez, at the end of a 17-mile dirt road that turns off the highway to the south of town, where it is possible to stay in a camp on the shore.

There are several ways to get to Guerrero Negro town: drive from San Diego (approximately 12 hours); take a commercial flight from one of several US, Canadian or Mexican cities to Loreto, then drive from there (five to six hours); or take a charter flight from San Diego or Ensenada. There is a whale festival in town every year, usually during the first half of February, to celebrate the annual arrival of the Gray Whales. The whale watching here is popular, even outside the Festival period, so do book in advance.

Magdalena Bay complex

The Magdalena Bay complex is the southernmost Gray Whale breeding ground. Consisting of an extensive array of narrow mangrove channels and wide-open waterways, some 125 miles long, it is divided into three main zones: the North Zone, or

Santo Domingo Channel, from the San Jorge Fish Camp to about 12 miles south of the ocean entrance Boca de Soledad; the Central Zone, which is Magdalena Bay itself; and the Southern Zone, which is Almejas Bay.

'Mag Bay', as it's often called, harbors far fewer whales than the other lagoons – on average, it accounts for less than 6 per cent of all Gray Whale births in Baja – but, in the narrow confines of the North Zone, they do congregate more densely than elsewhere. This is the area most favored by Gray Whales, with about 200 individuals at peak times, and not surprisingly it is where most whale watching takes place.

Puerto Adolfo López Mateos lies at the heart of this concentration and is the capital of whale watching in Magdalena Bay. The whales here are so densely packed at peak times – as many as 15 per square mile – that they are often found within minutes of departure. But the whale watching can be crowded (about 60 boats have permits altogether) and the boats are usually filled to capacity. Trips usually last for two hours.

There is a smaller sub-population of up to 100 whales in the Central Zone. Whale-watching trips to see them leave from Puerto San Carlos, overlooking the main bay. These are more of a wilderness experience than trips leaving from Puerto Adolfo López Mateos farther north. The combination of the large area (Magdalena Bay itself is 30 miles long and 19 miles wide at its widest point) and the relatively low numbers of whales in this zone means there are fewer sightings. On average, in recent years there has been only one whale for every 2 square miles of bay. There are about 35 licensed boats and they are rarely filled to capacity. Trips usually last for three hours. Puerto San Carlos hosts a Gray Whale Festival every winter.

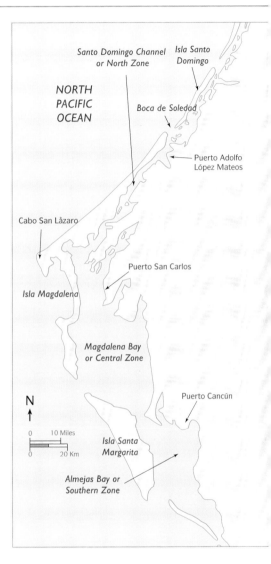

Mag Bay is a popular whale-watching destination, at least partly because of its proximity to international airports in Cabo San Lucas, La Paz and Loreto (the nearest major hub – Puerto Adolfo López Mateos and Puerto San Carlos are just a couple of hours drive away, on paved roads).

Pacific Coast

There is much more to Baja's wild Pacific coast than the Gray Whale breeding lagoons. The California Current, which flows nearly 2,000 miles southward along the Pacific coast of North America from southern British Columbia to the tip of Baja, supports a particularly vibrant marine ecosystem. Teeming with life, it attracts huge numbers of seals and sea lions, sharks and other large fish, sea turtles, seabirds and whales and dolphins.

There are feeding Blue Whales, migrating Gray Whales, breeding Humpback Whales, colossal schools of dolphins, and much more. It is one of those places where almost anything can turn up.

The easiest way to whale-watch along this coast is to join a 12-day marine safari on a live-aboard boat departing San Diego, California. These explore the entire 800-mile coastline, and beyond.

Alternatively, there are half-day boat trips from Ensenada, exploring the region around the Todos Santos Islands about 12 miles away. The main focus is Gray Whales, as they migrate past on their way to and from the Baja breeding lagoons, but Fin Whales, Humpback Whales, Pacific White-sided Dolphins, Long-beaked Common Dolphins, Short-beaked Common Dolphins and other species are frequently seen as well.

There are also half-day trips from the town of Todos Santos, farther south in the Cape region, to see Humpback Whales (best before mid-February and again in April – there are far fewer in March) and Gray Whales (mainly from late January to mid-March). Both species can readily be seen from shore here.

Overview

Main species: Blue Whale, Fin Whale, Humpback Whale, Gray Whale, Common Bottlenose Dolphin, Short-beaked Common Dolphin, Long-beaked Common Dolphin, Pacific White-sided Dolphin, Dall's Porpoise.

Occasional species: Sei Whale, Bryde's Whale, Minke Whale, Sperm Whale, Killer Whale, Short-finned Pilot Whale, Baird's Beaked Whale, Risso's Dolphin.

Other wildlife highlights: Northern Elephant Seal, Harbour Seal, Guadalupe Fur Seal, California Sea Lion, Osprey, Peregrine, Green Turtle, Loggerhead Turtle, Hawksbill Turtle, Pacific Ridley Turtle, Ocean Sunfish, Pacific Manta Ray, Munk's Mobula Ray.

Main locations: packages from San Diego, California; Ensenada, Todos Santos.

Types of tour: half-day tours; 12-day marine safaris on a live-aboard boats; most trips depart San Diego, California, travel down entire Pacific coast of Baja (stopping off for two or three days in San Ignacio Lagoon), spend nearly a week in Gulf of California, then disembark in Cabo San Lucas.

When to go: mid-December to late April.

Regulations and guidelines: official regulation NOM-131-SEMARNAT-2010; whale-watch boats require official permits.

Wildlife species are listed systematically (not in order of abundance) and frequency of sightings varies with location and season.

A Humpback Whale feeds incredibly close to a whale-watch boat.

Los Cabos & Gorda Banks

The bustling city of Cabo San Lucas – better known as a playground for movie stars and for its sports fishing and nightlife – is an unlikely whale-watching destination. But it's actually possible to see whales from beachfront hotel balconies and there are some outstandingly good trips here. Most trips last for two to three hours and they often encounter several different species. Some of the operators are first-class (with professional marine biologists

Overview

Main species: Gray Whale, Humpback Whale, Common Bottlenose Dolphin, Short-beaked Common Dolphin, Long-beaked Common Dolphin.

Occasional species: Blue Whale, Fin Whale, Bryde's Whale, Sperm Whale, Pantropical Spotted Dolphin, Spinner Dolphin.

Other wildlife highlights: California Sea Lion, Magnificent Frigatebird, Brown Booby, Green Turtle, Loggerhead Turtle, Hawksbill Turtle, Pacific Ridley Turtle, Whale Shark, Striped Marlin, Pacific Manta Ray, Munk's Mobula Ray.

Main locations: Cabo San Lucas, San José del Cabo.

Types of tour: two- to three-hour tours.

When to go: early December to mid-April.

Regulations and guidelines: official regulation NOM-131-SEMARNAT-2010; whale-watch boats require official permits.

Wildlife species are listed systematically (not in order of abundance) and frequency of sightings varies with location and season.

and hydrophones on board) but be wary of the many cowboys with zero knowledge of whales or whale watching.

Located on the southern tip of Baja, Cabo happens to be near a major Humpback Whale breeding ground. The whales traditionally gather around two seamounts (underwater mountains) called Inner and Outer Gorda Banks, some 25 miles northeast of town. Sometimes referred to locally as Wahoo Banks, they lie in deep water, some 5–7 miles from shore, and rise to within 130ft of the surface; this is a popular dive site, good for sharks and other pelagic fish as well as whales.

The whale-watching season runs from early December to mid-April and Humpbacks can be seen anywhere along the southern coast any time during this period. They are rarely inside Cabo San Lucas bay itself, but are often close to shore in the corridor between here and San José del Cabo. Los Frailes is another hotspot.

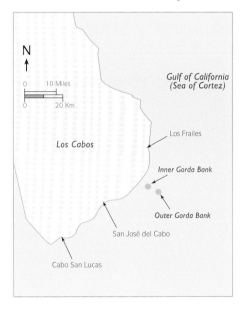

Most are winter residents (their numbers peak from late January to the end of February) but others pass through at the beginning and end of the season on migration to and from their wintering grounds farther south. What you are most likely to see depends on when you go: most mating activity (such as heat runs) is in late December and throughout January; baby Humpbacks are usually seen from early January onward; and, toward the end of the season, most encounters are with mothers and their calves.

One of the highlights at any time during the season is a chance to listen to male Humpback Whales singing their plaintive songs. Drop an underwater microphone, or hydrophone, into the water and, with a little luck, the air is filled with an unforgettable and haunting medley of moans, groans, snores, squeaks and whistles.

Gray Whales are the second most commonly seen species. Most Grays spend the winter in or around their breeding lagoons farther north, on the Pacific coast of Baja, but small groups of adults are often encountered within striking distance of

Cabo. They are usually present from January to mid-April (though they are rarely seen in El Niño years).

Dolphins are frequently encountered, too. Bottlenose Dolphins are the most common, with small groups (typically fewer than 10 animals) seen on more than half the tours. Pantropical Spotted Dolphins are also sometimes seen during late fall and winter – passing through in inquisitive groups of 10–20 – and, particularly later in the season, it is not unusual to see large pods of Short-beaked Common Dolphins and Long-beaked Common Dolphins.

Trips that venture farther offshore are sometimes rewarded with large pods of Spinner Dolphins, especially on calm days, and Sperm Whales (usually females with their calves) feeding in the deep-water trenches.

A number of other species turn up from time to time, including Blue Whale, Fin Whale and Bryde's Whale. These are all relatively common in the Sea of Cortez and off the Pacific coast, and are usually just passing through the Cabo region. Rarities include Minke Whales, False Killer Whales, Short-finned Pilot Whales, Rough-toothed Dolphins (often with Bottlenose Dolphins), Dwarf Sperm Whales and Pygmy Sperm Whales. Killer Whales (from the Eastern Tropical Pacific population) are seen roughly four or five times a season.

On 20 February 1996, during an aerial survey for Blue Whales, a single North Pacific Right Whale was observed some 9 miles south of Cabo (extending the known range of this species 336 miles south). It was only the third confirmed sighting of Right Whales in Baja.

Pantropical Spotted Dolphins are sometimes seen on trips from bustling Cabo.

Gulf of California (Sea of Cortez)

Rounding the Baja peninsula, and turning north, you enter an even more extraordinary world. This is the Gulf of California, or Sea of Cortez, which lies between Baja and 'mainland' Mexico. A large, semi-enclosed sea, covering approximately 100,000 square miles, 'the Gulf' is considered to be one of the most productive and diverse seas in the world. Visiting the more famous Gray Whale breeding lagoons without venturing into this marine paradise is like buying a book and then reading only the first chapter.

Dotted with uninhabited islands, it is home to an assortment of seabirds from Red-billed Tropicbirds to Blue-footed Boobies, weird and wonderful Elephant Trees, the world's tallest cacti, endemic Xantu's Hummingbirds, Munk's Mobula Rays that leap out of the water and flap their wings like birds (local fishermen call them 'flying pancakes'), several different species of sea turtles, and so much more. It is a hotspot for snorkeling with Whale Sharks and there is even an islet, called Los Islotes, that is probably the best place in the world to snorkel with friendly, inquisitive and playful California Sea Lions.

Blue Whales

But it's the whales that draw people back time and again. For a start, it's one of the few places in the world where Blue Whales are virtually guaranteed. Hundreds of thousands of them were killed by whalers and, although they

Overview

Main species: Blue Whale, Fin Whale, Bryde's Whale, Humpback Whale, Short-finned Pilot Whale, Dwarf Sperm Whale, Common Bottlenose Dolphin, Short-beaked Common Dolphin, Long-beaked Common Dolphin.

Occasional species: Gray Whale, Minke Whale, Sperm Whale, Killer Whale, Pygmy Beaked Whale, Cuvier's Beaked Whale, Spinner Dolphin, Risso's Dolphin, Pacific White-sided Dolphin.

Other wildlife highlights: California Sea Lion, Blue-footed Booby, Brown Booby, Magnificent Frigatebird, Red-billed Tropicbird, Xantus's Hummingbird, Green Turtle, Loggerhead Turtle, Hawksbill Turtle, Pacfic Ridley Turtle, Whale Shark, Blue Shark, Hammerhead Shark, Thresher Shark, Pacific Manta Ray, Munk's Mobula Ray.

Main locations: extended multi-day expeditions depart San Diego and La Paz; half-day to full-day tours depart Loreto; eco-lodge on Midriff Islands.

Types of tour: 12-day marine safaris on a live-aboard boats: most trips depart San Diego, California, travel down entire Pacific coast of Baja (stopping off for two or three days in San Ignacio Lagoon), spend nearly a week in Gulf of California, then disembark in Cabo San Lucas; also live-aboard boat trips departing La Paz, exploring primarily the Gulf (albeit sometimes with overland add-ons to one of the Gray Whale lagoons on opposite coast); half-day to full-day tours.

When to go: February–April for Blue Whales and some other species; Fin Whales, Bryde's Whales, Bryde's Whales and some dolphins are resident.

Regulations and guidelines: official regulation NOM-131-SEMARNAT-2010; whale-watch boats require official permits.

Wildlife species are listed systematically (not in order of abundance) and frequency of sightings varies with location and season.

were given official protection in the mid-1960s, most populations have never recovered. But there is one that seems to be thriving: dividing its time between Baja California, central and southern California, and a place called the Costa Rica Dome (an upwelling of cold, nutrient-rich water off the coast of Central America) it accounts for as many as one in four of all the Blue Whales left in the world. There are believed to be about 2,500 in the region altogether, and the numbers are slowly rising.

As many as 300 of these Blue Whales are in the Gulf during winter and early spring (they are known to be present from November–June, with a peak in February–April). Most sightings are along the southwest coast, between Loreto and Los Cabos, but they can be encountered almost anywhere. They are usually alone, or in pairs, and can sometimes be seen feeding on Pelagic Red Crabs and Krill. Mothers and calves are frequently around, too, suggesting that it is an important breeding ground (though it is still unclear whether the calves are actually born in Baja, or if the region is used as a nursery area).

Bay of Loreto National Park

About a third of the way north into the Gulf of California is the Bay of Loreto Bay National Park, which covers an area of 797 square miles (95 square miles of which is land). Ranging from Coronado Island in the north to Santa Catalina Island in the south, it includes three other islands: Carmen, Danzante and Montserrat. Declared under Presidential Decree in 1996, it became a

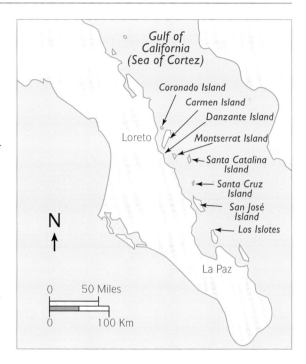

World Heritage Site in 2005. Local fishing is still permitted, but large commercial fishing boats and damaging fishing practices (such as drag-nets) are banned. The corners of Carmen, Danzante and Montserrat form the so-called 'Blue Triangle' – an important wintering ground for Blue Whales (though they also occur outside this region as well). A variety of whale-watching trips leave the historic town of Loreto in search of Blue Whales and a variety of other cetaceans that are winter or year-round residents. Most trips combine whale watching with snorkeling or hiking, and there are packages including trips to see the Gray Whales in Magdalena Bay.

It is also possible to stay at an eco-lodge on the Midriff Islands, in the north-central portion of the Gulf, where whale watching is one of the main activities. Blue Whales are seen regularly, along with a host of other species, including Fin Whales, Sperm Whales and Short-finned Pilot Whales. Nearby Bahia de Los Angeles is renowned for its Whale Sharks, which are present in fall.

No fewer than 33 cetacean species

While Blues are inevitably a highlight, no fewer than 33 cetacean species have been recorded in the Gulf of California altogether – about one third of the world's total. Indeed, it is home to one of the most varied populations of whales and dolphins anywhere. There are four main reasons for such impressive diversity: first, the Gulf has an exceptionally high rate of primary productivity that yields plenty of food; second, the complex topography of the seabed results in lots of different underwater habitats; third, conditions range from temperate in the north to tropical in the south; and fourth, the warm and relatively calm waters during winter and spring make it a perfect breeding ground.

There are resident Fin Whales in the Gulf, though the population seems to have declined from a high of 800 individuals in the early 1990s to some 300–400 today; it is unclear whether this represents a worrying drop in numbers or whether earlier figures were artificially high due to strong El Niños. During winter and spring the whales tend to be found close to shore mainly in the southern portion, between La Paz and Loreto, and they are rarely seen in deep water in the middle or on the other side of the Gulf. There is some evidence that they move farther north during summer and fall.

There is also a resident population of several hundred Bryde's Whales, and they are frequently seen throughout the Gulf. While Sei Whales are fairly common along the Pacific coast of Baja, they are rarely seen in the Gulf; most records are from the southwest. Minke Whales are also rarely seen, though there are records throughout the Gulf (from San Felipe in the north to La Paz Bay in the south) particularly during winter and spring. There is a significant breeding population of Humpback Whales off the southern tip of Baja, and quite a few wander farther north into the Gulf.

Some 300 Blue Whales enter the Gulf of California every winter and early spring.

A Sperm Whale dives in the Gulf of California.

The vast majority of the eastern North Pacific Gray Whales spend the winter in or around their breeding lagoons along the west coast of Baja, of course, but small numbers venture into the Gulf (usually solitary individuals or mothers with calves). There tend to be more when the sea-surface temperature is lower than normal, such as during La Niña events. Until 1984, a handful of Grays still visited two winter breeding lagoons on 'mainland' Mexico, on the other side of the Gulf: Yavaros-Tijahui, Sonora, and Bahía Santa María-La Reforma, Sinaloa.

There are believed to be several hundred Sperm Whales resident in the Gulf, though the frequency of sightings varies greatly from year to year. There is a known hotspot around Isla San Pedro Martir, in the central Gulf, and they are frequently seen above the San José Channel, farther south, but their distribution is tied to the presence of their favorite prey, Jumbo Squid, and the details of their movements are poorly understood. This is believed to be an important breeding ground: most encounters are with females and their dependent young, while adult males (and groups of subadult males) visit from time to time. There are significant

numbers of Dwarf Sperm Whales, too, especially on the western side, and they are frequently seen (mainly in calm weather – otherwise they are easy to miss). Strandings data suggests that Pygmy Sperm Whales are distributed throughout the entire Gulf, from San Felipe and Puerto Peñasco in the north to La Paz and Mazatlán in the south, but they are rarely seen.

Short-finned Pilot Whales are a common sight and they are found throughout the Gulf. There are occasional sightings of Killer Whales (typically in groups of five to six) and False Killer Whales, too, with Killer Whale sightings as far north as Bahia de Los Angeles.

The Gulf can be good for beaked whales, though they are rarely seen in anything but calm conditions. There are more records of Pygmy Beaked Whales here than anywhere else in the world; one particular hotspot, where they are encountered with some regularity, is in the southern portion between the islands of San José and Santa Cruz. Cuvier's Beaked Whales are not seen particularly frequently, but they are considered to be the commonest beaked whales in the eastern North Pacific, and are believed to occur in higher densities in the Gulf than elsewhere in the region; they can be encountered almost anywhere, but there appear to be two main areas of concentration: southwest of Los Frailes (the east cape region) and in the central Gulf (around Isla San Pedro Mártir).

The commonest dolphins are Bottlenose, Long-beaked Common and Short-beaked Common. Six other dolphins are seen from time to time: Risso's Dolphin, particularly in the central portion (south of the Midriff Islands); Pacific White-sided Dolphin, which is relatively common along Baja's Pacific coast, but much rarer in the Gulf (most sightings are in the southwest, roughly between Loreto and Cabo San Lucas, during winter and spring); Rough-toothed Dolphin, which is believed to occur in small numbers throughout the Gulf; Pantropical Spotted Dolphin, which is rare in the Gulf itself but is seen quite frequently in the mouth (especially off the coasts of the states of Sinaloa and Nayarit, in the southeast); Spinner Dolphin, which is sometimes seen in the southern Gulf (it is worth checking schools of Common Dolphins for lone individuals); and Striped Dolphin, which occasionally enters the southern portion.

In addition, there are single or sparse records of seven other species: North Pacific Right Whale, Melon-headed Whale, Baird's Beaked Whale, Longman's Beaked Whale, Blainville's Beaked Whale, Ginkgo-toothed Beaked Whale and Hubbs' Beaked Whale.

The Vaquita

The Upper Gulf of California is also home to one of the most endangered marine mammals in the world: the Vaquita, or Gulf of California Porpoise, which is in imminent danger of extinction.

The Vaquita was probably always a rare species (its population has never been particularly large and its range always limited) but entanglement and accidental drowning in gillnets for fish and shrimp have, for decades, been killing more than are born every year. The Upper Gulf of California and Colorado River Delta Biosphere Reserve was established in 1993; and a Vaquita Refuge was declared in 2005 – which included the positions of about 80 per cent of all verified Vaquita sightings. Unfortunately, a temporary gillnet ban in the Vaquita's range ends in spring 2017 and

Another dead Vaquita, caught in a gillnet.

there are fears that the species may not last long once fishing resumes. There is now a proposal to try to capture the last few survivors, to keep them safe.

But it may be too little too late. Scientists have long warned that anything short of eliminating all gillnets from the Vaquita's range *permanently* (requiring proper enforcement, as well as better efforts to help fishermen develop less harmful fishing methods and to establish alternative income-generating activities) would be insufficient to prevent its extinction. Sure enough, following a concerted visual and acoustic survey in 2015, and acoustic surveys in the years since, it has been estimated that as few as 30 Vaquita survive.

It is incredibly difficult to see a Vaquita, and there are no official tours. However, given that it has the most restricted distribution of any cetacean, there is only one small area to look. It occurs mainly north of 30°45'N and west of 114°20'W, and almost all encounters in recent years have been within sight of the granite outcrop Roca Consag (usually between Consag and San Felipe Bay).

Revillagigedo Archipelago

Lying approximately 250 miles southwest of Cabo San Lucas, this wild and remote archipelago of four volcanic islands (Socorro, San Benedicto, Roca Partida and distant Clarión) was declared a National Biosphere Reserve in 1994. Also known as the Socorro Islands, after the largest island in the group, it is well known for its rich waters teeming with sharks, Manta Rays and other big fish.

The reserve covers a total area of 949 square miles (including 67 square miles of land) and is a key Humpback Whale breeding ground. Relatively little is known about the whales in this sub-population and one particular mystery is why some of them have also been observed in Hawai'i, which is another distinct breeding ground. Recent research suggests that most migrate to feeding areas in the Gulf of Alaska but, in 2005, one individual swam all the way from Socorro to the Commander Islands, in Russia's Bering Sea (a minimum distance of 4,924 miles).

Special permits are required to visit Revillagigedo – surveillance posts on the

Overview

Main species: Humpback Whale, Common Bottlenose Dolphin.

Other wildlife highlights: sharks (including Hammerhead, Silky, Oceanic Whitetip, Silvertip, Galapagos, Tiger, Whale), Pacific Manta Ray.

Main locations: most trips leave from Cabo San Lucas.

Types of tour: no dedicated whale watching; extended multi-day live-aboard dive trips.

When to go: January to early April.

Regulations and guidelines: official regulation NOM-131-SEMARNAT-2010; whale-watch boats require official permits; special permits also required to visit the islands.

Wildlife species are listed systematically (not in order of abundance) and frequency of sightings varies with location and season.

islands enforce the regulations – and there are no dedicated whale-watching trips. However, it is possible to visit on a dive boat. It takes about 24–26 hours to get there from Cabo.

Divers sometimes encounter Humpback Whales underwater and, between dives, there are often chances to watch whales from the dive boat. But only some operators have whale-watching permits and no one is permitted to search for whales with the explicit purpose of diving, snorkeling or swimming with them. Nevertheless, the distant songs of Humpback Whales are a feature on many dives in the region and Bottlenose Dolphins are frequently encountered while travelling between dive sites. There is also at least one group of Bottlenose Dolphins that frequently takes an interest in divers.

Bottlenose Dolphins are frequently encountered while travelling between dive sites.

Banderas Bay

Banderas Bay, or Bahía de Banderas, within the states of Jalisco and Nayarit, is Mexico's main whale-watching location outside Baja. Covering an area of nearly 400 square miles, with a 60-mile coastline, it is one of the country's largest and deepest bays. The continental shelf is wide in the north, but narrow in the south (where there is a submarine canyon – the Banderas Bay Submarine Canyon – that lies parallel to the southern shore of the bay, dropping to a depth of 5,760ft). The Middle America Trench, where the water depth quickly drops to over 13,000ft, begins to the west of Banderas Bay. The main town, Puerto Vallarta, is a popular tourist resort and cruise ship port, and is roughly 320 miles southeast of Cabo San Lucas.

Banderas Bay is an important breeding ground for Humpback Whales, with an estimated 400–600 individuals visiting the bay each season. The whales were hunted intensively in the mid-nineteenth century (Banderas Bay was known as Humpback Bay in those days) but, after years of protection, numbers are slowly increasing.

In recent years, peak sightings have occurred from the full Moon in late December to the full Moon in February. The beginning of the season sees mostly adult Humpbacks, with new whales (males and females) arriving every day; this is also when most mating activity is observed. In good whale years, from late December until well into February, high energy groups are seen almost daily. Most of the mating is over by mid-February and the newly pregnant females begin their migration north. Most years, baby Humpbacks start to be seen

Overview

Main species: Humpback Whale, Common Bottlenose Dolphin, Pantropical Spotted Dolphin, Rough-toothed Dolphin.

Occasional species: Gray Whale, Bryde's Whale, Killer Whale, False Killer Whale, Pygmy Sperm Whale, Spinner Dolphin.

Other wildlife highlights: Magnificent Frigatebird, Red-billed Tropicbird, Brown Booby, Blue-footed Booby, Caspian Tern, Royal Tern, Elegant Tern, Forster's Tern, Black Tern, Laughing Gull, Heermann's Gull, Least Storm Petrel, Pacific Ridley Turtle, Hawksbill Turtle, Green Turtle, Pacific Manta Ray, Devil Ray.

Main locations: Puerto Vallarta, Nuevo Vallarta, La Cruz de Huanacaxtle, Punta de Mita, Sayulita; San Blas (just over 60 miles farther north), Mazatlan (190 miles farther north).

Types of tour: 3- to 5.5-hour tours; research programs.

When to go: official whale-watching season early December (exact date varies year to year from 1–15 December) to 23 March (peak whale numbers December and January); dolphins present year-round (most abundant March–April, when shoals of Sardines inside the bay); dolphin swimming May–November.

Regulations and guidelines: official regulation NOM-131-SEMARNAT-2010; whale-watch boats require official permits.

Wildlife species are listed systematically (not in order of abundance) and frequency of sightings varies with location and season.

in mid-December; by late December they are a common sight. Later in the season, after most of the breeding adults have left, is dominated by mother and calf pairs (together with a few persistent males).

There is strong evidence that the Humpback population here is thriving. Since

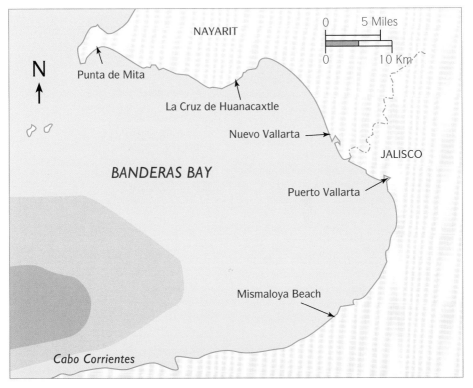

Rough-toothed Dolphins are being seen more and more frequently in Banderas Bay.

A Humpback Whale mother and calf in Banderas Bay.

the beginning of the century, researchers have observed more and more calves each season and a good diversity of age classes, including calves, yearlings, juveniles, sub-adults and adults.

There are a variety of tours to choose from, on everything from Zodiacs and pangas to catamarans and speedboats, running from the beginning of December to the end of March. Most last for a few hours to half a day. Several have marine biologists and hydrophones on board, one allows participants to help with research, and another uses a spotter plane to track the whales.

While Humpbacks are the main focus, Banderas Bay is the year-round home of a resident pod of Bottlenose Dolphins and they are seen on most trips (some companies also offer tours to snorkel with them, outside the whale season). Pantropical Spotted Dolphins are seen quite often, too, typically in groups of 10–50, and they regularly interact with Humpback Whales; however, groups of over 1,000 are sometimes seen from mid-March to mid-April. Rough-toothed Dolphins are being seen more frequently these days and are present year-round. They sometimes interact with the resident Bottlenose Dolphins and, during winter, often hang out with the Humpback Whales. There is often major interaction between the Rough-toothed Dolphins and Humpbacks – the whales produce loud trumpeting sounds and slash their tails, while the dolphins jump around them.

There are occasional sightings of Bryde's Whales and the peak period is between February–June, with some also in November and early December. Locally, they are known as 'Sardineras', as they usually appear whenever there is an abundance of Sardines. Gray Whales are often sighted in years when the water is colder.

Killer Whales visit the bay many times a year to feed on turtles, Manta Rays, dolphins and whales (there are transient groups from the Eastern Tropical Pacific population among them, but there are still many questions about which ecotypes are most commonly seen in the bay). Sightings of False Killer Whales vary from year to year, but some years they are seen throughout the winter. A recent investigative survey discovered a large nursery group of Sperm Whales only a mile from the Nayarit coast, though little is known about them. Pygmy Sperm Whales have been observed almost every winter since the mid-1990s, over the northern slope of the submarine canyon, and it's thought possible that they are present year-round. And there are also some Spinner Dolphins, which are frequently in deeper waters outside the bay, usually in large schools containing several hundred individuals.

There are also half-day tours from two locations farther north: San Blas and Mazatlan (which is due east of Cabo San Lucas). Mazatlan in particular, runs trips from mid-December to mid-April, focusing on migrating Humpback Whales. Other species are encountered from time to time. And there are trips year-round in Mazatlan to snorkel with Bottlenose Dolphins, Pantropical Spotted Dolphins and Spinner Dolphins in the bay.

It is worth noting that whale watching in the Banderas Bay region is greatly affected by El Niño and El Niña events. In years of great temperature abnormalities, the distribution and abundance of cetaceans can be very different to the 'norm'. For example, in 2015, Humpback Whale abundance was about 25 per cent of normal, but there were sightings of rarely observed Sperm Whales and Risso's Dolphins.

Bryde's Whales appear whenever there is an abundance of sardines.

Bahia de Petatlán

There is another significant population of Humpback Whales about 50 miles south of Puerto Vallarta, in Guerrero state. Within a few hours' drive of Acapulco, Bahia de Petatlán is a 75-square-mile bay with a long, pristine beach and a lot of whales and dolphins.

Several hundred individual Humpbacks have so far been identified on this important breeding ground, where they mate and calve, and it is believed that as many as 2,000 pass through the area on migration between Central America and the west coast of the US.

As well as the Humpbacks, Bottlenose Dolphins, Rough-toothed Dolphins, Pantropical Spotted Dolphins and Spinner Dolphins are seen regularly. Schools of more than 700 Spinner Dolphins have been observed on a number of occasions and researchers have so far cataloged about 150 Rough-toothed Dolphins (they are also investigating a little-known behavior in

Overview

Main species: Humpback Whale, Common Bottlenose Dolphin, Rough-toothed Dolphin, Pantropical Spotted Dolphin, Spinner Dolphin.

Occasional species: Short-beaked Common Dolphin.

Other wildlife highlights: American Crocodile, Leatherback Turtle, Pacific Ridley Turtle, Green Turtle, Hawksbill Turtle, Golden Cow-nosed Ray, Spotted Eagle Ray, Munk's Mobula Ray, Red-billed Tropicbird, Blue-footed Booby, Brown-footed Booby, Roseate Spoonbill, Wood Stork.

Main locations: residential research programs: Barra de Potosí; half-day tours: Zihuatanejo, Ixtapa and La Majahua.

Types of tour: half-day tours, week-long research programs.

When to go: January–March.

Regulations and guidelines: official regulation NOM-131-SEMARNAT-2010.; self-monitoring by trained boat operators.

Wildlife species are listed systematically (not in order of abundance) and frequency of sightings varies with location and season.

Spinner Dolphins are seen regularly in Bahia de Petatlán.

which the Rough-toothed Dolphins appear to molest Humpback Whales). Short-beaked Common Dolphins are encountered from time to time, too.

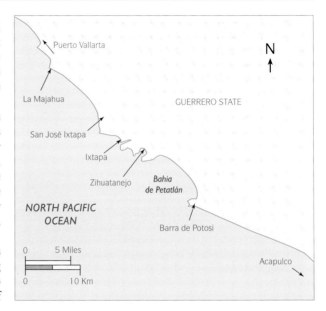

More unusual visitors have included Bryde's Whale, Sperm Whale, Killer Whale, False Killer Whale, Short-finned Pilot Whale and Cuvier's Beaked Whale (which is probably relatively common in Guerrero state, though farther offshore).

During the winter, it is possible to join week-long land-based expeditions to help with the Whales of Guerrero Research Project. Volunteers are based in Barra de Potosí, just south of Zihuatanego, and work mainly in Bahia de Petatlán. Project staff are also training local guides and fishermen, to enable them to run educational and responsible whale-watching trips in the future (the workshops cover everything from Humpback Whale biology to best boat practices and regulations). Now it is possible to join four-hour ecotours from Zihuatanejo, Ixtapa and La Majahua (focusing on whales and dolphins) with fishermen who have participated in these workshops. You can also pay extra to have a bilingual trainee biologist from the project on board.

Bahia de Petatlán is an important breeding ground for Humpback Whales.

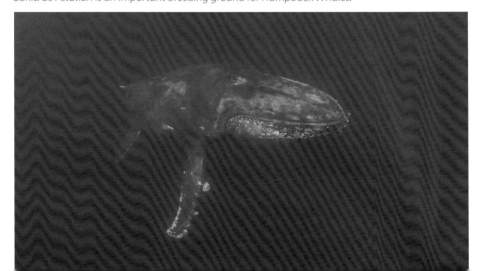

MEXICO: EAST COAST

Yucatán Peninsula

There is great potential for whale watching around the Yucatán Peninsula. No fewer than 30 species of cetacean have been recorded here altogether – including everything from Pygmy Killer Whales and Melon-headed Whales to Blainville's Beaked Whales and Fraser's Dolphins – although, admittedly, few of these could be considered common. It was also one of the last remaining strongholds of the Caribbean Monk Seal, which is now extinct.

Much whale and dolphin watching here is opportunistic, but there are tours to see Bottlenose Dolphins in the beautiful Sian Ka'an Biosphere Reserve, on the northeastern coast of the peninsula. Lying roughly halfway between Tulum and Majahual, and just 90 miles south of the mega-resort of Cancún, this is the largest protected area in the Mexican Caribbean. Sian Ka'an (which means 'where the sky is born' in Mayan) consists of 2,000 square miles of tropical forests, mangrove lagoons, fresh- and saltwater marshes, white sand flats and a large marine section intersected by a huge barrier reef.

The area is teeming with wildlife, including resident Bottlenose Dolphins. They are seen on most trips and often approach the boats closely. One famously jumped into a dolphin-watching boat in 2016 (it was returned safely to the sea).

Most visitors get to Sian Ka'an from Tulum, and enter the reserve through the main entrance at Boca Paila. From there, it is a rough drive (taking about an hour – though it takes longer and is more difficult

Bottlenose Dolphins are resident.

Overview

Main species: Common Bottlenose Dolphin.

Other wildlife highlights: West Indian Manatee, Magnificent Frigatebird, Jabiru, American Flamingo, American Crocodile, Morelet's Crocodile, Hawksbill Turtle, Loggerhead Turtle, Green Turtle.

Main locations: Sian Ka'an Biosphere Reserve.

Types of tour: half-day and full-day trips.

When to go: year-round.

Regulations and guidelines: official regulation NOM-131-SEMARNAT-2010; whale-watch boats require official permits.

Wildlife species are listed systematically (not in order of abundance) and frequency of sightings varies with location and season.

during the rainy season, from late May to October) to the remote fishing village of Punta Allen, which is where the trips leave from. Alternatively, arrange to get picked up from any of the towns along the coast (Cancún, Playa del Carmen, Akumal or Tulum) and use a boat to avoid the worst part of the road.

abyssal plain Ocean floor beyond the continental shelf, where the sea is generally more than 3,200ft deep.

amphipod Small, shrimp-like crustacean that is a food source for some whales.

balaenopterid *See* 'rorqual'.

baleen plate Dense, comb-like structure hanging down from the upper jaws of most large whales (baleen whales in the Mysticeti); formerly known as 'whalebone'; made of keratin (the same protein that makes hair, nails and rhino horn); hundreds of baleen plates packed tightly together, with fibrous fringes along the inner surfaces, form a giant sieve for filter-feeding on small prey.

baleen whale Member of the Mysticeti; a predominantly large whale with baleen plates instead of teeth.

beak Elongated snout of many cetaceans; anterior portion of skull that includes both the upper and lower jaws.

benthic Living in, on, or just above the ocean floor.

blow Refers both to the act of breathing – the explosive exhalation followed immediately by an inhalation – and to the misty cloud of water droplets (condensed water, a fine spray of mucous from inside the lungs, and seawater trapped in the blowholes) formed when a whale breathes; also known as a spout.

blowhole Nasal opening or nostril on the top of the head; baleen whales have two blowholes, toothed whales have one.

blubber Layer of fatty tissue between the skin and underlying muscle of most marine mammals; important for insulation, instead of (or as well as) fur.

bubble-netting Feeding technique used by Humpback Whales in which they produce fishing nets by blowing bubbles underwater.

bycatch Animals that are caught accidentally or incidentally during fishing operations (when they are not the target species of the fishery).

callosity Area of roughened, keratinised tissue on the head of a right whale, inhabited by large numbers of whale lice.

caudal fin Tail fin.

cephalopod Member of a group of molluscs including squid, cuttlefish and octopuses.

cetacean Any member of the Cetacea, a group of aquatic mammals that includes all whales, dolphins and porpoises.

continental shelf Gently sloping submerged shelf from shore to a depth of about 330ft, between a continental landmass and the ocean floor.

continental slope The stretch of ocean floor that drops between the continental shelf and the abyssal plain; like a giant cliff, ridge or steep-sided canyon, it is also known as the shelf edge and is often where cetaceans (and other wildlife) concentrate in greater numbers.

copepod Minute crustacean that occurs in great abundance in the sea and is an important food source for some whales.

crustacean Member of a group of nearly 70,000 invertebrates (animals without backbones) that includes lobsters, crabs, shrimps and barnacles; characterised by a segmented body, chitinous exoskeleton, jointed limbs and two pairs of antennae; mostly aquatic, crustaceans are an important source of food for many marine animals.

diatom Microscopic single-celled algae, abundant in marine and freshwater environments, with cell walls of silica.

dorsal cape Distinct dark region on the backs of some toothed whales, dolphins and porpoises, mostly in front of the dorsal fin (sometimes stretching to behind) and dipping onto the sides to varying degrees; not to be confused with the saddle patch.

dorsal fin Raised structure on the back of most (but not all) cetaceans (and various other, unrelated, marine and freshwater vertebrates); not supported by bone.

drift net Fishing net that hangs in the water, unseen and undetectable, and is carried freely with the ocean currents and winds; a gillnet that is not anchored; strongly criticised for catching everything in its path, from seabirds and turtles to whales and dolphins.

drive fishery Technique used to capture dolphins and other small toothed whales, usually using speedboats to herd them into a bay or shallow water; a net is then drawn across the mouth of the bay to prevent their escape, before the fishermen/hunters wade into the water to kill the animals.

echolocation Process of sending out high-frequency sounds and interpreting the returning echoes to build up a 'sound picture', as in sonar; used by many cetaceans to orientate, navigate and find food.

euphausiid Krill.

falcate Sickle-shaped or back-curved; often used to describe the shape of a dorsal fin with a concave rear margin.

fast ice Stable sea ice attached to land.

filter feeding Technique used by baleen whales to strain small prey animals from the water, using baleen plates.

flipper Variably shaped, flattened, paddle-like forelimb of a marine mammal (also known as the 'pectoral fin' or 'pec fin').

fluke Horizontally flattened tail of a cetacean (in contrast to the vertically flattened tail of a fish); two flukes comprise a cetacean's tail.

gill net A fishing net that is suspended vertically in the water and ensnares fish by the gill covers (or other parts of their body) as they try to back out of its meshes; usually used near the coast or in a river.

great whale Any large whale (including all the baleen whales and the Sperm Whale).

hydrophone Waterproofed, underwater microphone used to detect whale (and other) sounds.

infrasonic Low frequency sound, below the normal range of human hearing (lower than 20Hz).

keel Distinctive bulge (a deepening or thickening) on the tailstock near the flukes; it can be dorsal, ventral, or both.

krill Small, shrimp-like crustacean that is a major food source for many large whales; there are about 85 different species, ranging from 0.3–2.4 inches in length; also known as a euphausiid.

lactation Production of milk by a female mammal to feed its young.

longline A buoyed line up to tens of kilometers long, with many branch lines, each terminating in a baited hook; usually left to drift in the surface waters of the ocean (though sometimes anchored) to catch large pelagic fish such as swordfish, tuna and sharks.

mandible Lower jaw of the skull.

melon Bulging fatty tissue that forms the 'forehead' of toothed cetaceans, believed to be used to focus and modulate sounds for echolocation.

Mysticeti Group containing all the toothless or baleen whales (known as mysticetes).

oceanic Lives in deep water seaward of the continental shelf.

Odontoceti Group containing all the toothed whales, dolphins and porpoises (known as odontocetes).

pectoral fin *See* 'flipper'.

peduncle *See* 'tail stock'.

pelagic Waters of the open sea, beyond the continental shelf and away from the seabed; also used to describe the animals that live in these waters.

pelagic trawl Bag-like net that is towed through the upper part of the water column.

photo-identification Technique for studying cetaceans using photographs as a permanent record of identifiable individuals.

phytoplankton Planktonic plant life.

plankton Passively floating, or weakly swimming, plant and animal life that occurs in swarms usually near the surface of open waters.

pod Coordinated group of closely related killer whales; the term is also used for a group of any medium-sized toothed whales.

polar Region around either the North Pole or South Pole (ie the Arctic or Antarctic); characterised by cold and often ice-covered waters.

porpoising When members of the dolphin family (and, less commonly, some other cetaceans) travel at high speed and make low, arcing leaps clear of the water every time they take a breath.

purse-seine net Vertical curtain of netting set around a shoal of fish, then gathered at the bottom and drawn in to form a 'purse' to prevent the fish from escaping.

remora Type of fish that has modified its dorsal fin into a sucker (thus the alternative name 'suckerfish') to attach onto large marine animals such as whales and dolphins (and anything else in the water, from turtles to submarines).

rorqual Baleen whale of the family Balaenopteridae, characterised by a variable number of pleats that run longitudinally from the chin to the navel; the pleats expand during feeding to increase the capacity of the mouth; otherwise known as a Balaenopterid.

rostrum Beak-like projection at the front of the head of a cetacean; also used to describe specifically the upper jaw.

saddle patch Light colored saddle-shaped marking behind the dorsal fin of some cetaceans, which extends to a variable degree onto the sides; not to be confused with the dorsal cape.

school Term for a coordinated group, normally used in association with dolphins, that swims and feeds together; often used synonymously with 'herd'.

snout *See* 'beak'.

sonar *See* 'echolocation'.

spout *See* 'blow'.

stranding The act of coming ashore, intentionally or accidentally, alive or dead.

submarine canyon Deep, steep-sided valley in the continental shelf.

tail stock Muscular region of the tail between the dorsal fin and the flukes; also called the caudal peduncle, or peduncle.

temperate Mid-latitude regions of the world, between the tropics and the poles, characterised by a mild, seasonally changing climate.

toothed whale *See* 'Odontoceti'.

tropical Low-latitude regions of the world, between the Tropics of Capricorn and Cancer, characterised by a warm, seasonally stable climate.

tubercle Circular raised protuberance, or bump, found on some cetaceans (usually along the edges of pectoral and dorsal fins, but also on a Humpback Whale's head).

turbid Term used to describe water with poor visibility because of the presence of sediment or other suspended matter.

ultrasonic High frequency sound, above the normal range of human hearing (higher than 20kHz).

upwelling Process by which ocean water rises from the depths, forced by currents, winds or density gradients, bringing nutrients to the surface (normally resulting in increased production); it occurs most often along the edges of continental shelves and submarine canyons.

whalebone *See* 'baleen'.

whale louse An amphipod crustacean (not an insect) adapted for living on the skin of cetaceans.

zooplankton Planktonic animal life.

FURTHER READING

There are too many wonderful books on whales, dolphins and porpoises to list them all. But here is a small and varied selection more relevant to North America and whale watching:

Brakes, Philippa, and Simmonds, Mark Peter, *Whales and Dolphins: Cognition, Culture, Conservation and Human Perceptions*, Earthscan, 2011.

Baird, Robin W., *The Lives of Hawai'i's Dolphins and Whales: Natural History and Conservation*, University of Hawai'i Press, 2016.

Darling, Jim, *Humpbacks: Unveiling the Mysteries*, Granville Island Publishing, 2009.

Ford, John K. B., *Marine Mammals of British Columbia*, Royal BC Museum, 2014.

Higham, James, Bejder, Lars, and Williams, Rob, *Whale-watching: Sustainable Tourism and Ecological Management*, Cambridge University Press, 2014.

Hoyt, Erich, *Marine Protected Areas For Whales, Dolphins and Porpoises* (2nd edn), Earthscan, 2011.

IFAW, *Whale Watching Worldwide: Tourism numbers, expenditures and expanding economic benefits*, IFAW, 2009.

Jefferson, Thomas A., Webber, Marc A., Pitman, Robert L., *Marine Mammals of the World: A Comprehensive Guide to Their Identification* (2nd edn), 2015.

Kraus, Scott D., and Rolland, Rosalind M., *The Urban Whale: North Atlantic Right Whales at the Crossroads*, Harvard University Press, 2007.

Perrin, William F., Wursig, Bernd and Thewissen, J.G.M. (eds), *Encyclopedia of Marine Mammals*, Academic Press, 2008.

Shirihai, Hadoram, and Jarrett, Brett, *Whales, Dolphins and Seals: A Field Guide to the Marine Mammals of the World*, A & C Black, 2006.

Swartz, Steven L., *Lagoon Time: A Guide to Gray Whales and the Natural History of San Ignacio Lagoon*, The Ocean Foundation, 2014.

Wilson, Ben, and Wilson, Angus, *The World Guide to Whale & Dolphin Watching*, Colin Baxter, 2006.

Wilson, Don E., Mittermeier, Russell A., *Handbook of the Mammals of the World: 4. Sea Mammals*, Lynx Edicions, 2014.

Würsig, Bernd, Jefferson, Thomas A., and Schmidly, David J., *The Marine Mammals of the Gulf of Mexico*, Texas A&M University Press, 2000.

ACKNOWLEDGMENTS

Many wonderful people have helped with this book – answering my endless questions, providing information and commenting on early tentative drafts – and it couldn't have been written without them. Their generous contributions have helped me to make fewer mistakes than I would have made on my own (incidentally, any errors that remain are entirely down to me) and I'd like to thank them all for their time, enthusiasm, generosity and support. It is very much appreciated.

In particular, I would like to acknowledge the expertise and invaluable assistance of Erich Hoyt (Senior Research Fellow, Whale and Dolphin Conservation), Vassili Papastavrou (Whale Biologist), and the staff at Whale and Dolphin Conservation (in particular, Alison Wood, Courtney Vail and Cathy Williamson). I am also deeply grateful to all the whale-watch operators, whale scientists, friends and colleagues listed here:

UNITED STATES

HAWAI'I
Robin W. Baird (Research Biologist, Cascadia Research Collective, Affiliate Faculty, Hawai'i Institute of Marine Biology www.cascadiaresearch.org)

SOUTHEAST ALASKA
Fred Sharpe (Principal Investigator, Alaska Whale Foundation – www.alaskawhalefoundation.org)

NORTHWESTERN GULF OF ALASKA
Craig Matkin (Executive Director, North Gulf Oceanic Society – www.whalesalaska.org)

COOK INLET
Greg Balogh (Field Office Supervisor, NOAA Fisheries, Anchorage alaskafisheries.noaa.gov/pr/belugas)

ALEUTIAN ISLANDS & PRIBILOF ISLANDS
Melissa Good (Alaska Sea Grant Advisory Program, Unalaska – www.alaska.edu)

SAN JUAN ISLANDS & PUGET SOUND
Elizabeth Seely (Soundwatch Boater Education Program, The Whale Museum, Friday Harbor www.whalemuseum.org)

WESTPORT & THE OLYMPIC COAST
Phil Anderson (Westport Seabirds www.westportseabirds.com)

OREGON
Luke Parsons (Interpretive Ranger, Depoe Bay Whale Center, Newport www.oregonstateparks.org)

CALIFORNIA
Robert L. Pitman (Marine Ecologist, Marine Mammal and Turtle Division, Southwest Fisheries Science Center, NOAA swfsc.noaa.gov)

MONTEREY BAY
Nancy Black (Captain/Marine Biologist/Owner, Monterey Bay Whale Watch www.montereybaywhalewatch.com)
Robert L. Pitman (Marine Ecologist, Marine Mammal and Turtle Division, Southwest Fisheries Science Center, NOAA swfsc.noaa.gov)

NEW ENGLAND
Mason Weinrich (Executive Director / CCS, Adjunct Scientist, Whale Center of New England www.whalecenter.org)
Laura Howes (Head Naturalist, Boston Harbor Cruises – www.bostonharborcruises.com)
Jessica K. D. Taylor (Whale Researcher)

EASTERN SEABOARD: NEW YORK TO GEORGIA
Arthur H. Kopelman (President, Coastal Research and Education Society of Long Island www.cresli.org)
Paul L. Sieswerda (President & CEO, Gotham Whale – www.gothamwhale.org)
Jessica Taylor (President, Outer Banks Center for Dolphin Research – www.obxdolphins.org)
Jessica K. D. Taylor (Whale Researcher)

FLORIDA & THE GULF STATES
Randall S. Wells (Director, Chicago Zoological

Society's Sarasota Dolphin Research Program www.sarasotadolphin.org)
Jessica K. D. Taylor (Whale Researcher)

CANADA

VANCOUVER ISLAND (JOHNSTONE STRAIT)
Alison Wood (Policy Integration Manager, Whale and Dolphin Conservation – uk.whales.org)
Jackie Hildering (Marine Educator and Whale Researcher – www.TheMarineDetective.com)
Jim and Mary Borrowman (Telegraph Cove)

VANCOUVER ISLAND (SALISH SEA)
Amanda Madro (Captain, Sidney Whale Watching www.sidneywhalewatching.com)
Liz Calhoun (Captain, Orca Spirit Adventures www.orcaspirit.com)

VANCOUVER ISLAND (WEST COAST)
Toddy Landry (Archipelago Cruises www.archipelagocruises.com)

BAY OF FUNDY
David Welch (Founder, Fundy Tide Runners Whale Watching and Nature Tours www.fundytiderunners.com)
Laurie Murison (Senior Scientist and Executive Director, Grand Manan Whale & Seabird Research Station – www.gmwsrs.info)
Moira Brown (North Atlantic Right Whale researcher)

NEWFOUNDLAND
Dave Snow (President, Wildland Tours www.wildlands.com)

THE GULLY
Rick and Karen Miles (Wanderbird Expedition Cruises – www.wanderbirdcruises.com)

ST. LAWRENCE RIVER & GULF OF ST. LAWRENCE
Richard Sears (Mingan Island Cetacean Study www.rorqual.com)

NUNAVUT
Graham Dickson (Founder & CEO, Arctic Kingdom – www.arctickingdom.com)
Nate Small (Expedition Leader, One Ocean Expeditions – www.oneoceanexpeditions.com)

CHURCHILL (HUDSON BAY)
Grant MacNeil (Executive Director, Churchill Northern Studies Center www.churchillscience.ca)

INUVIK
Kylik Kisoun Taylor (Owner/Guide, Tundra North Tours – www.tundranorthtours.com)

MEXICO

BAJA CALIFORNIA
Mike Keating (Owner/Captain, Spirit of Adventure www.spiritofadventurefishing.com)
Brian Evans (Captain, Spirit of Adventure www.spiritofadventurefishing.com)

OJO DE LIEBRE (SCAMMON'S LAGOON)
Edgardo Maya (Mario's Tours www.mariostours.com)
Florin Botezatu (Manager/Lead Guide, Miramar Adventures – www.miramar-adventures.com)

LOS CABOS & GORDA BANKS
Peter Wilcox (Owner, Whale Watch Cabo www.whalewatchcabo.com)

GULF OF CALIFORNIA
Pamela Bolles, Naturalist/Whale Guide, Loreto Blue Whales – www.loretowhalewatching.com)

BANDERAS BAY
Oscar Frey (Oceanologist and Chief Researcher, Deep Blue Conservancy, Puerto Vallarta www.deepblueconservancy.org)
Peter Wilcox (Owner, Whale Watch Vallarta www.whalewatchvallarta.com)
Isabel Cárdenas Oteiza (Oceanographer, Vallarta Whales – www.vallartawhales.com/tours/whale-watching)
Liz Perry (Vallarta Adventures, www.vallarta-adventures.com)
Nicky Ransome (Zoologist, La Orca de Sayulita www.laorcadesayulita.com)

BAHIA DE PETATLAN
Katherina Audley (Founder and Director, Whales of Guerrero Project www.whalesinmexico.com)

YUCATAN PENINSULA
Rogelio Velasco (Wild Dolphin Tours www.dolphinstour.com)

Special thanks go to the brilliant and gifted cetacean artist Martin Camm, who provided all the illustrations; we have collaborated on more whale books than either of us can remember, over more years than we dare admit, and it's always a great pleasure. And huge thanks to Stephen Johnson of Copyright Image Ltd for so kindly and diligently preparing all the artwork for reproduction. A very big thank you to Rachel Ashton, my outstandingly efficient manager, for her never-ending patience, perseverance, encouragement, enthusiasm and general brilliance. My literary agent, Doreen Montgomery, has been a huge support, too, as always over the past quarter of a century (how can it have been so long, Doreen?). I am particularly indebted to Jim Martin at Bloomsbury, without whom this book wouldn't have happened at all, for his unwavering belief in the whole idea and for his genuine love and passion for the natural world. Thank you, also, to the wonderful Jane Lawes (Bloomsbury's Senior Editor) who smoothed the way so calmly; Jane, it's been a pleasure working with you. And many, many thanks to copy editor Emily Kearns for her enthusiasm and diligence.

I'd like to thank my dear friends and family, who have enthused with me when things have been going well and cheered me on when I've been flagging: in particular, Peter Bassett and John Ruthven, for those welcome interludes over coffee in the Clifton Lido (I was going to dedicate the book to them: 'For John and Pete, without whom this book would have been written in half the time'); and Roz Kidman Cox, for her knowing sympathy and good counsel.

I'd also like to give my wonderful, kind, encouraging parents, David and Betty, a special mention. Thank you for everything. Thanks to Adam, Vanessa, Jessica and Zoe for all the food and entertainment. And last, but by no means least, a huge heartfelt thank-you to my co-conspirator in life, Debra Taylor, who always makes things better.

IMAGE CREDITS

All photographs are © Mark Carwardine, except: Back Cover (Killer Whale) © Hiroya Minakuchi/Minden Pictures; p25 (top), p81, p97 © João Quaresma; p29 © Steven Kazlowski/www.naturepl.com; p35 © DejaVuDesigns/Shutterstock.com; p45 © Martha Holmes/www.naturepl.com; p65 © wildestanimal/Shutterstock.com; p67 M Baran/NOAA Fisheries/ SEFSC Permit 779-1633; p73, p231 © Brandon Cole/www.naturepl.com; p75, p296, p307 © Todd Pusser/www.naturepl.com; p77 © Unalaska City School; p79, p253 (bottom) © Gorka Ocio/verballenas.com; p83 © Marina Milligan; p85 John Durban/NOAA Fisheries; p99 Sergio Mtz A/IWC; p101, p143 © Sophie Webb; p107 © Tobias Bernhard Raff/Biosphoto/Minden Pictures; p109 © David Fleetham/www.naturepl.com; p111 © Malcolm Schuyl/FLPA /Minden Pictures; p113, p129, p159 © Doug Perrine/www.naturepl.com; p115, p141 Jessica Taylor/IWC; p121 © Shane Gross/Shutterstock.com; p123, p220 Robert Pitman/NOAA Fisheries; p125, p157, p224, p233, p271, p275, p283, p301 © Flip Nicklin/Minden Pictures; p127 Paula Olson courtesy Southeast Fisheries/NOAA; p145, p237 © Jenny Varley; p147 © Thomas A. Jefferson/VIVA Vaquita; p149 © Nick Hawkins/www.naturepl.com; p152 © Artie Raslich/Getty Images; p160 © Joe West/Shutterstock.com; p161 © Manamana/Shutterstock.com; p173 © Visuals Unlimited/www.naturepl.com; p177 photo Don Graves, courtesy Reid Brewer; p183 © Ralph Lee Hopkins/NGCreative/Minden Pictures; p186 © JulieC@the toursanjuanisland.com; p207 © Chase Dekker/Shutterstock.com; p209 Jennifer L Keating/NOAA Fisheries; p215 © Moira Brown; p232 Doptis/Shutterstock.com; p248 Marianna Hagbloom/New England Aquarium; p253 (top) © Hilary Moors-Murphy; p259 © Wildnerdpix/Shutterstock.com; p263 © Gremm/Québec Tourism; p266 © Marc Loiselle /Québec Tourism; p281 © Doug Allan/www.naturepl.com; p304 © Robin W Baird/Cascadia Research; p305 Vallarta Adventures/www.vallarta-adventures.com

INDEX

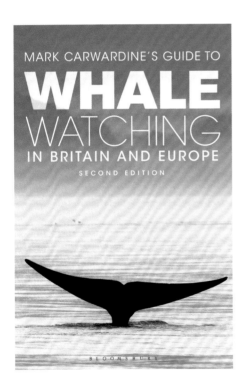

Also available

Mark Carwardine's sister guide – in the same series as *Whale Watching in North America* – covers everything you need to know about where, when and how to watch whales, dolphins and porpoises in Europe.

Whether you want to watch Blue Whales in Iceland, Bottlenose Dolphins in Wales, Narwhal in Greenland or Sperm Whales in Greece, this comprehensive and authoritative book tells you everything you need to know.